NO TIME TO
THINK

NO TIME TO
THINK

The Menace of Media Speed and the 24-hour News Cycle

HOWARD ROSENBERG
CHARLES S. FELDMAN

continuum

NEW YORK • LONDON

2008

The Continuum International Publishing Group Inc
80 Maiden Lane, New York, NY 10038

The Continuum International Publishing Group Ltd
The Tower Building, 11 York Road, London SE1 7NX

www.continuumbooks.com
http://notimetothinkbook.com

Printed in the United States of America on 50% postconsumer waste recycled paper.

Library of Congress Cataloging-in-Publication Data
Rosenberg, Howard, 1938-
  No time to think : the menace of media speed and the 24-hour news cycle /
Howard Rosenberg and Charles S. Feldman.
    p. cm.
  Includes bibliographical references and index.
  ISBN-13: 978-0-8264-2931-5 (hardcover : alk. paper)
  ISBN-10: 0-8264-2931-9 (hardcover : alk. paper) 1. Journalism—United States.
2. Television broadcasting of news—United States. 3. Journalism—Objectivity—United States.
4. Journalism—Social aspects—United States. I. Feldman, Charles S. II. Title.

PN4867.2.R67 2008
071'.3—dc22
                                        2008025488

Contents

I'd like to dedicate this book to my mother, Martin Jay, and Erik Carlson.

—Charles S. Feldman

For Carol, Kirsten, and the late great Margaret, Claire, and Getzel.

—Howard Rosenberg

Prologue

A tale of two realities . . .

It is the best of times; it is the worst of times.

It is the age of media wisdom; it is the age of media foolishness.

It is the epoch of belief in technology; it is the epoch of incredulity in technology.

It is the season of light; it is the season of darkness, of 24-hour news and schmooze, of talk radio histrionics, of jerks and knee-jerks.

It is the spring of hope; it is the winter of despair, of newspapers collapsing like the U.S. dollar; of virtual unreality and YouTube, YouNews, and Facebook sprawl; of phone-photo and home-video hordes, of high-tech gizmos galore; of key-stroking masses and Internet cascades of citizen journalists ordained as democratizing saviors liberating society from the tyranny of competence and expertise.

We have before us, at our fingertips, all possibilities; we have before us bloggers whipping up hyperbole like meringue, and hyperventilating news anchors, ad-libbing reporters, instant nonexperts and hair-trigger pundits shooting from the hip with bombast blazing on the Fox News Channel, CNN and MSNBC.

We have before us stirring high-definition pictures of global human wreckage that stamp our brains with the bloodbaths of war and terrorism, as they should; we have before us the manipulative, pulsating theater of live TV, screaming headlines, gimmicky instant polls, rumor, innuendo, opinion and speculation . . . along with Paris Hilton, Perez Hilton, and Britney Spears redux.

We have before us amazing news technology and fantastic speed; we have before us technology washing over us like a tsunami, velocity trumping veracity, frenzied pack reporting and fiery crashes waiting to happen as news zooms out of control around slippery hairpin curves on perilous fast tracks.

We have before us, warns veteran TV journalist Dave Marash, news and faux news traveling faster than "the speed of thought."

We have before us potential disaster.

Acknowledgments

It began for us at bustling Art's Deli in Studio City, where we first hashed over the concept for *No Time to Think* (this was before it acquired a subtitle), and where we would return many times to incubate, discuss, and shape the book that was to occupy us for more than a year. If not our L.A. office, this was our unofficial home base. Thank you, Art's, for that, and for the potato latkes, too.

Like most books, this one was a collaborative effort, with many fingers in the pie.

A standing ovation is due the many souls who bravely submitted to our interviews, including those who did not share our hypothesis about the perils of media speed and Internet excess.

Locating some of our interviewees took a bit of effort. Assisting greatly in that endeavor were Jennifer Siebens, London bureau chief for CBS News; Taylor Ansen and Josh and Julie Dorkin, whose Web wisdom and research also proved enormously helpful. Greg Woolway gave us valuable Internet assistance, too. And Russ Poldrack of UCLA was generous with his advice.

We're also greatly indebted to world-class Diana Forman, who not only transcribed nearly all of our interviews but heard them with an acute ear, and to gifted columnist Colleen Cason, who pointed us in the right direction at her newspaper, the *Ventura County Star.*

Applause, also, for our staff linguist, Kelley Riffenburgh, who lent us her 14-year-old's cellphone sensibility. And finally, to David Barker and everyone else at Continuum for their insights and for giving us this opportunity.

CHAPTER 1

"Why Is Speed So Bad?"

They stumble that run fast.
—William Shakespeare, *Romeo and Juliet*

They wouldn't have *him* to kick around anymore.

Two weeks before leaving office in 2007, British Prime Minister Tony Blair aimed a withering attack at his nation's news media. Taking no prisoners, Blair charged that journalists had created a supercharged atmosphere driven by 24-hour news technology and an emphasis on "impact" and "heat." He said they stressed "sensation above all else."

He declared, "We are all being dragged down by the way media and public life interact." He equated news media to a "feral beast, just tearing people and reputations to bits."

Blair claimed that loss of audiences by traditional newspapers and evening news broadcasts to 24-hour cable news and the Internet created an environment that required media to increasingly compete for attention and forced politicians into a mode of perpetual reaction that served no good purpose.

He said that when he campaigned for election in 1997, "we took an issue a day." But "in 2005, we had to have one for the morning, another for the afternoon, and by the evening the agenda had already moved on."

The prime minister noted that nuances become casualties in news coverage that paints issues in black and white. In the shrill, hyperbolic vocabulary of "mediaspeak," he added, a setback becomes "a policy in tatters," mere criticism a "savage attack."

The relationship between public life and the news media "is now damaged in a manner that requires repair," he continued. "The damage saps . . . confidence and self-belief . . . it reduces our capacity to make the right decisions, in the right spirit, for our future."

Blair did not come away unscathed from his assault on media; the counterattack was swift and understandably harsh. Skeptics dismissed his remarks as self-serving payback for aggressive media investigations of scandals in his government and their criticism of his unwavering support for President George W. Bush and the U.S.-led invasion and occupation of Iraq.

Indeed, inescapable here was the irony of Blair, the ardent media spinner, now outraged by media spin; Blair, the maestro of manipulation, now complaining bitterly of being manipulated by media.

Yet Blair was on to something as he prepared to leave 10 Downing Street. His hypocrisy notwithstanding, the much-maligned 24-hour news cycle had already shrunk to something like 24 minutes by the time he delivered his blistering critique of UK media, and some of his remarks had bulls-eyed a deserving target. In his crosshairs—transcending nations' borders, partisan rhetoric, and the usual back-and-forth between the outgoing Blair and his critics—was something that continues to beguile and bedevil U.S. media at least as much as it does their counterparts on the other side of the Atlantic.

That something is speed.

Reckless speed.

The speed of media pushing their pedals to the metal at any cost while racing blindly into today's new-age data stream.

Blair's farewell flip-off—regarding pressures on newsmakers to respond to the accelerated news cycle—was reinforced in the

United States five days before the 2008 Texas Primary and Caucuses. The occasion was Democratic presidential hopeful Hillary Clinton's attention-grabbing "dangerous world" TV ad that aired in Texas at 7 A.M. It pictured kiddies slumbering peacefully as a dangerous crisis broke, and a voice declaring, "It's 3 A.M. and your children are safe and asleep. Who do you want answering the phone?" Last scene: It's Clinton who has answered—calm, confident, in command.

A guns-blazing assault on her Democratic foe Barack Obama's slender foreign policy credentials, the Clinton spot immediately rocketed across the blogosphere, followed later that day by a superswift rebuttal from Obama's campaign.

By noon Obama's people had whipped up a 30-second response ad that was quickly sped to broadcast and cable networks and uploaded to YouTube—*before* that evening's newscasts. This was significant, for as Brian Stelter wrote in the *New York Times,* "This may be the year politics finally moves at the speed of the Internet."

He was right. Created to make news, Obama's catch-up counterattack was a response not only to Clinton, but more essentially to the media's own stunning pace that, in many ways, had already been shaping the 2007–2008 presidential election campaign.

Nor is obsession with speed exclusive to U.S. media. As Blair noted, Brits, too, are bonkers for it. In his book *Flat Earth News* prominent UK journalist Nick Davies describes the manic, high-speed "churnalism"—a hybrid of churn and journalism—that he says has overtaken news websites in his country, notably that of the BBC. The clash of traditional journalism and this new "churnalism" echoes loudly in the official BBC guide distributed to online staff, he writes. "On the one hand, it urges: 'Your story MUST be accurate, impartial, balanced and uphold the values of BBC News. . . . NEVER publish anything that you do not understand, that is speculation or inadequately sourced.' And then, as if there were no contradiction at all," Davies adds, the guide continues: 'Get the story up as fast as you can. . . . We encourage a sense of urgency—we want to be first.'"

The message? Like the all-powerful wiz pushing levers behind a curtain in *The Wizard of Oz*, speed is calling the shots.

Why should anyone bloody well care?

For one thing, "it is absolutely true, and anybody who says otherwise is slinging bullshit, that every mistake that's made in the news business is made because of speed," says Keith McAllister, former executive vice president and managing editor for CNN's national newsgathering.

For another, the faster-and-faster crowd is gaining ever more stature with the public, with surveys showing that most Americans (especially those under 30) have lost faith in traditional media and prefer the Internet as a primary news source.

For another, media and inaccuracy, after a flirting through the ages, are now in a steamy lip lock. "Even when the first read (of a story) is not always true," notes Washington, D.C.–based talk radio host Bill Press, "that doesn't stop it from spreading like wildfire."

Examples abound, as when a powerful politician was cut down prematurely by the Fox News Channel in runaway madcap overdrive. It began on the morning of March 10, 2008 after the *New York Times* website reported that New York Governor Eliot Spitzer—a former hooker-busting prosecutor—had been linked to a Washington, D.C.–based prostitution ring.

The 24-hour news channels immediately pounced and began speculating wildly about Spitzer and his future. But it was Fox and its anchor Shephard Smith who blew like Vesuvius. The sequence began with Smith quoting "sources" that Spitzer was expected to resign "just minutes from now." Then came Smith's announcement that Spitzer *had* resigned during a brief televised statement he'd made to the media. "He came in, he resigned and that was it," said the ever-emphatic Smith, who then began speculating with his guests about what the administration of Spitzer's successor, Lieutenant Governor David Patterson, would be like. Very relevant, very incisive—and above all, very fast.

Except that Spitzer had not resigned.

Minutes later Smith corrected himself, blaming the mistake on two sources, one a Fox executive. Some 45 minutes after that, a Fox headline reported, *"N.Y. Gov. Eliot Spitzer Expected to Resign Later Today."* It was another misfire, as was Fox's entire push-it-out-fast-and-faster approach to the story that morning (actually, the governor would wait two days before announcing he would step down), which also included reporting that Spitzer had been "indicted."

Also not true, Greta Van Susteren, the attorney who hosts Fox's *On the Record* legal series, told Shephard later. After quickly thumbing through legal documents that had been released to the media minutes earlier, she warned, "I think we gotta really dial back on this, Shep."

Dialing back is not is in the electronic media's DNA, especially when it comes to sex scandals that threaten the high and mighty. The speed of that coverage shoves offenders out the door—witness the instant vaporization of Spitzer's political career because of that alleged tryst with a high-priced call girl. With little time to regroup, today's scandalized politicians are usually gone like *that*, so fast does news travel in the Internet era. That speed "forces [them] to make decisions more quickly. You can't sit back and reflect," Harvard University lecturer Tom Fiedler told the *Washington Post.*

Nor is reflection usually a media priority when reporting celebrity news. Take the online hysteria and sheer pandemonium that greeted the death of young actor Heath Ledger on January 22, 2008, at once a minuscule footnote of history and microcosm of the challenges brought on by new media.

Stories of Ledger's death that first raced across the Internet were riddled with confusion and errors, with the celebrity news website TMZ and even the *New York Times* City blog, for example, both posting the erroneous tidbit that he had died in the New York apartment of actress Mary-Kate Olsen. It turned out both had been misinformed by a spokesman for the New York Police Department, and they rushed to update the story after the spokesman corrected himself.

"But here's the problem," David Sarno wrote afterward in the *Los Angeles Times,* comparing media generations. "Stories have never arrived to the world fully formed or vetted. Journalists have generally had hours—not minutes or seconds—to craft a story from the blast wave of facts and factoids that come in the wake of a bombshell. What people are seeing now is an old-fashioned process—reporting—as it unfolds in real time."

Did he say "minutes or seconds" to vet a story? Journalists might as well walk a slippery high wire in snowshoes.

Tech-minded new media do it all the time, their sped-up news cycle often granting urgency and credibility even to the silliest of rumors and half-truths. Take the Great Toilet Paper Flap that that centered on popular Grammy-winning singer/songwriter Sheryl Crow.

In the spring of 2007, the planet became intimately acquainted with Crow's preference for sanitary cleanliness. At least, it thought it had when Crow, an outspoken environmentalist, was widely quoted as saying that, in the interest of conservation, people should use just one square sheet of toilet paper for each bathroom visit. From this spark, the Crow story ignited and spread across 24-hour news channels and the Internet faster than a wind-swept wildfire.

One very minor detail, hardly worth mentioning, really. It wasn't true.

Not that Crow hadn't made the remark; but she'd said it as a lark. As she told *The New York Times Sunday Magazine,* "It was always a joke. It was part of a shtick. It was part of a comedy routine that Laurie (Laurie David) and I were doing on the 'Stop Global Warming College Tour.'"

Nonetheless, as she was about to fly out of Washington, D.C., the next day, Crow said she saw the following headline on a CNN monitor in the airport: *Sheryl Crow has proposed that we legislate toilet paper to one square.*

A better idea: Flush impulsive media.

Contrary to Malcolm Gladwell's best-selling *Blink* treatise on the validity of first glances and snap judgments, instant response is not necessarily wise response. Plus, the stakes become greater— quickness at times leading to quackery—in a higher- and higher-tech society that urges us to move faster. Not such a good idea.

"The collective pressures of technology and the marketplace have ratcheted up the expectations that we can think at the same pace we can press the send button," writes syndicated columnist Ellen Goodman. "We are expected to make sense of information as fast as we can communicate it."

But expectations and reality don't necessarily coincide, especially when the issues before us contain subtleties or intricacies easily missed at first glance. "Reality demands that you pay attention to both complexity and detail and nuance, and that takes the time in the telling," says Dave Marash, formerly an anchor for the English-language Al Jazeera network in Washington, D.C. "Also, there has to be cognitive time for the viewer to absorb detailed, complex nuanced information," adds Marash, whose pedigree also features years of reporting for *Nightline* on ABC. "So you have to pace stories so that they can be ingested efficiently. Understanding complex and rapidly changing events . . . cannot be done in an instant."

Speed-caused missteps are not exclusive to journalism, of course. Was speed a culprit when the U.S. Supreme Court stiff-armed Democrat Al Gore and handed the 2000 presidential election to Republican George Bush? Jeffrey Toobin hints as much in *The Nine: Inside the Secret World of the Supreme Court.*

Toobin, an attorney and CNN regular, writes that historically the High Court nearly always denies litigants' requests for speedy treatment. "But in the matter of the election of 2000, the justices departed from their usual roles. There was no order, no regularity, no procedure. The justices decided them on the fly." Most of the justices were not even in the building on Wednesday, November 22, he adds, "so their clerks and the Court staff had to track them down to give them the Republicans' briefs. Many of the law clerks had already left for the Thanksgiving holidays, so the decision on Bush's cert petition [writ of certiorari, which asks the High Court to reverse a lower-court decision] went to the justices alone. And they did not wait to hear from the Democrats to issue their decision."

You can just about pick your field, including government, where speed makes a difference, often for the worse. "I've never heard a decision made on the run or off the cuff or quick that's better than one that's thoughtful," says Marlin Fitzwater, who ran press relations for presidents Ronald Reagan and George H. W. Bush. "I've never heard a first response better than a considered one."

That also applies to the medical field, where mistakes potentially do the ultimate damage: they can kill. "The majority of errors (in medicine) are due to flaws in physician thinking, not technical mistakes," oncologist Jerome Groopman writes in his collection of essays *How Doctors Think.*

"In order to think well, especially in hectic circumstances," Groopman notes, "you need to slow things down to avoid making cognitive errors." He cites "cognitive cherry-picking," a shortcut in thinking by doctors who judge their current cases by past cases, latching on to a diagnosis by selecting only those symptoms that confirm their original hypothesis, while ignoring contradictory ones. This "skewed reading of the map," Groopman says, "confirms your mistaken assumption that you have reached your destination."

Edward H. Tenner, a Princeton University historian of technology, calls this "the bias of convenience," which closely resembles the "law of least effort" theory set forth in 1935 by mathematical linguist George K. Sipf, who believed that people tend to be satisfied by answers that are the easiest to obtain. So much so that they are unlikely to pursue other options.

And that's especially the case, we can safely assume, if they are in a rush.

The parallels of this speed-driven "cognitive cherry-picking" with journalism are especially striking. "There's a cynical expression—'too good to check,'" says Ron Nessen, who was an NBC correspondent before becoming President Gerald Ford's press secretary. "Some stories, you don't want to spend too much time checking because you don't want to find out you're wrong."

In one high-profile example of speed-driven perilous reporting, "the rush to air" without sufficient probing was behind a later-discredited *60 Minutes Wednesday* report on CBS in 2004, according to the findings of an independent panel. Relying on memos it said were authentic, the report claimed President George W. Bush had skirted some of his duties during his earlier National Guard service and that a commander felt pressured to sugarcoat Bush's record.

"In retrospect, we shouldn't have used the documents," then CBS News president Andrew Heyward acknowledged at the time, "and we clearly should have spent more time and more effort to authenticate them." The blunder forced Dan Rather, who fronted and initially defended the report, to relinquish his *CBS Evening News* anchor job earlier than he had planned.

More recently, ABC News legal reporter Jan Crawford Greenburg speculated in her blog that U.S. Supreme Court Justice Ruth Bader

Ginsburg was ready for retirement after she was seen taking a long time rising from her seat after a hearing. That thesis hurtled through the blogosphere before *New York Times* Supreme Court reporter Linda Greenhouse put it to rest, reporting that Ginsburg had gotten up slowly because she couldn't find a shoe she had kicked under the table.

In a higher-profile case of blog bungling driven by extreme haste, reporter Ben Smith's 2007 story about the candidacy of John Edwards briefly flamed before crashing thunderously on Politico, a well-regarded Washington, D.C.–based website staffed largely by migrants from traditional news organizations. Smith, a former *New York Daily News* staffer, reported that presidential hopeful Edwards would announce at noon that day his plans to suspend campaigning for the Democratic nomination because his wife, Elizabeth, had suffered a recurrence of cancer. Preferring not to wait until the news actually broke, Politico posted it— "EDWARDS TO SUSPEND CAMPAIGN"—on its front page shortly after 11 A.M.—less than an hour before a scheduled press conference with the candidate and his wife.

Cyberspace linkage immediately toggled on, and within seconds Smith's blog was headlined on the widely monitored *Drudge Report* website, then picked up with varying qualifiers by CNN, the Fox News Channel, and MSNBC, which gave it a "breaking news" marquee. NBC News Anchor Brian Williams told viewers, "We will know more just a few moments from now when we hear it from the source, but reports have been circulating all morning long that Senator Edwards is, indeed, about to end or suspend his campaign for president." Meanwhile, Smith was being interviewed about his "scoop" by three radio stations—and no wonder, for it was a big story, an important story.

And oh, yes—a wrong story.

Things were moving swiftly, for shortly after Politico posted Smith's story a disclaimer came in from the Edwards camp that the website added to the story but without changing the headline (something the *Drudge Report* site did do after learning of the error).

Smith acknowledged his mistake in another Politico piece posted later that evening. "I've done much of my reporting on blogs and have developed an instinct to let my readers know whatever I know as soon as I know it," wrote Smith, stating the high-risk, news-in-an-eye-blink mantra of bloggers everywhere. But his single "good" source had been wrong, he added.

Actually, Smith and his source, and everyone who followed Politico's lead, turned out to be right. They were just 10 months early. Edwards did drop out—on January 30, 2008, when it was obvious he had no chance of getting the nomination.

Smith was apologetic when asked about this episode months later, acknowledging that he had blown it. Of course, all he had to do was wait an hour to hear what Edwards had to say, hear it from the candidate's own lips instead of getting it wrong from an anonymous source. One lousy hour—why *not* wait? Even now, Smith doesn't appear to quite get it.

His reply: "Why is speed so bad?"

It's not necessarily bad, just dangerous when there's no time or inclination to seek a second "good" source.

One can see how lethal to truth and accuracy the Tenner-titled "bias of convenience" can be when reporters do hurried research while gathering news on the run. Tenner sees the Internet as "flattering people into thinking they know something" and making it "easier to be satisfied with an incomplete or misleading answer (that) can convey a false sense of empowerment." And, he wonders, "Are young journalists who are used to finding what they need on the Web going to be equally zealous in using other sources?"

In other words, it's the old tree-falls-in-the-forest argument: if it isn't instantly accessible online, it must not exist.

Another aspect of this—the echo chamber effect—demands scrutiny as well. As a research tool, the Internet's possibilities are prodigious if not infinite. Tap, tap, click, and you're there; it's all before you, encyclopedic universes opening up like petals on a blossom. Or is it? Is it possible that, in its most prevalent use, the Internet is less a source of diverse and contradictory views than one echoing opinions that its users already hold?

The "overarching crisis of memory and knowledge" that Susan Jacoby describes in *The Age of American Unreason* refers to a general condition of unknowing in the United States. But her comments about famed 19th-century agnostic Robert Ingersoll, when interviewed by Bill Moyers on PBS, evoked a striking parallel with Internet usage.

Ingersoll often spoke to audiences who rejected his beliefs, "but they wanted to hear what he had to say," Jacoby said. "And now what we have is a situation in which people go to hear people they already agree with. What's going on is not so much education as reinforcement of the opinions you already have."

Hence, the echo chamber—in a sense, speaking to oneself. *The Wizard of Id* cartoon strip nailed it years ago when it had Spook, a hairy character held interminably in a dungeon, spruce up for visitor's day. In the next panel, he's sitting, legs crossed, in front of a large mirror, asking, "So, how's the family?"

○ ○ ○

You can blame Al Gore—sort of.

He didn't invent the Internet, but he was an enabler. It was Gore, when he was a U.S. senator and not yet Bill Clinton's vice president, who provided legislative support to help transform what was essentially a private plaything for the military and academia into a worldwide Web available to the masses.

As far back as 1988, Gore had helped introduce legislation to pump money into the National Science Foundation, which spearheaded software developments with the full backing of the U.S. military. "With greater access to supercomputers," promised Gore at the time, "virtually every business in America could achieve tremendous gains."

Nice thought, with some truths attached to it. But incomplete vision. What Gore and other early advocates of this technology hadn't realized was this: The uncurbed rapidity of its flow of news and other kinds of information would have unexpected consequences that were beneficial only to the very few. One of them, for example, was that a teenager would be able to post for the planet to see, in an instant, a video of his chums and him guzzling beers in a contest to see who could upchuck in the shortest time.

Oh, *that*.

More recently, Gore wrote in *The Assault on Reason* that he puts his trust in the Internet to rescue us from television's capacity to immobilize reason and stimulate a primitive "visceral vividness" not "modulated by logic, reason and reflective thought."

The Internet, he argues, "is perhaps the greatest source for hope for re-establishing an open communications environment in which the conversation of democracy can flourish."

To which *New York Times* columnist David Brooks responded, "Has Al Gore actually looked at the Internet?"

○ ○ ○

Well, get used to this fireball that Gore and others see as a messiah; think "meteor shower." Those are the words of Tom Brokaw, the former *NBC Nightly News* anchor whose long career arcs many epic changes in journalism. "I think we are in the middle of another Big Bang," he says about the Internet's exploding growth. "We've created this universe in which all these planets are suddenly out there colliding with each other. We are trying to determine which ones will support life, which ones will drift too close to the sun and burn up, which ones will meld with another. And the effect of it all is bewildering, both to those of us in this end of the spectrum and those who are on the receiving end. It's a big dilemma and we haven't given enough thought to the consequences."

Not that contemporary media were beyond reproach prior to the Internet's cosmic firing up for prime time. There had been plenty to complain about for years. Even when Walter Cronkite addressed America from Mt. Olympus way back when, it was the nature of newscasts to skim surfaces and render events equal, like flipping cards in a Rolodex. It was 30 seconds of fluff giving way to 30 seconds of bigger fluff followed by 30 seconds of global crisis, with no gradations of relative importance.

And Cronkite's CBS News colleague Eric Sevareid once equated the speed of contemporary TV news with a "spotlight in the darkness. It focuses on what's moving, and everything else is blotted in the darkness."

Could it get any worse than that? Possibly. The Internet and 24-hour news channels have built on that situation and escalated it, affirming technology as both a blessing and a scourge. "Satellites changed everything," notes Michael Gartner, a former newspaper editor and president of NBC News. "Satellites have made it so you can see the airplane crashing and the dictator being toppled." And presidents called on the carpet and humiliated? "You could see everything," Gartner says, "but Bill Clinton getting a blow job."

And see it all simultaneously. If, in a time warp, Abraham Lincoln had issued his document that freed the slaves in rebelling states in the era of all-news channels instead of in 1863, they would have split the screen, half to him, half to some Hollywood celebrity appearing before a judge or a YouTube video of Clinton indeed being serviced in the Oval Office by *you know who.*

Priorities have always been a problem for news media, especially for those on the electronic side. Along those lines was a newscast on KCBS in Los Angeles that shamelessly granted a quarter of the screen to one of those routine cops-chasing-fugitive freeway adventures as President George W. Bush addressed the nation live on federal funding of limited embryonic stem cell research. Little did Bush know that while opining on this significant hot-button issue, he was being undermined in Los Angeles by embryonic intellects at a TV station owned and operated by CBS.

"And then," says Gartner, "the Internet took it one step further." If not two or three.

"Isn't it thrilling," observes a character in Garry Trudeau's wonderfully ironic *Doonesbury* strip, lying in bed in the dark of night. "A roomful of technology in standby mode, ready to leap to life and serve us."

Technology is wonderful if it's beneficial, and where would the news business be without its remarkable advances? In 1481, a letter reporting the death of a Turkish sultan took two years to reach England, Mitchell Stephens writes in *A History of News.* And in 1841, he notes, it took three months and 20 days for Los Angeles to learn of President William Henry Harrison's death in the east.

Moreover, beaming events to the multitudes as they happen is indispensable on occasion. Live cameras are peerless when covering some kinds of breaking stories, from massive shootouts and volatile civil disturbances to raging wildfires, devastating natural disasters, and truly epic catastrophes like the terrorism of 9/11. You don't twiddle your thumbs and wait for the morning paper to tell you what happened. You turn on TV or the radio, or, increasingly these days, the Internet.

On the other hand . . .

"The sort of ad absurdum extremity of faster and faster is *live*," says Marash. "More and more of the television news networks, particularly the American news channels, have become addicted to the added emotional engagement of live because of its unpredictability and, therefore, the potential for high drama or high intimacy."

So what's the problem with this touch of show biz?

"When you are live, you literally have no time to reflect and damn little time to think or consider," Marash says. "So a lot of times we get live coverage with a lot of disorganized information, some of it turning out to be true, some of it turning out to be untrue. But it has already shaped the discussion; it has already sent that river down stream colored by whatever the first impressions of the live coverage were. So one of our big problems is not so much what people don't know but the wrong stuff that they think they do know because they saw it presented in an early pre–first draft."

What about that old saw about news being the first draft of history? "This precedes even that," says Marash. "This is often the shocked ramblings that precede the first draft." Or the raw notes . . . scribbled in crayon.

Live reporting—instant news without safeguards—is the ultimate journalistic gamble, in many cases not only a device to seduce and sucker viewers but more significantly, a risky game. And that game— played ever more by newscasts in the last three decades—is Russian roulette, TV's high rollers squeezing the trigger and hoping no bullet is in the chamber.

Want a smoking gun? Try this, still vivid in many memories.

The year was 1998. And in the quintessential Los Angeles TV story, an obviously disturbed motorist, Daniel V. Jones, was being pursued by a bevy of patrol cars across the city's freeways when he stopped his truck on an overpass, stepped out without pants and walked around. So edgy, so exciting, so *now*. Then Jones placed a shotgun to his head and pulled the trigger, leaving his brains on the pavement as seven TV stations beamed the full public splatter to their viewers. *Live*.

Oddly enough, it was a media stunt. However poorly he was thinking, Jones knew TV choppers would be there. Why else would he have prepared a hand-scrawled banner lambasting HMOs and spread it out on the ground near his truck before ending his life?

How did he know that TV choppers would be there? Because it's TV, dummy, and they're always there, creating gridlock in the skies while beaming live pictures of freeway chases to inquiring minds with a yen for the instantaneous.

Why do experienced journalists telecast unscreened material in volatile situations? Because they can, and because they are driven by a powerful, rush-to-report herd instinct, the one commanding them to beat or at least keep astride of the competition and not be left behind. Just as their competitors answer the same call of the wild in trying to keep pace with them.

News on TV is driven largely by technology, the human contribution limited increasingly to flipping on the switch and letting everything rip. Mostly, events are covered live not because they're worthy of that coverage but because the equipment to do it exists. The rule of thumb is to go live not necessarily because it makes journalistic sense but because you have all the toys, all the technological goodies at your command.

"Everyone," says Keith McAllister, "is doing this at the speed of light."

This affirms what political philosopher John Gray writes in *Straw Dogs:* "Technical progress leaves one problem unsolved: the frailty of human nature. Unfortunately that problem is insoluble." This we've learned through the years.

Former CNN correspondent Charles Bierbauer recalls what happened when the Philadelphia station he worked for in the mid-1970s acquired its first microwave truck that could beam pictures live from anywhere in town. Station executives were buzzed, exhilarated, hopped up and revved up. Something was wrong with this picture, though. Instead of using this exciting new technology to support or enhance stories, the station sought to make its new microwave truck the centerpiece of newscasts and design coverage around it.

"Technology gets so far ahead of us," says Bierbauer, now dean of journalism at the University of South Carolina. "Journalistically, we should be focusing on what the content is and how we use the tools. But the damned tools get in the way."

These are the power tools that speed up the news and send it out in all directions.

"Never has falsehood in America had such a large megaphone," John Carroll commented in a *Los Angeles Times* op-ed piece when he was still editor of that paper.

Rob Silverstein, executive producer of the syndicated TV series *Access Hollywood,* has similar thoughts. "There is so much stuff that's first but wrong. All these websites are guilty of that," said Silverstein, vowing to the *New York Times* that his own show's website would be different.

The primordial gut urge of media hordes to take off and sprint toward the finish line with any baton handed them has not gone unnoticed by those with special agendas. In 2004, partisan TV commercials making unproved charges that Democratic presidential candidate John Kerry inflated his Vietnam War record had a small run in a handful of states. But the accusations, made by Swift Boat Veterans for Truth, hit 10 on the Richter scale after relentless media coverage that seriously wounded the candidacy of Kerry, who responded slowly after underestimating the speed and influence of 24-hour news and right-wing radio talkers and bloggers.

In the Spring of 2007, moreover, a Democratic operative, who later claimed he had acted independently, posted at no cost an anonymous YouTube video picturing presidential candidate Hillary Clinton as "Big Brother" from George Orwell's futurist tale *1984.* A week after airing, the anti-Hillary spot had already been viewed 2.7 million times and played repeatedly on 24-hour news channels, getting millions of dollars worth of free political advertising.

As did attack videos showing Republican presidential candidate Rudy Giuliani in drag (he was doing it as a gag) and Democratic presidential hopeful Edwards, whose expensive coif had been ridiculed by political foes, appearing to primp as he very carefully combed his hair.

So behold the era of *McNews:* spatulas of information carelessly splattering the hot grease of half-thoughts and half-truths on camera and online, instantly blabbing what is whispered to them or slid under the kitchen door anonymously, creating what journalist

Jeff Greenfield once called, in another context, a "maelstrom of semi-informed, uninformed windbaggery."

In earlier times, editors and news directors "had time to digest before disseminating," says Gartner. "Now it's regurgitation—fact, rumor, innuendo, often with no context and no distinction between fact and rumor or important fact and irrelevant fact. You have to be a lot smarter to be a news consumer these days than you did a generation ago." Well, good luck with that.

Packed off for early retirement are cool deliberation and thoughtful discourse, now cobwebbed relics banished to the attic along with hula hoops and old photos from the horse-and-buggy age.

The *public's right to know* has been supplanted by the *public's right to know everything, however fanciful and even erroneous, as fast as technology allows.*

This can have benefits. It was a stinging blogger swarm that, in effect, drove Mississippi Senator Trent Lott from his position as Senate majority leader in 2002 after he had made a speech appearing to endorse his elderly colleague Strom Thurman's early support for segregation.

Former Virginia Senator George Allen also learned what it was like to be tripped up by technology. His front-running quest to be the Republicans' 2008 presidential nominee collapsed almost instantly in 2006 when amateur video caught him uttering what many believed to be a racial slur in a speech to supporters.

Yet, for every revealing Lott meltdown or George Allen *macaca* moment YouTubed through cyberspace, dozens more of these are malicious cheap shots or outright deception, putting pressure on just about everyone. As a consequence, for the media and government leaders pledged to make carefully considered decisions on their behalf, there is literally *no . . . time . . . to . . . think.*

Speed was not invented by this generation's technophiles. The rush to report has been in journalism's bloodstream surely since humankind first felt the itch to pass on information, when prehistoric cave dwellers wrote on walls, early Romans gathered in the forum to hear the latest gossip and roving reporter Herodotus recorded what he saw in his fifth century B.C.E. travels in lands along the Mediterranean and Black Seas. One can also envision scoop-hungry medieval town criers competing to be the first to report "All's well!"

In modern times, though, no event epitomized speed as the heartbeat of breaking news coverage more than the assassination of President John F. Kennedy in Dallas on November 22, 1963. The frantic scene went like this: United Press International White House reporter Merriman Smith outfought rival Associated Press reporter Jack Bell for a radiophone in their wire services limo so that he could be first to report that the president's motorcade had taken fire.

In fact, 68 percent of Americans learned that Kennedy had been shot within 30 minutes of the attack. And Smith's historic "beat"—in arguably the biggest spot news story since Japan's attack of Pearl Harbor on December 7, 1941—was an example of ends justifying means. The two highly competitive wire services were at each other necks, carnivore to carnivore, giving no quarter, and filing first on such an epic story did matter greatly at the time. However, *Smith vs. Bell* was also a dark omen of what was coming. It foreshadowed media's present speed-for-speed's-sake mania, a mindless phenomenon that has its contemporary TV roots in a seminal event of 1980.

The occasion was the creation of the Cable News Network known as CNN—releasing into our biosphere a chain-reaction force and media-mushroom cloud whose fallout would become the 24-hour news cycle.

Well, why not 24-hour news? Our modern culture is not just up-tempo, its tempo is up, up, and away! Do we not bow down to, pray to, and worship speed as if it were a cult, even a religion? And are we not its acolytes and zip-along roadrunners, speedaholics addicted to things fast and faster? Isn't Carl Honore, author of *In Praise of Slowness,* correct in saying "modern life is stuck in fast-forward?" Isn't James Gleick on point when noting in *Faster: The Acceleration of Just About Everything,* "We've reached the epoch of the nanosecond"?

That includes drinking instant coffee while listening to instant analysis of instant polls. It includes not only speed dialing and speed reading, but speedier dialing and speedier reading, living life by a stopwatch, cramming more and more into less and less. We want faster food and faster orgasms. And these days, says actress/writer Carrie Fisher, even "instant gratification isn't fast enough."

Gleick likens this to a drug: "We've chosen speed and we thrive on it—more than we generally admit. Our ability to work fast and play fast gives us power. It thrills us. If we have learned the name of just one hormone, it is adrenaline."

This speed obsession intersects every aspect of contemporary life, including politics. "I wish we had 10 days instead of five," former President Clinton said in early 2008, lamenting the newly narrowed gap separating the Iowa Caucuses and the New Hampshire Primary, where his wife was pushing her bid for the Democratic presidential bid.

Even resurrections are fast tracked in this 24/7 Interneted-to-the-max, cable-newsed world in which we live to purchase new software updates seemingly every few days.

Take the case of New York–based Don Imus, the infamous radio talk show host who plummeted from grace like a meteor after he and his longtime producer made racially and sexually disparaging comments about the Rutgers University women's college basketball team. Those slurs, including Imus calling the African American players "nappy-headed hos," were instantly YouTubed across cybersphere. Almost immediately, Imus's CBS Radio show and MSNBC simulcast were history, his career in ruin.

At least it seemed so in April 2007, when this incident occurred. But some eight months later Imus was back on the air, on a different New York City station and syndicated by a different radio group—with many if not most of the advertisers who abandoned his ship now pleased passengers once more.

Even big-name politicos, along with other VIPs who frequented Imus's old radio and cable TV show, returned to bathe in his somewhat diluted venom.

Talk about fast comebacks. What happened?

Speed is what happened.

CBS News correspondent Bob Schieffer, a former Imus regular and one of the "old-timers" to rejoin the once-tainted radio personality on his new station, told the *New York Times*: "It seems like in this age of instant communication, they fall faster and they rise faster. . . . It used to be, before the Internet, it took a while for this stuff to go around. Now, it goes around in a nanosecond. Maybe what we're seeing is that it's possible to come back just as quickly."

Times writer Jacques Steinberg summed it up best, saying that Imus's speedy move "from transgression to redemption is—to some—a reflection of the country's collective attention span, which these days can be measured by the time it takes to watch a video on YouTube or to scan a blog item on the gossip site Defamer.com."

This is a national attention span that transcends age, for even toddlers are becoming addicted to the *faster-faster-and-faster* drug. Honore laments the arrival of the book *One-Minute Bedtime Stories,* which "condense[s] classic fairytales into 60-second sound bites." He says there's a backlash, that "everybody today wants to slow down." That's good news. But here's his punch line: "They want to slow down really quickly."

So *of course* 24-hour news—*One-Minute Bedtime Stories* for adults.

Frank Sesno, who spent 17 years at CNN before joining the faculty of the George Washington University, opens his speeches by announcing, "I'm from the media, and I'm here to help." Then he adds, "Here's the deal. If you're not born with attention deficit disorder, we'll teach it to you." He's kidding, of course, but on the square. And what better example of ADD than multitasking?

That long commute—isn't it such a drag? The radio or DVD player is not enough of a diversion. Your view of outside is the same-old, same-old. And the gridlock has you dozing anyway. So why not put your time to good use?

Why not—*yes*—read a book!

Multitasking is almost second nature to us now, even though recent studies show that the human brain can't do two things at once, that when we try doing that performance is impaired. And that those speaking on a cell phone while driving are more likely to crash than other motorists.

They don't call it *distraction* for nothing.

Yet 24-hour news channels continue to impose multitasking on their viewers in the form of screen clutter. It's Internet-driven, of course, as 24-hour news executives look beyond their traditional 50-plus age base to a younger generation of viewers more at ease with multitasking and reading from computers.

Talking 24-hour news anchors are sometimes relegated to an upper portion of the screen, as small as a third, while competing

for viewers' attention with layers of computer graphics and superficial, tabloidy, factoidy headlines (not the tip of the iceberg but
the tip of the tip) that run continuously near the bottom of the
screen. Known as crawls, these truncated stand-alone summaries
compete for viewers' attention while speaking a clipped idiom
that trivializes critical issues.

Experiencing this is a bit like driving in another country—say,
Italy—and coming to a crossroads where there are a dozen
confusing signs pointing each direction, then having to make
an immediate decision before the honking speedsters behind you
run up your back.

At one point during its early coverage of the assassination of
former Pakistan Prime Minister Benazir Bhutto at the end of 2007,
for example, the Fox News Channel had all of this on screen at
one time:

In the upper left corner, "LIVE."
Below that, news anchor Bret Baier
To the right of him, taped footage of chaos in the city of Rawalpindi
Below that, "BREAKING NEWS."
Below that, a headline.
Below that, a crawl.
Below that, "ALERT!"
Below that, another headline.
Below that, another crawl.
To the left of that, the Fox logo.

But even this kind of news jigsaw may not deliver information
fast enough for speed-burning caffeine heads too juiced for headlines, and even crawls.

"Crawls are almost antiquated," says Jon Klein, president of
CNN/US. "They seem almost sluggish in comparison to how quickly
a website loads or changes pages. So it's funny, our body clocks have
all sped up so much in the last 20, 30 years, thanks to the advent of
computers in every phase of our life, to the point that, you know,
when you tap in your secret code into the cash machine, doesn't
your foot start tapping in the three seconds it takes for the cash to
actually pop out? Or when you get that hourglass on the screen
when you've clicked on a website or when you turn your computer

on? Our bodies are so revved up now that the crawl itself feels almost stately. It tells you something about the pace of life in general these days. And we try to acknowledge that by cutting our cameras more quickly, putting up more images. That doesn't hurt the processing of information. I think it helps the processing of information if you're now moving at the same speed your audience is moving."

But are CNN and its 24-hour news siblings reflecting the speed culture or shaping that culture by increasing speed? Or are they joining other media in trying desperately to match the pace of the Internet?

Talk radio surely is. Radio host Press believes that his medium has been "left in the dust" by the blogosphere: "The pace keeps getting faster and faster and faster. I get caught up in it and find myself having to say sometimes, this is what the bloggers are saying, we're not really sure here. I caution myself and my listeners to slow down, but I'm not sure it works."

Rendering talk radio of all political stripes irrelevant has a certain appeal. But is it possible that reading books has also been "left in the dust"?

Reading, and reading proficiency, are declining dramatically in the United States, notes a 2007 study by the National Endowment for the Arts (NEA) that covered "all kinds of reading," including reading done online. The decline was especially pronounced among older teens and young adults, and as of 2005, scarcely more than a third of high school seniors read at or above the proficient level.

NEA chairman Dana Gioia called the data "alarming." The study did not say why reading had declined, but Gioia pointed to what the *New York Times* called "the proliferation of digital diversions on the Internet and other gadgets." Think smartphones, iPhones, iPods, iPlayers, and video games.

The Internet, Gioia told the *Washington Post,* "is the most powerful informational tool ever developed by humanity, except perhaps the phonetic alphabet. But it doesn't seem to nourish the sustained, linear attention" that good old-fashioned print media do. In fact, online use may have already surpassed even television in shortening attention spans, given that its users troll mostly for wee nibblets of information.

"There are more students who struggle with the ability to focus than there were 30 years ago," a high school English teacher said in the PBS *Frontline* documentary "Growing Up Online" in 2008. "They are so overexposed to the quickness of things and the immediate responses. It's just all at their fingertips. So when you have to reverse that and have them be quiet and give answers and carve out meaning, I think it's difficult for a lot of students."

One of these teen students had this to say in the documentary: "I can't remember the last time I read a book. Nowadays people are so busy that they need to get summaries of it like SparkNotes [a Web-styled knockoff of Cliffs Notes]. You can go on, it's a legitimate source (and) it pays enough attention to detail that you can get the assignment right and you can read the whole book in a matter of pages. So when it comes to reading, I read all online. I actually never read, like, *Romeo and Juliet* till I read it yesterday in five minutes."

In a *Los Angeles Times* story about publishing, a bookseller recalled being told by a browser in his shop that he wasn't really interested in books because "they're too slow a form of delivery." In other words, *Very nice prose, very nice dialogue, Mr. Dostoevsky, but please speed it up a little.*

And if not online, perhaps on cellular.

The latest literary boom in Japan is just that—cell phone novels composed on tiny keypads in ticlike short sentences characteristic of text messages, minus components like the plot and character development—*borrrrring*—found in traditional novels. They're aimed at a younger crowd that welcomes tiny stories with tiny themes that appear on tiny screens.

Whether cell phone novels represent Japanese literature's new dawn or its decline is in the eye of the beholder. A wild guess: the latter? However, it's worth noting that Japan's top-selling novel in 2007 was first speed-tapped on a cell phone and then republished in book form, according to the *New York Times,* which quoted one such author as saying conventional novels don't appeal to her and her young peers. "They don't read works by professional writers because their sentences are too difficult to understand, their expressions are intentionally wordy, and the stories are not familiar to them."

Yes, keep it simple, keep it snappy. Here, as provided by a teenager with a gift for cell phone gab, for example, is how the two preceding paragraphs would read in cell phone text:

omg did u hear? l8est in japan . . . novels 4 cell phones w/text msging . . . no plot or char dvlpmnt! its 4 yger ppl who wanna read tny stories with tny themes on tny screens. lol!

could b good, could b bad. Wld guess, latter . . . did u no japans top-selling novel in 07 wuz typed on a cell b4 being put in2 book form? ny times said 1 author said she n yg ppl don't like regulr novels cuz the sentences r 2 hard, 2 wordy n the stories suck.

And omg (oh my God), no one is snappier than star Fox News Channel anchor Smith who, according to one count, often belts out 50 stories an hour.

In accordance with that, new media are producing and nourishing a Google generation of information consumers—those who want news fast, so that they can receive it without breaking stride the way a marathon runner grabs a cup of water on the run. And hitting the refresh button won't change the way these people think.

Loyola Law School professor Laurie Levinson knows the feeling. A former federal prosecutor, Levinson is frequently asked by the Los Angeles media to comment on court cases and other issues related to the judiciary. And asked by radio and TV to do it fast. "People know that the world is looking over their shoulder because there is such a quick dissemination of information," she says.

But isn't she part of that process? "Oh, yeah. But it makes me extraordinarily nervous, primarily because the last thing the media want to hear is someone like me say what I often say, which is, 'I don't know' or 'it depends.' With 24-hour news coverage, everyone wants the latest angle. Whether or not it's right, seems irrelevant. They just want the gut answer."

Or the gut anything. Security was tight around the publication of Alastair Campbell's memoir *The Blair Years,* with media getting no advance access. "Twelve minutes after it went to shops," says Campbell, who was Tony Blair's official spokesman from 1994 to 2003, "some guy on one of our TV stations said, 'There's nothing new in this book.' A book that was nearly 800 pages, and

12 minutes to discover there's nothing in it? That's the kind of endless chatter factory where journalists don't have the desire to check. There's a slogan about (Rupert Murdoch's) Sky News: 'Not wrong for long.'"

These excesses aside, there is nothing intrinsically bad about speed.

As for the speeding up of news cycles, "I consider it mostly to be a panacea," says Andrew Breitbart, who operates his own website while helping run the *Drudge Report* from Los Angeles. "The only people who are complaining about it are the people in newsrooms whose jobs are dependent on it." Breitbart finds it "great" that the Internet has become such a force in news and information and that a vast array of blogs is now competing with traditional news organizations.

"I think the word *revolution* is justified," says news historian Stephens. "This is the most profound change we've seen in journalism since the invention of the printing press. Certainly never in my lifetime, and not in centuries, have I seen such a dramatic change in the way people get their information, with such dramatic consequences for the news organizations from which they get their information. And we're right smack dab in the middle of it. It's going to get worse for traditional media; it's going to get better for new media, clearly. And it's going to continue to reshape our lives to a large extent, and our politics to a large extent."

No one disputes that. It's the nature of the impact that's in question.

Some years ago, British critic Malcolm Muggeridge created the term *Newzak* to describe the drone, the constant buzz of omnipresent media in which one news source can't be distinguished from another. But that noise is many decibels louder today, thanks to the explosion and growing crescendo of media voices.

This torrential cascade of news and nonnews, of fact and faux, of punditry and posturing, is staged in a way that appears to demand from us a response while giving us nothing that empowers us to respond.

Comments PBS journalist/commentator Moyers, "I do sense information coming at me from all sources with no filter. They— whoever they are—keep adding to the rush without adding to the number of hours in the day. And it does seem that one journalistic exposé happens after another but no one has the attention span to act on them. So more information doesn't seem to equal reform."

Media writer Howard Kurtz talks about the "digestible chunks" on today's menu of fast-food news and its impact at his paper, the *Washington Post*. He adds, "The pace has gotten dizzying for me and my colleagues, just in the last few years. You know, everybody wants it now-now-now. And that's understandable in a wired world, but the sacrifice clearly is in the extra phone calls and the chance to briefly reflect on the story that you're slapping together."

For example . . .

"I often laugh," Kurtz says, "when I see some cable reporter standing in a live location, doing live shots all day, and then the anchor says, 'So what's been the reaction?' I would just want to say, 'How would I know? I've been standing here talking to you for the last hour.'"

The problem for cable news reporters, NBC correspondent Pete Williams feels, is there's little time for "reporting" between live shots. "God help you should you get out of your office and go ask someone something. The best you can hope for is to get in a few phone calls between live shots or you hope that there's someone working with you who can be out pounding the hallways to get you information. That is a constant problem for cable folks. But all broadcasters face the same issue at some point. When the networks go wall-to-wall coverage, like we did the first time during 9/11, you have that same problem. You're stuck in a live shot, and if you're outdoors in a live shot, then you're really in bad shape because all you can do is pick up your cell phone and hope you can find someone. It's not a new problem. Radio folks faced that as well, before television. The problem is, it used to come up just once in a while, but now it's constant."

Flash back to the night of December 12, 2000, the evening that Toobin wrote about in his book, when the U.S. Supreme Court issued its historic ruling on Bush vs. Gore. "We were handed 65 pages without benefit of any preliminary indication of what even the justices themselves had voted," Bierbauer recalls. "We had to sort of parse that as we went through it. But the pressure was such that if you said, 'Well (news anchor) Bernie (Shaw), give me 30 minutes to read this,' everybody would have been clicking channels to see what Pete Williams had to say on NBC."

And the pressure on 24-hour news reporters is much greater now than it was in Bierbauer's day. "There are so many avenues where we put our journalism—radio, TV, podcasts, and blogs—(that) what suffers is reporting," CNN veteran Candy Crowley told a Flagler College audience in St. Augustine, Florida. "You almost don't have time to figure it (a story) out before you're on the air with it."

What's more, televising events as they occur also nourishes collusion between news media and newsmakers, something that hardly benefits the public. This unhealthy union of agenda finds the traditional editing function of news programs cast aside in favor of meandering news conferences and various TV-tailored events that are covered live, usually for the wrong reasons.

Here's how this mutual embrace works. The all-news channels receive programming they can stretch across hours of airtime in exchange for allowing newsmakers to address their target audience unedited and unfiltered by professional journalists. All-news channels appear less interested in imparting useful information to ordinary viewers than in filling gaping potholes in their schedules.

But didn't such wire services as the Associated Press and United Press International face the same pressure in the old days?

"But here's what changed," says former journalist Nessen. "On cable television you've got 24 hours a day, 60 minutes an hour to fill up, and there isn't that much news. So what do you fill it up with? You fill it up with the correspondent on the scene and the anchorman having this conversation. And the anchorman says, 'What is going on down there. How does the situation feel? How do you predict this is gonna come out? What's your reaction to what so-and-so just said?' It's chitchat in which the reporter tells what he thinks, how he feels, what his reaction is, and so forth."

No wonder that well-crafted stories, with clearly defined beginnings and endings, may now be one of TV's most endangered species. A 2003 survey by the Washington-based Project for Excellence in Journalism found that 62 percent of stories on all-news channels were presented live (either in interviews or reporter stand-ups), downsizing the role of the reporter as a thoughtfully observant middle person connecting the event for the audience. Given the tenor of today's media, that percentage has surely increased, resulting in even more news gathering in the raw.

This goes as well for distortion through replication, for the same survey reported that round-the-clock news channels succumb to the pressure of filling their news holes by repeating themselves 68 percent of the time. They recap their recaps. They cling to breaking news that isn't breaking. They distend the bellies of stories, grafting on thick layers of fat to disguise their anorexia.

It's a kind of popular theater that permeates the culture, something that all-news channels call "feeding the beast," a beast so ravenous that one can almost hear CNN, the Fox News Channel, and MSNBC belch at the end of each 24-hour news cycle.

Abetted by talk radio and the Internet, it's the belch heard around the country, if not the world, as former Democratic presidential candidate Howard Dean learned to his dismay after he addressed supporters following his disappointing third-place finish in the 2004 Iowa Caucuses. Dean's televised concession—an emotional *Yee-ha!* call to arms dubbed the "I Have a Scream Speech"— swiftly gained cultlike status on 24-hour news and the Internet. The Associated Press took a count and found that it was replayed 633 times on national broadcast and cable news programs in the next four days.

The cumulative impact—Dean's 23-second clip was shown out of context, mostly omitting the screaming, hooting crowd he was speaking and reacting to—made him sound like the unstable madman that he wasn't, an act of media recklessness that added to his problems as a candidate.

Even the most inane nonnews stories can take on lives of their own once they've been inflated and repeated again and again in the echo chambers of 24-hour news channels, talk radio, and the Internet.

Try this not-so-farfetched scenario:

It begins at 8 A.M. with a Fox News Alert!
Anchor: "This information coming in fast and furious."

Two minutes later, CNN and Headline News run identical headlines: "Gastric Calamity!" A minute later comes MSNBC: "Belching and Bloating Blues!"

All three have the same story: Unconfirmed reports are circulating that George Walker Bush, the 43rd president of the United States, has been sidelined by severe gas.

At 8:11, bannering the headline "Cheney in Charge?" the Drudge Report runs a story speculating that the president may be incapacitated. By 9:00 the three all-news channels have had reporters on the White House lawn doing stand-ups about Bush's rumored gas. Experts are quoted: "Flatulence, also known as farting," one says, "is the act of passing intestinal gas from the anus." The word "allegedly" is used.

A half hour later, countless bloggers have weighed in on the president's gas, with fart.com demanding an investigation. No longer treated as a rumor, it assumes the aura of fact.

At 10:00, Fox News convenes a special edition of its Beltway Boys with Morton Krondracke and Fred Barnes, who reports grimly, "Here's what's on the inside track today."

Fifteen minutes later, CNN brings in Wolf Blitzer early, to moderate a panel of experts on flatulence and its global implications, during which a crawl on the screen reports that Britney Spears has "found Jesus."

It's noon, and by now grainy "caught on tape" pictures are surfacing, appearing to show Bush on the toilet, grimacing. And on radio, Rush Limbaugh and Sean Hannity have attributed the president's gas to a liberal conspiracy.

Despite what MSNBC's Keith Olberman calls "suspicious" White House denials, the story winds its way toward evening, where it makes the flagship newscasts of ABC, CBS, and NBC, gets a going over by Chris Matthews on MSNBC's Hardball, and on CNN is linked to "our loose borders" by immigration hardliner Lou Dobbs.

On Fox, Bill O'Reilly delivers a stinging rebuke of "gaseous pinheads." On CNN Larry King and a blue ribbon panel—a defense lawyer, a tabloid reporter, a psychic, a body-language expert, and CNN house fanatic Nancy Grace—weigh rumors that Bush's gas is connected to the unsolved murder of JonBenét Ramsey.

Later, CNN's Anderson Cooper will ask viewers to take part in the evening's instant poll: "Do you think gas should disqualify a president from serving?"

And on and on the story speeds through the evening, with newspapers updating their webpages with the story to avoid being left behind, and Jay Leno and David Letterman mocking it in their "Fartgate" monologues.

Bush's gas is written in stone for the ages by the time America hits the sack that evening only to learn in the morning that the story is false. No gas, no conspiracy.

Are those who burped up this fantasy embarrassed? Not in the least, for they have achieved what they set out to do, to hell with the consequences. They have filled space and filled time, the phoniness of it all not mattering to them.

That evening, King convenes a panel of media types, as he usually does after high-profile journalistic debacles, and asks: "Did we go too far?" And the panelists will stroke their chins thoughtfully and agree that, yes, perhaps the media did go too far this time.

After which these amnesiacs will go home, get a good night's sleep, and do the same thing again.

The new media, Brokaw observes, are "both a blessing and a curse because of the range of information that you can now get with just a keystroke. But the downside, the consequence is that just pushes everybody, both the journalists and the consumers, the viewers, the readers of information, to make snap decisions, to not connect the dots, to very seldom see what's happening in a contextual basis."

What's more, the Internet has transformed not only news media, but also the newsmaker. The extreme speed of the Internet and 24-hour news—as well as their frequent reckless, freewheeling nature and willingness to report anything, true or not, confirmed or not—inevitably alters the behavior of those they cover. Their subjects develop siege mentalities and feel they have to move faster and faster and make decisions faster and faster to avoid being drubbed by media tormentors. And in fact, they do.

Amen, veteran London political operative Ceri Evans would surely echo about media on his side of the Atlantic. "People who enter politics should, for the most part, be given the benefit of the doubt that they actually want to do it to make a difference," says Evans, former communications chief for the chairman of the Blair government's Strategic Rail Authority. "Sometimes, as we know, when you're making a difference on complex issues, you're going to get things wrong, you're going to be blown off course. And when that happens now, with 24-hour news, you're not allowed to make a mistake. You're not allowed to be blown off course. You're not allowed to have a rethink because of any of those things is regarded as a failure."

Evans says UK politicians and their staffs traditionally turn the other cheek but long ago should have demanded, "Enough is enough!" But they haven't, he says, partly because of tradition, partly because of fear they wouldn't be able to get their message out if they stiff-armed the press. "What happens is they think, well, we're going to need some reaction to that in time for the lunchtime bulletin or in time for the evening bulletin or let's make sure that we catch the early edition of tomorrow's *Telegraph* or tomorrow's *Guardian*. And what I would like to say is, Why? Why? Find other ways to talk to people."

Just what those ways are is yet to be determined in the U.S. as well as the UK, and the emergence of instant communications as a pressurizing influence worsens the dilemma. It didn't used to be this way.

Today's realignment of the media cosmos has Hodding Carter recalling when he was U.S. State Department spokesman during the Iran Hostage Crisis in 1979–81. "I look at the simple stuff with which we wrestled, cameras showing the same mob marching in the same constricted circle around the former embassy [in Tehran]," he says, referring to the daily media events staged by militant Iranians. "And you know, we had no more business responding to them than to the man in the moon. And yet, there I was, out there doing it every day, playing earnest responder to the terrible thing—which was, of course, utterly unchanged day in and day out."

The pressure to respond would be still greater today," Carter says, "because the present media rules of the game destroy the ability of government to move at all rationally."

One reason? Rationality appears to be incompatible with new media's attention deficit disorder. Marash, a frequent Internet user himself, says, "the overwhelming proportion of information [the Internet offers] is as drastically encapsulated as what has become conventional news coverage. That is to say, you rarely see podcasts or reports for video that are more than two minutes in length.

"On the other hand," he adds, "you could also rightly argue that the Internet has a wealth of extensive material filled with detail and nuance, and that you can use the Internet to obtain greater detail and depth of information than ever before in history."

So Charles Dickens had it right, says Marash: "It is the best of times and the worst of times."

Two Revolutions:
French and Mexican

Our invention can perhaps be exploited for a certain time as a scientific curiosity, but it has no commercial future.
—Auguste Lumière in 1895, describing the motion picture projector

Innovation in mass communication has always gone hand in hand with speed. And in one instance, specially trained pigeons.

In 1850, Paul Julius Reuter used them to fly news and stock prices from Germany to Belgium in just four hours, undercutting delivery of such stories and related data by the railroad, which took six hours to cover the same distance.

Across the Atlantic, increasing news-delivery speed was as much a goal in the still-callow United States as in Europe. That was achieved with great flourish when Western Union finished the first transcontinental telegraph line across North America in 1861.

Nor did television's omnipresent 24-hour news cycle surface in a vacuum. Ted Turner's Atlanta revolution, which redefined and sped up news dramatically, would not have been possible without the French and Mexican revolutions. Of course, this French revolution was not bloodied by the guillotine, and this Mexican revolution did not star Pancho Villa.

Regardless, what do French and Mexican revolutions have to do with the blazing speed of today's communications, to say nothing of 24-hour hair-triggers and breaking news that hasn't broken? The French answer lies in the closing years of the 19th century and, to be more specific, the Lumière.

Some may be surprised to learn that Lumière Brothers was not the name of a cough drop. On the contrary, in 1895 brothers Auguste and Louis Lumière made history in France (you see, this whole communications-speed thing is really the fault of the French) by doing something that had not been done before . . . ever!

The brothers shot the world's first news film, and then showed it to an invited audience two days later.

The "news event" captured by the Lumières was nothing for them to write home to Lyon about. Nor did what they shot—the annual holiday trip of the Congress of the National Union of French Photographic Societies—qualify for the front page or perhaps any page of *Le Figaro* or *Le Temps*. But it did have the dubious dual distinction of being not only the first news event covered on film, but also the first filmed news event all but forgotten in the swirl of time.

Three months later, the Lumières filmed another event that historians generally agree kicked off the age of cinema. This time the Lumières' subjects were their own workers. Imagine how groundbreaking, how breathtaking: Moving pictures of hundreds of Lumière employees (along with at least one dog and a horse) doing something they were extremely pleased to do, something they did every day, routinely. But now, for the first time, they were doing it for a camera lens and all the world (or at least a tiny part of it) to see, for what the Lumières had achieved so historically that day was capture these workers and their animals, yes . . . leaving the building!

This is not regarded as the first filmed "news" footage, however, because even then workers pouring out of a building at workday's end apparently seemed much less newsworthy than shutterbugs frolicking on holiday.

And in today's newspeak as well, the holiday excursion would be likelier than plant workers to earn "team coverage," a titillating "BREAKING NEWS!" headline and gratuitous live shots in the dark of night with a reporter announcing, "It was at this location just eight hours ago that members of the photographic society embarked on their journey."

So it was the holiday trip footage that opened the age of newsreels that led to television news as we know it today. By 1911, Charles Pathé had inaugurated the first weekly silent newsreel in Europe, as high-tech advances in both transportation and film greatly slashed the time between a news event being filmed and developed and then shown to gathered onlookers.

Audiences still had plenty of time to think about and digest the news they were viewing, but this luxury wouldn't last long, as the frequency and sheer numbers of newsreels increased dramatically in just a few short years.

Speed was as much a driving impulse in the past as now. There must have been something about the way humans were hard wired even then that drove them to seek news at an increasingly faster pace. The filmed weekly newsreel was just three years old in 1914 when Pathé sought to speed things up by offering a daily one. What made this possible was the use of what came to be called "safety film," which, unlike film made from nitrate, was nonflammable. That meant daily newsreels could be dispatched through the mail while the news itself was hot, without anyone worrying that the film stock would be, too.

This daily newsreel service was short lived, though. World War I, while fueling a global appetite for speedier news, made it too dangerous if not impossible, to ship newsreels globally on a daily basis. This setback for daily newsreels turned out to be historical, too, marking perhaps the last time delivery of news actually slowed. In fact, only weekly newsreels would come through the Great War unscathed.

The newsreel was gaining popularity and influence, though. As early as 1914, one newsreel company had almost 40 cameramen in the U.S. alone and operated out of 60 offices in Europe and the United States. The industry's size and competitive fervor—though not as intense as action on the Western Front—were growing. And by the time they found their voice in 1926 with the addition of sound, weekly newsreels were being produced by five big movie companies: Paramount, Fox Movietone, Universal, Warner-Pathé, and Hearst Metrotone.

Who could have guessed that the fate of these newsreels would be tied, in a tragic way, to global calamity?

The year was 1929, the historic tragedy to be known as the Great Depression, which most historians agree was touched off in the United States by the October 29 stock market crash. Overvalued stocks, often bought on credit, had started a precipitous decline in September that extended well into October. Those who bought on credit saw their stock investments collapse, and had no money to repay the lenders who gave them the money to buy in the first place. And so, near the end of that month, the market dove catastrophically, taking the nation's optimism down with it.

Naturally that received bold banner headlines. Just three days into these tumultuous happenings, however, a seemingly insignificant event took place that attracted little notice. With their lives falling apart, with their futures instantly wiped out, with their world in panic and chaos, why *would* so many New Yorkers pay attention to the new attraction at an elegant, ornately appointed, high-toned movie house on the ground floor of an office building? Only it wasn't Gloria Swanson or Charlie Chaplin's Little Tramp who lit the marquee on November 2, 1929, at the Embassy Theatre at 1560 Broadway in Manhattan; it was news.

The 544-seat Embassy had become the nation's—surely the planet's—first theater showing newsreels and nothing but newsreels, and showing them all the time. Without the usual out-of-town tryout in Chicago or Boston, all-news had proceeded straight to Broadway.

It was (depending on one's opinion of cable's 24-hour news) a date that would live in either nobility or infamy, one that would foreshadow the epic all-news radio and television transformation of decades later. Included on the Embassy's first newsreel bill, at 25 cents a pop, was sound film of tired, unshaven wife murderer William E. Peters slowly confessing to Philadelphia police. And there, too, was young Prince Umberto of Italy surviving an assassination attempt in a Brussels street, and footage of a crowd pouncing on the anti-Fascist shooter.

So popular was this Embassy Theatre experiment, so packed with newsreel patrons was this converted movie house, that scores more would be established throughout the United States, even though the financial crisis had spread like a raging infection.

This was the Depression, after all, and only a relatively well-heeled news junkie could scrape together the change for a ticket to these continuously running 45-minute shows that bundled a week's worth of competing newsreels from the five major newsreel companies.

But what these consumers received for their two bits, virtually 24/7, was quite extraordinary for the times. Never before had images and sounds of distant places and foreign intrigues been available so quickly—weeks, if not days, after being filmed. Year after year, through the early 1930s and 1940s, on came these flickering images showing the world's greatest achievements as well as its massive failures, often in new movie houses built with newsreels in mind.

One of the most extravagant was Detroit's streamlined Telenews Theatre, which opened in 1942 as part of a national chain. As the Cinema Treasures website describes the opulent 465-seat theater,

> The main feature of The Telenews was the large glass globe above the vertical marquee which advertised the fact this was a newsreel cinema. The façade was decorated in bright blue and orange terra cotta, separated by bands of glass blocks, which made for a bold and very modern looking building at the time.
>
> In the basement, a radio station once broadcast behind large windows from behind which people could sit on benches and watch the news being read live. In the lobby, a teletype machine clicked away, giving patrons up to the minute news.

The all-newsreel-all-the-time movie theater proved so success-ful as a business concept that by the late 1930s several other companies had established chains of theaters showing only news and information. Nor was this just an American phenomenon. Brits loved it, too, and by 1940 there were more newsreel theaters in London than in all the United States.

Throughout World War II, newsreel movie theaters had stood ready around the clock to add sight to the sounds of the conflict that rapt listeners were hearing on their radios. However, the war's end also signaled the beginning of the end for newsreels.

They had not been without controversy, and some were accused of an antilabor bias in their coverage of labor-management disputes that surfaced in the early postwar period. An even greater threat were the mahogany boxes with tiny screens that began showing up in homes increasingly after the war, transfixing Americans and gradually addicting them to the rudimentary black and white pictures that were now so easily accessible.

It wasn't long before the nascent alternative—this much-speedier thing called TV news—had rendered newsreels and newsreel theaters obsolete. The economy was booming, consumers energized, TV sets plentiful. Why bother leaving home and buying a ticket to get video news that was now available in your living room, more current and at no cost?

When the last newsreel was shown on December 26, 1967, with big-voiced announcer Ed Herlihy doing the farewell honors, some 72 years had passed since Auguste and Louis Lumière had created that first news film of vacationing French photographers at play and snapping photos of each other. Public expectations had been raised, and the race to deliver news at greater speed was again heating up.

○ ○ ○

That was how it went in France. But flashing back to the Mexican revolution first requires a side trip to Texas. The town was Paris, some 100 miles northeast of Dallas–Fort Worth. The year was 1921, the date was June 8, the event was the birth of Gordon Barton McLendon.

Following his early formative years, McClendon went to Yale University, he went off to World War II, he went to Harvard Law School, and then, most crucially, he went to Palestine. No, not in the Middle East; he went to Palestine, Texas, where in 1946 he bought into a small radio station and, simultaneously, bought his way into the history books.

As the father of 24-hour news. Well, at least the stepfather.

McLendon was an innovative radio pioneer and visionary who performed magic with radio formats. By the 1950s he had acquired numerous radio stations across the U.S. and was considered a frontiersman in the development of what came to be called format radio. He also is credited with creating in Dallas one of the nation's first "Top 40" stations; it endlessly played the 40 hottest singles each day, in effect putting disc jockeys on something like automatic pilot. It was McLendon, too, says the Radio Hall of Fame, who created the "beautiful music" format, at a San Francisco station in 1959.

Soon, he would widen his broadcast repertoire. As a student of radio and its eclectic maze of formats, he must have known that another San Francisco station, with the KFAX call letters, had introduced the nation's first all-news format in 1960. He was also aware, surely, that the growing popularity and availability of FM broadcasts and receivers—with their cleaner high-fidelity sound—would render many AM radio station formats obsolete. Why listen to music with static when you can listen to music that sounded like . . . well, like music?

AM radio, as the common wisdom went, was better suited to the spoken word than to the music revolutions in pop and rock that were sweeping the United States. Logically, then, what better format for an AM station like KFAX than news radio?

Its format was certainly unique: 25 minutes of news every hour on the hour, 15 minutes of news on the half hour. The rest of the time? Informational filler.

Nice plan. However, KFAX did not attract enough listeners to propel it to profitable elite status on the city's radio charts. As a result, in barely more than six months the station wound up in the red to the tune of a $250,000. Many sponsors had left and many more hadn't bothered to sign up in the first place, making the format a commercial flop. Before the year was out, KFAX was broadcasting music, and all-news radio was dead.

Or was it?

Enter Gordon McLendon.

His radio empire growing, McLendon did not lack for confidence as he sought new formats to transfer to his AM radio stations. He liked to think he could do radio better than anyone, and had the track record to back that claim up. Thus, it wasn't surprising that he would regard KFAX's failure as a challenge, not as a sign that all-news was a format to avoid.

So it is no wonder that on May 6, 1961, McClendon launched an all-news format at a station he controlled in Mexico just south of the U.S. border. The station and its new identity were good to go, all right. He had changed its call letters to XTRA (as in *Extra! Extra! Read all about it!*) and given it a snappy slogan (*All the news, all the time. The world at your fingertips.*) as part of a catchy promotional campaign aimed at Southern California.

XTRA was a "border blaster" whose strong signal reached vast portions of that region, including San Diego and Los Angeles, while having the advantage of being immune to restrictions placed on radio stations by the U.S. Federal Communications Commission.

All the news, all the time took off, putting more profits at McLendon's fingertips.

Of course, XTRA was much more than KFAX south of the border. Unlike the San Francisco station's failed experiment, XTRA was formatted on the assumption that listeners would "turn over" regularly, dipping in and out as the day progressed instead of remaining nonstop with an all-news format. No long-form programming for XTRA. In the manner of the Bill Murray film *Groundhog Day,* the day's most important news was played and replayed every few minutes. This allowed a listener to tune in anytime and get headlines, weather, and sports.

McLendon had his template, and by 1964 was so confident in his all-news philosophy that he converted his Chicago station to that format, changing its call letters to WNUS. A year later, WINS in New York City and KYW in Philadelphia joined the party, and in 1968 all-news radio also opened for business at KFWB in Los Angeles, as all across the United States, stations began falling like dominoes to the appeal of this format.

Yet was there a market for all-news radio on a national scale? Did the entire nation need to know, as a single unit, what was happening as it happened?

In a bold move, NBC sought to find out when it created the NBC News and Information Service (NIS) in 1975. NBC got its answer swiftly. The market was there, all right, but NBC also learned that an all-news national radio network ran up intolerable costs while placing an enormous burden on its news correspondents, who were not used to the second-by-second deadlines imposed on them by all-news radio. After two years, NIS shut down.

The stage had been set, though, for a wealthy America's Cup winner in Atlanta to make a 30-second telephone call to New York that, for better or for worse, would revolutionize not just how the United States but the entire planet would receive news—and at what highly accelerated speed.

The 39-year-old maverick yachtsman was Ted Turner, and the call he made was to a 47-year-old journalist who was as much of a visionary and independent thinker as he and relished his reputation as an outsider. Reese Schonfeld was a crusty but brilliant TV newsman with a dream. He had already created the Independent Television News Association (ITNA), a nonprofit syndication service that for years supplied low-cost news coverage to nonnetwork stations that didn't have at their disposal the fully financed news divisions that network stations enjoyed.

But Schonfeld wanted something more. Following in the steps of the groundbreaking Lumière brothers and McLendon, he aimed—he ached—to create the first all-news television network.

Oh, sure, all-news TV. And who would watch this . . . *news*? Shut-ins? Eggheads? A handful of news fanatics? And why, exactly, was it needed? Giant broadcast networks ABC, CBS, and NBC produced nightly 30-minute newscasts and weekday morning shows, and therefore had national and global TV news largely to themselves. And the networks—this club of corporate elites—wanted to keep it that way.

Nonetheless, Schonfeld pitched his idea to every network TV news executive who would listen. And damned if they didn't listen. Then they all said no.

So it was perfect timing for Turner to make his call. Hardly a full-time yachtsman, he was in the television business himself as owner of WTBS, a nonnetwork Atlanta station that had made history of its own. It had been the first station to utilize new satellite technology to beam a station's programs (mostly antique, dustbin network reruns) to cable television viewers nationwide.

Turner knew of Schonfeld's all-news cable channel dream. Who didn't know of it, given how aggressively and widely Schonfeld had pushed the idea? Turner also liked it, and had the money, guts, and—some would argue—insanity to pull it off.

Which was why he made the 1978 call to Schonfeld that, according to several sources, went something like this:

> *Turner:* I'm thinking about doing 24 hours of news for cable. Can it be done?
>
> *Schonfeld:* Yes!
>
> *Turner [coyly, though surely knowing what the answer would be]:* Do you want to do it?
>
> *Schonfeld:* Yes.

Just like that, egg and sperm had found one another. From this union would come the Cable News Network, which arrived on June 1, 1980. And the rest is history—some exhilarating, some of it downright bad.

Part of that history was the race to catch up with the early leader.

CNN lacked the money, high-priced talent, and production values of the three broadcast network news divisions, but its potential was apparent almost from its inception.

Two years after CNN's launch, ABC joined with Westinghouse Broadcasting to create the Satellite News Channel (SNC) on cable. No novice in this area, Westinghouse already owned WINS, an all-news radio station in New York.

But in SNC, the ABC and Westinghouse broadcasting giants were establishing a Yankee version of CNN that was based in Stamford, Connecticut, far from the Atlanta headquarters of its older archrival.

Another civil war had begun. But a brief one, for less than a year later, SNC was out of business—bought out and shut down by Turner, who added its slim subscriber list to CNN. This time Atlanta didn't fall to the Yanks, the Yanks fell to Atlanta.

The traditional Western wire services—the Associated Press, Reuters, and United Press International—serviced newspapers, television and radio. In contrast, CNN immediately established its brand as the *viewers'* wire service. There was no middle person or filter; news—or at least whatever CNN defined as news—went nonstop, directly to the consumer. And when it came to velocity, instantaneous CNN left even the speed-driven traditional wire services in the dust.

Looking back at CNN's genesis, Schonfeld says today that he underestimated how much faster CNN would push the speed of communications, most notably in terms of drastically truncating the news cycle. "The idea was to move it up a half cycle, a half day ahead [so that] you'd see the same news in your newspaper on CNN. Now, it's much faster than that!"

This all came at a cost, as the aftershocks of CNN's speed mentality continue to reverberate and rock the newsgathering landscape all across the globe even today, from small journalistic venues to large.

Tom Brokaw, a White House correspondent for NBC before becoming its superstar evening news anchor, recalls wistfully those earlier days of the 1970s when he'd have the luxury of stretching out the process of contacting sources for a story that would not appear until the next morning on NBC's *Today* program. He'd also have much of the day, if needed, to gather material and prepare his report for the evening newscast. "Now," says Brokaw, *Meet the Press* moderator, "our correspondents don't have that time."

What began with CNN, meanwhile, has now expanded into a lively cable-news throng that includes NBC-operated MSNBC and Rupert Murdoch's Fox News Channel in the U.S. and his Sky News in Great Britain. All-news players are far flung and also include Istanbul-based CNNTurk and Arabic Al Jazeera and Al Arabiya.

All of which may seem a long way from the revolutionary Lumière brothers and McLendon, but not when we connect the dots. What drove them—as it does their new-media progeny on the Internet as well as cable—is perfectly captured in a line spoken by Tom Cruise's hotshot pilot in the movie *Top Gun:*

"I feel the need for speed."

Our expectations shaped by media, don't we all feel that need intensely, even narcotically? Don't we require a speed fix increasingly and depend on this generation's new media to shoot us up? In union with that is the imposing challenge that cable's 24-hour daredevils faced from the start in filling news holes that seemingly could not be filled, and certainly not by going faster and faster.

But the extraordinary manner in which they tried to it would turn out to be as revolutionary as the technology responsible for their very existence.

CHAPTER 3

All the News before
It Happens

May a love-starved fruit fly molest your sister's nectarines.
—Johnny Carson, as the all-knowing, farseeing Carnac the
Magnificent on *The Tonight Show*

It's the morning of December 27, 2007, several hours after the assassination of former Pakistani Prime Minister Benazir Bhutto, and across the media moonscape serious journalism is breaking out. How serious? This serious:

"If you are Secretary of State Condaleeza Rice and President Bush," CNN anchor Heidi Collins asks White House correspondent Ed Henry, "when you get the news about Benazir Bhutto, what would you be thinking?"

Yes, Ed, read their minds; climb inside their heads and tell us what's there.

And yes, crank up the speculation and roll that tape, again and again and again, so you and the media's other esteemed chin strokers can mass in front of the camera and apply your pop psychology and guesswork to world events as sportswriters and sportscasters do to the World Series and the Super Bowl.

Is that news?

Or this? It's the evening of January 30, 2008, right after a CNN/Politico/*Los Angeles Times*–sponsored debate with the remaining GOP presidential candidates at the Ronald Reagan Presidential Library in Simi Valley, California. On CNN, Anderson Cooper, Gloria Borger, Roland Martin, Bill Bennett, and John King—the self-proclaimed "best political team on television"—are analyzing the debate. Well, not quite, really. Actually, what they are doing is playing the strategy game, the consultant game, giving their sage views on what each of the candidates needs to do to gain an edge or win, as if they were the candidates' paid advisers.

Is that news?

Or this? It's the evening of January 31, 2008, six minutes *before* a CNN/Politico/*Los Angeles Times*–sponsored debate with Democratic presidential candidates Senator Hillary Clinton and Senator Barack Obama at the Kodak Theatre in Hollywood, California. On CNN, Kitty Pilgrim, subbing for news anchor Lou Dobbs, is asking her two guests, "Is this a turning point?"

And three minutes *before* the debate, Wolf Blitzer is commanding reporter Candy Crowley to "tell our viewers what they can expect tonight."

All of them are analyzing an event—applying all of their great tarot-card wisdom, expertise, and clairvoyance to it—*before* it occurs.

Is that news?

Or this? It's February 13, 2008, shortly after major league baseball pitching great Roger Clemens has testified under oath before the House Committee on Oversight and Government Reform, repeating his strong denials that his former trainer, Brian McNamee, had years earlier injected him with steroids and human growth hormone, despite McNamee presenting blood-stained gauze and syringes as alleged evidence.

Fox News Channel anchor Shephard Smith—giving his best impression of a rocket starting to lift off—is livid, almost shouting:

> I've just spoken with not one but three legal experts within this
> building with whom I would trust with the lives of my families,

and these legal experts say, Are you *kidding* me? Gauze and needles alleged to have come from five years ago? With no information about chain of custody, absolutely nothing? What judge is going to admit that in a court of law? The truth is, we're not in a court of law. There are no criminal accusations, there can be none, for the statute of limitations for the use of a prescription drug without a prescription expired long ago. And today the United States congress—which says it's on top of the economy, it's on top of the war, it's on top of the mess that either is or is not a recession—spends its time with this. And at the same time, Senator Arlen Spector of Philadelphia is bringing before his esteemed committee the commissioner of the National Football League to talk about some VHS tapes made by [coach Bill] Belichick and his staff for the New England Patriots. We think we got problems in the nation. "Congress—how ya doin'?"

This is more than not news, dudes, it's *way* not news. In fact, it's soapbox commentary—more precisely, a tirade. And of course, to give Smith his due, he had a point. The hearing was rather futile, despite CNN and the Fox News Channel deciding to air it live in its whopping four-hour, eyelid-closing completeness, surely because it helped fill their gaping news holes; even committee chairman Henry Waxman said later he regretted holding it, as much as admitting that the hearing exposed Capitol Hill's public servants at their partisan, pedestrian worst.

But Shep—how ya doin'?

Since when is it the proper role of a news anchor to deliver an emotional lecture on camera to the viewing minions? Since late in the 20th century, unfortunately—perhaps most egregiously these days at NBC-run MSNBC, which still badly trails Fox and CNN in viewers despite dramatically increasing its weekday prime-time audience.

Some NBC reporters who appear on MSNBC have concerns about its almost-anything-goes atmosphere, as Phil Griffin, NBC News senior vice president in charge of the cable channel, acknowledged to the *Los Angeles Times* in 2008. What Griffin called "'liveliness and richness'" in the MSNBC news product was clearly a euphemism for strong, in-your-face, kick-butt opinion. But he added that "'people feel more comfortable with the crossover'" than ever before.

This is the great danger, for if defining opinion as news becomes the accepted mainstream standard, then anything *does* go.

How quaint now to hear Ron Nessen—as if he'd just beamed down from Pluto—repeat the admonition he received from then NBC News president Reuven Frank years ago when Nessen, then a young journalist, had uttered something on camera that his boss felt was an opinion: "Ron, nobody cares what you think."

What a difference four decades make, for the guiding principle of today's media increasingly is *everyone* cares what they think.

In fact, the standard for gathering and presenting news is "faster, looser and cheaper" than ever, reports the highly reliable media watchdog group Project for Excellence in Journalism (PEJ). Blogs and cable news programs foster a "journalism of assertion" that relies less on reporting than on personal opinion, it finds. Some bloggers, it says, couldn't care less about accuracy, their self-correction philosophy being, "Publish anything, especially points of view, and the reporting and verification will occur afterward in the response of fellow bloggers."

As if "fellow bloggers" necessarily know what's up, a dicey assumption given that too many of these correctors are informed by other bloggers. Yes, the echo chamber again.

Not that you need a study to affirm what former CNN correspondent-turned-academic Frank Sesno says is true: "Much of what is defined or presented as news today is opinion, interpretation or speculation." More bluntly, FCC Commissioner Michael J. Copps dismisses it as "baloney passed off as news."

Perhaps he had in mind satellite exchanges like the one Captain Queeg–like *Hardball* host Chris Matthews had with guest Dee Dee Myers, former press secretary to President Bill Clinton, during MSNBC coverage of the New Hampshire Primary that Senator Hillary Clinton was to win.

> *Myers:* A year ago, nobody expected Hillary Clinton to be the front runner.
> *Matthews:* Excuse me, Dee Dee. Everybody thought Hillary was going to win the nomination. The national betting odds have been clear for years now.

Myers: That's wrong.

Matthews: That's a fact. Everybody has been betting that Hillary would be the nominee. When they put money on it, people bet on Hillary being the nominee. This has been going on for years now. Why do you say she wasn't the front runner?

Myers: I think a year ago, in the spring of last year, that wasn't the story line at all. And I think what people thought—

Matthews: Who was the front runner if it wasn't her?

Myers: I don't think there was a front runner. I think that—

Matthews: This is revisionism, Dee Dee. This is revisionism.

Myers: You know, you ask me a question. If you let me answer it I would—

Matthews: You are answering it and you're wrong. It's—

Myers: You can disagree with your guests. But don't shout at them on your show.

Matthews: No one believed that Hillary wasn't the front runner.

Myers: I do. I think that she showed over the course of the last year, a lot of grit, a lot of . . . she ran a better campaign than people expected her to run. She was able to get it. People could take a second look at her . . . in a way that they hadn't. And I think she became the inevitable—

Matthews: I look at the polls. You look at the polls. Which poll have you looked at in the last several years that hasn't made Hillary Clinton the front runner?

Myers: Chris, I don't think a year ago she was the front runner. It's been the result of a well-run campaign over many months. That's my opinion.

Matthews: Okay, I think she's been the front runner a long time.

It didn't end there. Matthews and MNSBC's Keith Olbermann (who agreed with Matthews about Clinton) continued to toss it around long after Myers had departed.

Olbermann to NBC correspondent Andrea Mitchell: "At some point was Hillary Clinton a front runner in this Democratic nominating process, or did we dream it?" Mitchell agreed that they hadn't dreamt it. But of course, Myers had never claimed Clinton wasn't the front runner "at some point," only that she wasn't "a year ago."

Not that this joust over Clinton's frontrunnership seemed to matter to anyone beyond Matthews, Myers, and Olbermann. But it was a nice way to fill time.

There's more than one way to look at this, of course. A broader view comes from Mitchell Stephens, author of *A History of News*. "News itself is being devalued again," he says. "News which became, for a period of time, something you could sell, is rapidly no longer that. Now it's sort of going back to what it used to be, the analysis of news. That's a really revolutionary change."

Revolutionary it may be. But one person's analysis is another's anathema.

Former newspaper editor John Carroll could have been describing a Hollywood set or make believe from Jim Carrey's movie *The Truman Show* when he wrote in 2004, "All across America, there are offices that resemble newsrooms, and in those offices there are people who resemble journalists, but they are not engaged in journalism."

Instead, his target was rapidly expanding "pseudo journalism," whose practitioners regard the audience "as something to be manipulated." He said he had in mind not only the Fox News Channel (generously sparing CNN and MSNBC) but also "a broad array of talk shows and websites that have taken on the trappings of journalism but, when studied closely, are not journalism at all."

Carroll likened this to the aftermath of Orson Welles's famous 1938 radio dramatization of *The War of the Worlds,* which depicted Martians invading the town of Grover's Mill, New Jersey, in such realistic news style that many listeners bought it and went cuckoo. In their hysteria, they ran out into the streets, jammed police switchboards, and gathered in churches to pray.

"It didn't sound like fiction; it sounded like journalism," Carroll wrote. "The actors who described the unfolding events at Grover's Mill had the same stylized cadences and pronunciations as broadcast journalists of the time."

Carroll's fakery metaphor hits home in the present millennium's broadcast and web-news milieu. As in, *I'm not really a journalist, but I play one on TV and the Internet.* Or to borrow a line from the late Cleveland Amory, some of these people are journalists "in the sense that a woodpecker is a carpenter."

The "pseudo journalism" that Carroll describes inevitably leads to faux news—hardly a new phenomenon, but one that comes in many exotic varieties.

It includes the video press releases that companies and even the U.S. government have distributed to local TV stations for years. They're made to look like a real news report: an anchor or coanchors reciting propaganda or throwing it to a pseudoreporter in the field. Most viewers probably wouldn't know the difference, and it's unethical for stations to run these without labeling them for what they are.

A few years ago, the Bush administration was caught red-handed distributing to stations a so-called news story touting a new Medicare drug plan. It looked like a news story. It sounded like a news story. But it wasn't a news story. It was slick propaganda, underwritten with taxpayer money.

White Houses will be White Houses, Republican or Democrat. But the real guilt is on the part of stations—dozens of them ran the phony Medicare drugs story—that know what they are getting, and look the other way and air it anyway.

Another kind of faux news is meant to be entertainment, not propaganda, a prime example being Comedy Central's *The Daily Show with Jon Stewart*. It's designed to make viewers laugh. Nonetheless, in 2004 the Pew Research Center for the People and the Press found that 21 percent of viewers between the ages of 18 and 29 used *The Daily Show* as their primary source for election news. That was so even though the TV show is clearly labeled as satire.

The talk used to be about the blurring of news biz and show biz, with news increasingly aping entertainment. But now a bit of the reverse also appears to be true—as news edges toward entertainment, some entertainment moves closer to news. Isn't it true, in fact, that the road to the White House now leads through Jay Leno and David Letterman, and that it's essential for candidates to be seen mixing it up on TV in ad-lib situations, even if the ad-libs are written for them?

All of this is part of what some have called this era's "news and schmooze" explosion. Actually, much less news than schmooze.

John Morton had it right when describing the basis for *Broken News*, a 2005 satirical TV series he cocreated for the BBC: There's "an onslaught of nearly news—endless two-way speculation live by satellite about what might have happened, what might be about to happen, or what might possibly be happening right now—although, of course, it's impossible to say what's happening for sure until whatever it is has finished happening."

So, you see, the Martians *have* landed, for the nasty little truth about 24-hour news—whether cable TV or the Internet—is that most of it is not news. Looks like news. Sounds like news. Smells like news. But nope, ain't news.

One view: rarely is there enough actual news to fill a 24-hour broadcast or unlimited Internet space. A less charitable assessment is that cable news channels and the Internet haven't the inclination to pursue it, preferring instead to rely on pseudo or Martian news.

When the very first all-news radio stations hit U.S. airwaves in the early 1960s, they were minimalists, intending to deliver nothing more than a few headlines, sports scores, and weather to their urban listeners, usually repeated every 15 or 20 minutes. (In New York, WINS radio still boasts, "You give us 22 minutes, we'll give you the world!") It was assumed that most of the audience would be in cars and uninterested in a steady diet of news while languishing in traffic.

But then along came CNN as the first 24/7 all-news television channel, and things took a dramatic turn.

Unlike radio listeners, TV audiences (at least in the days before it was possible to download video programming onto iPhones), were rarely on the move except for occasional snack and bathroom breaks. They were mostly inert couch potatoes with beer bellies watching from home, eyes glazed over while juggling munchies and the remote control. So economically, rolling over the audience every 15 minutes or so just didn't work as well for television as it did for radio, where production costs were much, much lower. Madison Avenue wanted viewership to consistently expand, and that meant keeping eyeballs forward on the programming.

From the very first, CNN founders recognized the potential problem. There was not enough news they wanted to cover on a given day—barring some catastrophic event—to fill 24 hours. Don't forget, this was long before the media bottom-feeding days of bad girls Paris Hilton, Lindsay Lohan, and Britney Spears.

So a smorgasbord of separate units was created within CNN to produce soft, feature-type pieces that although not breaking news were deemed to have some informational value; there were medical units, nutrition units, science units, fashion units, business units, political units, unit units, and you-name-it units. To be sure, this myriad of units did at times manage to dig up something that generously could be defined as news in the traditional sense. But for the most part, they produced only "filler"—material designed to consume space, hold an audience and, most important, keep advertisers happy.

Yet even that was not enough to plug an hour, let alone 24 hours. So what to do if you're an all-news network with, of all things, a shortage of news? Throw in the towel? Pack up your headlines and hairspray and call it day? No.

You change the definition of news! The twisted logic goes this way: If you call yourself an all-news network, then by definition, everything you air, minus commercials, must be news.

In other words, going live for the sake of going live is now news. Going live when there is no valid journalistic purpose to go live is now news. Going live because you know the "live" label turns on viewers is now news. Going live solely because you have the technology to do so is now news.

Why? Because you, an all-news network, say it is.

Although local TV news operations from Atlanta to Altoona had been using live shots as cheap theatrical gimmicks to fill space and titillate viewers for years, rigidly formatted national news-casts on ABC, CBS, and NBC rarely did so before the advent of live news–dominated CNN.

In CNN's early years, insiders would joke that it didn't really matter whether something was news or not. The punch line? If it moved, CNN would try to cover it live, however inane. The most trivial nonevent could be elevated to lofty *BREAKING NEWS!* status by virtue of CNN carrying it live.

It was CNN, also, that pioneered the now commonplace live coverage of routine news conferences, often in their entirety, for no other reason that these fatties filled time. CNN welcomed and embraced them, dissected and autopsied them: 20 minutes of live coverage with some public figure babbling or drooling for the cam-era was 20 minutes CNN needn't to try fill with something else.

This, too, influenced nightly newscasts on ABC, CBS, and NBC, which, prior to the arrival of CNN, did not grant live coverage to press conferences unless they were related to something dramatic like a plane crash or political assassination—or better still a political assassination involving a plane crash.

But for CNN, and later its 24-hour progeny MSNBC and the Fox News Channel, the agenda was to consume time by creating the illusion of covering important news.

What's more, going live meant that stories from just about any spot on the planet would be transmitted back to TV screens almost as they occurred, giving news a fuzzy homogeneity that largely erased editorial boundaries separating global stories from national stories and national stories from local stories. All stories, as far as CNN was concerned, became local stories. That point was driven home to viewers because all stories arrived at about the same time and were about the same length, no matter their origin. This dramatic compression of time, while now standard, was flat-out revolutionary in 1980 when CNN made its debut.

Changing the definition of news also meant branding self-promotion as news, a signature deception that had characterized local newscasts for years and something CNN and other 24-hour news operations have embraced enthusiastically and creatively.

CNN greeted 2008, for example, with a nighttime hour titled *I Report: Caught on Camera* that was nothing more than self-serving, wall-to-wall testimonials for the amateur footage it uses, replete with pulsating car-chase music, a razzle-dazzle set lit up like a room full of Las Vegas slot machines, and an anchor in Rick Sanchez who nearly jumped out of his skin (this guy needs to chill).

"Whatever the story, wherever it is," he boomed, "CNN can cover the story better and faster because I Reporters are there!"

Really now, was *that* news?

Or was CNN star Larry King's worshipful, hourlong interview of CNN anchor Anderson Cooper about his just-published memoir?

Or CNN airing an hour special on *Time* magazine's "Person of the Week"—arguably not even worth the paragraph or two it usually gets in newspapers—only because CNN and *Time* are both owned by Time Warner?

Or CNN mingling "CNN: the most trusted name in news" with news headlines in its continuous "crawl" at the bottom of the screen?

Or the relentless self-adulation by CNN anchors and presidential campaign reporters after being commanded by their bosses to refer to themselves on camera—Wolf Blitzer did it a dozen times during CNN's New Hampshire Primary coverage—as "the best political team on television"? Not to be outdone, Fox News anchor Brit Hume later trumped that, calling himself and his Fox News colleagues "the best political team ever."

And they are, if not that, surely the best—along with CNN—at patting themselves on the back.

TV's robust self-celebration movement has a long and dubious history, most notably with anchors being prominently installed as gleaming hood ornaments on the body they defined (at times generously) as news. There's a reason why news anchors from New York to Walla Walla are paid more than anyone else on the staff, and it's not because they are necessarily smarter or better journalists than their colleagues. Don't be shocked if the opposite is true; send them out to do a story in the field and they might step into an open manhole and injure themselves.

Yet the aura of anchor omnipotence persists, affirming an unhealthy worship of personality in TV news, where style and charisma remain a passport to longevity.

The fact is, both national and local newscasts are built largely on personalities, with focus groups and other high-priced audience research as bricks and mortar. Their mere presence is meant to rivet viewers to the screen. Even that iconic Mt. Rushmore, Walter Cronkite, wasn't paid top dollar by CBS all those years because he strapped on a parachute and dove into Normandy with U.S. troops during World War II. He became our Uncle Walter because he was magnificently avuncular; there was something indefinable in his face, voice, and manner that earned much of America's trust and made you want to climb upon his knee and rest your head on his chest like a kid would with Santa Claus.

The personality aura is widespread and widening, nourishing even the success of news programs as celebrated for their journalism as their glitz. For example, the success of *60 Minutes,* television's longest-running prime-time hit, has always been due as much to its reporters' network-nurtured stardom as to the stories they skillfully tell on CBS.

The problem comes when the glamour and renown of celebrity journalists elevate them above the stories they are assigned to cover, the messenger shining brighter than the message.

And when that happens, is *that* news?

What better example than the promotional blitz granted Anderson Cooper and his new *360* newscast in 2006 when CNN plastered his mug across blogs, billboards, and print media coast to coast? Some of the ads featured multiple shots of Cooper in the field, always contemplative, always with furrowed brow. One of them showed him sitting on a curb in Beirut taking notes, CNN's very own selfless Ernie Pyle, with Cooper promising in an accompanying text to "hold the people in power accountable for their words and their actions."

But who would hold CNN accountable for this extravagant personality worship?

Or CBS, for its outlandishly high-profile search for a successor to Dan Rather, a 2006 transfer of leadership so heavy with pomp, tingly suspense, and high drama that you might have thought a new pope was being chosen instead of someone to front a 22-minute newscast? Leslie Moonves, chairman of CBS and copresident and CEO of its parent, Viacom, had issued a command saying he said he didn't want the "voice of God" anchoring the *CBS Evening News.* Instead he raided NBC's *Today* program and snapped up the voice of gosh. Her name: Katie Couric.

It was a digitally slenderized Couric who arrived at CBS. At least it seemed that way based on her first official network photo, which carved some 20 pounds from her figure. In contrast, the network's nonstop glorification of her was a potbelly of excess—all Katie, all the time—as if she alone would be able to rescue the *CBS Evening News* from its third-place ratings sinkhole. That included two days of Couric taping 10-minute interviews with 50 publicity-seeking news anchors from affiliate stations—an orgy of symbiotic self-promotion for them as well as her—amid speculation that she was changing her "look" to something more dignified befitting a network news anchor who was being paid a reported $15 million annually.

What any of this had to do with journalism was not immediately apparent.

It's what former CNN man Frank Sesno calls "hypercelebrification" of news. "A TV correspondent I really respect told me he was told by his boss that what he had to understand was, 'If you're going to play the ratings game, you have to understand that when you stand up there in front of the cameras, it's not about the news, it's all about you.' So shows are all named after people now."

It's not only TV, though. "Every columnist has a picture in the newspaper or online," Sesno notes. "Everybody is available to e-mail. Newspapers have whole PR divisions that try to get their reporters on television or elsewhere. The *Washington Post* and other papers have put studios in their newsrooms so that all you have to do is sit in front of the camera and you can talk."

As Aaron Altman, the principled TV reporter in James L. Brooks's dark comedy *Broadcast News,* says caustically, "Yeah, let's never forget, *we're* the real story. Not them."

CNN hasn't forgotten.

When assuming leadership of CNN, personality-promoting Jonathan Klein announced that he wanted more "passion" from his anchors and field reporters. He said he wanted viewers to witness the "real them." Take *that,* Fox and MSNBC!

Of course "passion"—which Cooper immediately began wearing like a chest full of medals—and the "real them" may not be what you want from newscasters since it's already available, and in your face, from Oprah Winfrey. What's more, "passion" translates to opinion, already a destructive force in TV news, along with swelling musical soundtracks that manipulate viewers as much as they do moviegoers. And instead of the "real them," how about the real story, with "them" marginalized or even omitted?

Fat chance.

Sesno flashes back to CNN's coverage of Hurricane Katrina. "There was this scene when you had two correspondents and two cameras at this place in New Orleans and the winds were picking up to about 90 miles an hour. And the two cameras and two correspondents were taking shots of each other being buffeted around."

So memorably outrageous, almost surreal was this scene, that former NBC News correspondent Nessen recalls it, too. "These two CNN crews are yelling at each other, 'Watch out, those shingles are falling off that roof! Be careful there, that wave is gonna get you!'" He paused for a brief sigh. "That's the coverage."

CNN kept its eye on the prize, though. For a time, it assigned a camera crew to follow its new star, Cooper, and cover him covering Katrina, as if it took his presence to validate tragedy.

"Because the ratings-driven world by which the cable networks now measure themselves feeds on the culture of celebrity," Tim Rutten wrote in his *Los Angeles Times* column, "each now has a signature personality—Bill O'Reilly on Fox, Keith Olbermann on MSNBC and the neopopulist Lou Dobbs on CNN."

Oh, yes, that self-inflating gasbag O'Reilly, the smirking, snickering, mocking Olbermann and the smug, sermonizing, fulminating, self-appointed folk spokesman Dobbs, who scolds and talks over guests who dare disagree with him.

CNN gives Dobbs virtual carte blanche to do whatever he wants, which includes wielding like a truncheon those hastily designed, unscientific, manipulative, instant-opinion, quickie polls that newscasts increasingly deploy to hold viewers' interest.

Is it any wonder that his viewers always overwhelmingly agree with him?"

Here, right after he had questioned "just where your government *does* work for you," was Dobbs's poll for one evening: "Do you believe that elected officials in Washington are truly working in the national interest?"

Here, right after he had lambasted media coverage of the presidential race, was a Dobbs poll on the night of the New Hampshire Primary: "Are you tired of the national media reporting on the presidential race in terms of charisma, change, dynasty, momentum, and likability, instead of candidates' positions on the issues?"

To which he immediately added, further stacking the deck: "I'd like to ask you a secondary question: Do you mean it when you say no?"

And is *that* news? Or the predictable results that overwhelmingly support Dobbs's positions? Or what the Washington, D.C.–based PEJ calls the "answer culture," which it says is supplanting the "argument culture"?

The "argument culture" is a synonym for what Michael Crichton once called the "Crossfire Syndrome," named for the former CNN show featuring battling cohosts from the Far Right and Near Left. The agenda of *Crossfire* and like-minded series and segments within newscasts was the conflict and verbal violence of Jerry Springer journalism, not illumination. For years, cable news channels have liked nothing better than filling time by splitting the screen and letting foes shout at each other as the anchor or host takes a break much like the rest of a jazz ensemble does during the drummer's solo.

"With 24-hour news and instant deadlines," says Nessen, "you fill up a lot of time with people in the studio debating. Which is not necessarily bad, but it seems to me that some of the networks choose somebody on the Far Right and somebody on the Far Left and put 'em in front of a microphone and say, 'Yell at each other,' the theory being that every story has two sides. That's crazy. Some stories have one side, some stories have 20 sides."

Yet this era of "pie-throwing," as R. W. Apple of the *New York Times* once termed it, may be fading, said the PEJ in its 2007 report "The State of the News Media." Its "answer culture" replacement, it says, has journalists and news outlets "offering up solutions, crusades, certainty and the impression of putting all the blur of information in clear order for people. The tone is just as extreme as before, but now the other side is not given equal play." And "the most popular show on cable," it adds, "has shifted from the questions of [CNN's] Larry King to the answers of [Fox's] Bill O'Reilly. On CNN, his rival, Anderson Cooper, becomes personally involved in stories. Lou Dobbs, also on CNN, rails against job exportation."

And they call it news.

Says CNN cofounder Reese Schonfeld about the 24-hour news environment he helped pioneer on TV, "I don't think there is a real news network in the U.S. right now. They have far too many experts who aren't expert on anything. All of them are so full of opinion."

Indeed, and how the news industry's attitude toward it—and the public's tolerance of it—has changed through the years. There was a time when media watchers worried about the impact if a powerful news anchor like CBS's Cronkite or NBC's David Brinkley raised an eyebrow while reading a story on camera. Would that convey an opinion or point of view to millions of viewers and influence public opinion?

That sounds quaint today when the line separating news and opinion, most notably on TV and in the blogosphere, is buried to the extent that you need a Geiger counter to find it. And not by accident.

One insider reports attending a 24-hour news staff meeting "where people were essentially told there has to be more opinion and interpretation in programming because viewers get the news and the facts elsewhere."

Of course, it's often tricky deciding where news interpretation stops and flat-out opinion begins. But Rutten of the *Los Angeles Times* has a good idea. Writing about the 2007–2008 election campaign, he noted "CNN's descent into hyperbole and histrionics" and castigated the "shamelessly high-pressure pitch machine that has replaced [CNN's] once smart and reliable campaign coverage." He went on to call CNN's political reporting a "traveling wreck of a journalistic carnival" and lament "cable's descent into partisanship."

Cable's all-news networks, he observed, "have aligned themselves with a point on the compass. Fox went first and consciously became the Republican network; MSNBC, which would sell its soul to the devil for six ratings points, instead found a less-demanding buyer in the Democrats. Now, CNN has decided to reinvent itself as the independent, populist network cursing both sides of the conventional political aisle—along with immigrants and free trade, of course."

Dobbs made these his signature issues long ago, extending CNN's history of substituting opinion for news. But that was merely Deception 101, low-level duplicity, faux news at its most elementary level, foreshadowing a phenomenon that was to be far more exotic, far more creative, and again related to speed.

CNN's rise began in the 1980s, a decade that soon would see such tabloid-style TV series as *A Current Affair, Hard Copy,* and *Inside Edition* gaining popularity on U.S. airwaves. Much like their tabloid newspaper cousins these series, along with the equally fatuous *Entertainment Tonight,* became skilled at covering and giving false gravitas to the most trivial and sensational stories by pumping them up with music and gaudy graphics to make audiences believe they were watching real news and information, not just candy for the eyes.

And CNN closely followed that template, imitating the shallowness of these TV shows while being faster on the trigger. After all, the speed of communications had accelerated dramatically, thanks to technology. So, of course, use it, profit from it, get high on it.

But ultimately, ordinary speed began to seem so . . . *yesterday,* so not fun anymore and not nearly enough to satisfy 24-hour news executives with their eyes on the future. For them, speed no longer was just a goal. It had become their intoxicant, one taste leading to another and another and another until they were sloshed on the stuff, falling off their barstools.

In other words, once microwave and satellite trucks became ubiquitous, news executives had to devise other ways to beat their competition. Being able to transmit a story as fast as or faster than the TV guys down the block just wasn't good enough anymore.

But what to do? They were already transmitting news as fast as the technology allowed. They couldn't do it faster than live. Or could they?

Very gradually, the solution crept into their minds, perhaps without any level of consciousness. It was intuitive, even organic, and they responded obediently to this call like dogs to a whistle too high-pitched for humans to hear. What they had to do was really so simple. The solution had been in front of them all the time. They couldn't report the news any faster than delivering it live, couldn't do it—that is, unless they created their own news. In other words . . .

Report it before it actually happened.

How innovative. How revolutionary. How *tomorrow*. Plus the ramifications for the news industry, and the news consumer, would be nothing less than transformative.

And how to do it?

Armies of "guests," otherwise known as talking heads, had to be recruited to speculate about domestic and world events, telling the future as if gazing into a crystal ball, giving the impression that forecasting what lay ahead was news. They had to be groomed. They had to be available. And here was the most important part, these CNN-anointed swamis had to be willing to work free. Yes, not even for as much as *bupkes*.

Actually, there would be payment, but without money being directly involved. Instead, an informal quid pro quo, the same symbiotic process guiding talk show guests and their hosts, would be in play: The guest forks over his presumed expertise for free, receiving national exposure in return, whether for him as a personality or for a book or movie or any other product dear to his heart. In other words, even news sound bites would now be commercialized, for the only reason someone would be up at 4 A.M. talking to an anchor a thousand miles away was to sell a product.

Perhaps nowhere is this penchant for predicting news more on display than in television coverage of jury trials in the U.S. The 24-hour news programming clock is relentlessly ticking and the mouth of the beast always open wide. What better way to feed it than to cover long trials—in their entirety—with minute-by-minute analysis from guest experts galore?

Media stars were made that way, one of them Greta Van Susteren, an energized Washington, D.C., attorney who had made a CNN name for herself during the network's coverage of the 1991 William Kennedy Smith trial as someone who could size up matters quickly on camera and deliver an immediate incisive opinion.

Later, Van Susteren would become a virtual workhorse for CNN, seemingly on call around the clock for trial and other legal punditry with a former federal prosecutor named Roger Cossack, with whom she would cohost a show called *Burden of Proof*. She was a fast study, swiftly learning the demands of TV. If a judge as much as dropped a gavel, CNN knew it could immediately plug Van Susteren and her instant analysis into that trial.

Yet 1995 was the year Susteren went big time on CNN, a year in which attorneys appeared to spend as much time on TV as in law offices, thanks to O. J. Simpson.

As much of the nation joined CNN in playing Can You Guess the Verdict?

On June 12, 1994, Los Angeles County prosecutors claimed that one-time-football-great-turned-B-movie-and-TV-commercial-star O. J. Simpson murdered his former wife Nicole Brown Simpson and her friend Ronald Lyle Goldman.

The criminal trial that followed in 1995—quickly dubbed "The Trial of the Century" and later elevated to "The Biggest Trial Ever" by one ABC anchor—was weighted with more than 130 days of testimony that was televised to a seemingly eager world, thanks to California's policy of allowing cameras inside state courtrooms at the option of judges.

Both CNN and Court TV opted to cover the entire trial every day from start to finish, a move that proved highly beneficial to CNN's economic future. Coming off of the audience highs of the first Gulf War in 1991, CNN's ratings had taken a virtual nosedive. Something needed to be found, and found quickly, to spike the ratings. The heads of key CNN executives would be on the chopping block if audience numbers did not rise quickly. And they did, the Simpson case proving an Oh m'Godsend. Ratings not only climbed, they hit the roof, went through it and kept on soaring.

Simpson may or may not have killed his ex-wife and Goldman, but the double homicide became a savior for CNN and its beleaguered executives—the goose that not only laid the golden egg but also provided the bacon and home fries to go with it.

News organizations poured money into coverage of the criminal trial at rates that would make the Federal Reserve blush. Reporters and producers from not only across the United States but from across the globe were jetted to Los Angeles to take part in the spectacle. An entire media city was constructed around the courthouse like a giant erector set, and hotel rooms and executive suites were booked in such volume as to actually create a shortage of accommodations in the nation's second largest city.

Television and radio were not the only carpetbaggers. Newspapers and magazines also dispatched entire delegations, often including highly paid, widely known "celebrity" writers, to cover the trial. The Internet as we know it today did not exist, and so was not a factor. Yet the coverage foreshadowed what was to come, given the dizzying speed at which the media assembly line researched, wrote, mass produced, published, and aired O. J.–related stories, spiked by rumors and innuendo, during the entire length of the criminal trial.

There's an old media axiom about expenses: If you spend big bucks to cover a story, there had better *be* a story. And the bucks spent on covering the Simpson criminal trial were very, very big, and had to be justified. That meant there was no such thing as a nonnews day during this period, no matter if there was no news, no matter how boring and uneventful the day's testimony might be. In fact, even on weekends, when the court was not in session, the pressure on reporters and producers to come up with (translation: *invent*) stories was unrelenting.

Perhaps never before had so much time, talent, and money been spent on something that had such little real significance (except, of course, to the Simpson and Goldman families).

Another old axiom is that media don't necessarily tell news consumers what to think; they tell them what to think *about*. That certainly held true with their soaring-over-the-top O. J. coverage. When CNN and others were criticized for it, they replied that they were merely catering to public demand. But what had created that demand if not the glut of coverage, a virtual Super Bowl of media excess? And who but the media had titled it "The Trial of the Century" in order to justify their swollen coverage of it?

Of the multitudes of wild-speculating, fantasizing, rumor-mongering media covering the criminal trial, television was without doubt the least patient. The appetite of 24-hour news proved voracious. Think of a shark, a virtual eating machine cruising the depths for something—anything—to devour. So virtually every hour, if not every 30 minutes, there had to be fresh material on the trial or on personalities associated with the trial or on personalities associated with personalities associated with the trial.

On any given day or night of coverage, oraclelike former police detectives predicted what evidence would likely be revealed. As if possessing psychic powers, defense attorneys and former prosecutors predicted what courtroom tactics would be employed by each side. Taking their cues from Johnny Carson's all-knowing Carnac the Magnificent, former and current forensics specialists speculated on how the wounds to the two victims might have been obtained and from what knife angles. Equally prescient politicians of all stripes, eager to get their mugs on camera, predicted how various segments of the city's diverse population might react to whatever the verdict might be. And many of these, along with authors, reporters, C-list personalities, bystanders, and just about anyone else capable of uttering some form of human sound, predicted the verdict.

All this before the trial had even begun.

In the United States alone, the criminal trial was simulcast on ABC, CBS, NBC, three cable channels, and six local Los Angeles stations—coverage so overblown that the case became a common denominator, a shared national language by which Americans communicated.

There was media precedent, of course, and trying aggressively to beat the other guy to a story is part of the American journalistic heritage. When the infant son of iconic aviator Charles Lindbergh was kidnapped and killed in 1932, for example, the press went wild. Newspapers assigned teams of their finest reporters to hunt for clues before the body was eventually discovered.

And when accused kidnapper/murderer Bruno Hauptmann was tried three years later (in an earlier "Trial of the Century"), newspaper headlines convicted him even before the jury did. And press coverage of the trial, including newsreels, was so overzealous and obtrusive that cameras were barred from the courtroom—a prohibition that continues today in federal, and some state, trials.

What had changed when newscasters began guessing about the Simpson verdict was the sheer enormity of the media undertaking, the relentless 24-hour coverage, and the power and inclination of television to make even the silliest of "experts" appear to be profound legal thinkers.

Echoing the tone of the media coverage, many of these prognosticators forecast a guilty verdict for Simpson. Week after week they said that he was doomed by the weight of the evidence against him. Perhaps that is why so many viewers were stunned when the jury, after deliberating only about three hours, returned a verdict of not guilty.

It turned out the experts weren't wrong, ultimately—just premature, for in a subsequent civil trial (for which the bar of evidence was lower) Simpson was found liable for the deaths of his former wife and Goldman. But that trial wasn't televised.

Murder trials of Simpson-like notoriety are rare. However, the media compulsion to predict is not limited to sensational court cases. The *What do you think will happen?* question pervades all of 24-hour news coverage. It's asked and answered many times daily as these news operations buckle under self-imposed pressure and report news before it happens.

In a sense, they're much like local weathercasters on TV and radio. Don't these human weathervanes also predict the news before it happens? Do they not assume the role of chatty, breathless telepaths and ask us to trust them and their bombast about wind advisories, crisp cool nights, and warm fronts? Do they not at times employ sensationalist scare tactics while issuing one false alarm after another—most notably in Southern California, where weather patterns make such forecasts notoriously unreliable?

Yes. However, meteorology, not phony clairvoyance is the basis for their forecasts. Is that news? Yes. Is guessing what will happen before it happens, based on hunches? No. Yet, 24-hour news and bloggers do it all the time.

CHAPTER 4

Blog On!

One by one, Marshall McLuhan's wackiest-seeming predictions come true.
> —Author Tom Wolfe, on the 10th anniversary of the blogosphere

Posted 11/8 7:49 A.M.

Cut the ribbon and pop the bubbly. This blog is launched, open for business and poised to soar through cyberspace.

Posted 11/8 8:00 A.M.

Bill Press, a talk radio host based in Washington, D.C., likens blogs to "ejaculations." That would explain why so many are premature.

Posted 11/8 8:05 A.M.

Not interested at all, says author Walter Isaacson, who heads the Aspen Institute and earlier ran CNN and was managing editor of *Time*. "I've never been a blogger partly because I like to write my thoughts down and do it in a way that takes quite a bit of time and revision and polishing. So I'll write a piece for *Time* on charter schools, as I did this week, but that takes me, you know, three weeks of thinking. It's not something I could have blogged before I went to work one day. Blogging rewards speed, and there's a value to instant blogged opinions, but blogging does not reward taking your time for judicious reflection."

Judicious reflection? Get real. That's for lumbering dinosaurs. Can't be bothered. Gotta run. Gotta go. Gotta blog. Gotta post.

Posted 11/8 8:20 A.M.

What a place, what a crowd. Your blogmeister is checking in from the massive Las Vegas Convention Center, rubbing elbows with the elite bloggerati, one face in a very large throng of multitaskers attending the first annual BlogWorld & New Media Expo. It's the morning of November 8, 2007, and your blogmeister is waiting for this sucker to open while seated at a table just outside the exhibition hall beside blogophiles who appear to be doing exactly what Press described: at laptops, ears to ground, minds on pointless drivel, eyes on screen, fingers on keys . . .

Ejaculating.

Posted 11/8 8:30 A.M.

Greetings again, with more news and musings from BlogWorld.

First thoughts: Boy oh boy, this place is a city within a city, a regular blogopolis pulsating with bloggers, vloggers, and God knows what other kind of weird oggers, along with podcasters and tradespeople who have bought booths in the South Hall to advertise and sell their wares.

Oh, yeah, lots of buzz. The expo is a trade show plus an educational gathering with lots of panel discussions in large conference rooms featuring topics ranging from blog branding and blogging for dollars to marketing strategies and Internet partisan politics.

Posted 11/8 8:40 A.M.

Late breaking: Speaking of politics, Arianna Huffington, who famously operates the *Huffington Post* website (www.huffingtonpost.com), something approaching a Web newspaper or salon, was billed as participating in one of the panels but canceled at the last moment. Yet the Huffster smiles at conventioneers from the cover of the expo issue of *Blogger & Podcaster* magazine that yours truly picked up outside the South Hall, affirming her omnipresence as the Oprah of blogging. Just call her Bloprah.

Posted 11/8 8:49 A.M.

Like Starbucks, bloggers are everywhere these days. And some of them—such as Middle Eastern bloggers who take great risks by reporting repression in nations where they live—do epic work that puts them at great risk. No doubt about it. Don't see that type here, though.

Vegas is known for topless; at BlogWorld, few are laptopless. The PR people here say more than 2,000 bloggers have showed up for the convention. Been looking around, and yup, they're overwhelmingly white, about 80 percent male. Not many have the stereotypical string-bean, big-eared, geek-in-white-socks look that nonbloggers associate with blogdom. As Chris Mooney reported in the *Columbia Journalism Review*, bloggers are a diverse bunch: "Grouping them isn't just grouping apples and oranges, but apples and oranges and bananas and the occasional kumquat." However mainstream many look, they don't talk it.

Posted 11/8 9:16 A.M.

My God, are these kumquats speaking in tongues? Not quite, but close. The alien sound heard throughout the hall is is *Blogese,* an emerging odd language of the arcane ("love your domain name") and spoken by a burgeoning counterculture that genuflects at the mention of new technology the way Elvis worshipers light candles and go glassy-eyed on the anniversary of his death.

First thought: Is this an alternative universe or what?

Second thought: Or is everyone else now the alternative universe?

Third thought: Whatever the universe, Jon Klein, the president of CNN/US, embraces it tenderly, even though it's his competitor. In a pre-BlogWorld chat, he said, "I like the surprise that blogs offer, that any given moment on any particular story you might find yourself heading down an avenue that you would never have explored on your own. I enjoy the process of seeing where the paths are going to take you, and that element of surprise. Because in mainstream media, there's sameness, you know; the formula was figured out years ago and a lot of journalists take pride in just executing the formula, and I think the audience is on to it."

And this from Geneva Overholser, a former newspaper editor and *Washington Post* ombudsperson and now journalism director at the University of Southern California: "In the old days there was a much neater, tighter circle and there was less speculation and less gossip; there were also fewer voices heard and a much narrower view of what kinds of knowledge counted and what kind of experience counted and what kinds of thought. It's now a much richer, yeastier mix, and I think that is welcome in a democracy."

Last thought: Richer, yeastier, maybe. Louder, definitely.

In fact, someone once called the blogosphere "the loudest corner of the Internet." In other words, *All the noise that's fit to blog.*

Posted 11/8 9:52 A.M.

Noise? There's plenty of it, says Andrew Keen, the Silicon Valley entrepreneur and author of *The Cult of the Amateur* who sees blogs as a new take on the old saw that monkeys pounding on a keyboard will ultimately produce something literary, perhaps even Shakespearean.

Monkeys, yes, says Keen. Shakespearean, no way. "Today's technology hooks all those monkeys up with all those typewriters," he writes. Except they're not typewriters but personal computers, and instead of monkeys the new millennium's typists are Internet users. "And instead of creating masterpieces, these millions and millions of exuberant monkeys . . . are creating an endless digital forest of mediocrity." At the center of this forest, Keen argues, is the ubiquitous blog. And he says its present prolific rate of expansion will give the planet more than 500 million blogs by 2010, "collectively corrupting and confusing popular opinion about everything from politics, to commerce, to arts and culture."

And as a bonus, doing it at blinding speed.

Posted 11/8 9:55 A.M.

A forest of fast food caught your blogmeister's eye. Had a doughnut and black coffee for breakfast. Overpriced. Lousy. Used the bathroom. First thought: Feel much better now.

Posted 11/8 10:00 A.M.

Update: I'm at the opening keynote address now, sitting in front of a bald blogger in shorts with a head as large as Vegas icon Wayne Newton's—think beach ball—and a name tag identifying him as Mr. Fabulous.

Is there a metaphor here? Nope, don't think so, for blogging is not just for Mr. Fabulous and the young. The tall, genteel man beside me, from Montreal, is 83 and looks it. Says he's been blogging for a year, wants to increase his blog's visibility, and came here hoping to pick up "the odd tip."

Thumps up, your blogmeister tells him, "Blog on."

Posted 11/8 10:03 A.M.

Buzzword: *borrrrrrring.* The keynote speech is a bomb. Keynote speeches should be against the law.

Posted 11/8 10:05 A.M.

The buzzword is now *ethics.* Yours truly is now at a discussion of blogging ethics. How interested is the BlogWorld crowd in ethics? This interested: the room holds 188 seats, 13 of them are occupied. First thought: *Uh-oh.*

Which brings up this question: "Blogging ethics"—is that an oxymoron?

For a take on that, flash back to an earlier chat with Marlin Fitzwater, who was press secretary for presidents Ronald Reagan and George Bush the Elder. Fitzwater called bloggers "the first cousin of speed."

Meaning, Marlin?

"Bloggers bring to the table a point of view. But they also bring a demand for action, demand for allegiance, demand for speed, and it forces everybody to operate in a more unthoughtful way. First of all, they have no training, no experience, no system of ethical education that they received." And here's the irony, Fitzwater said. "It's the [traditional] media who have empowered them. They [bloggers] have a very small audience. Even though the Internet reaches millions of people, most bloggers are not read by huge audiences. But they are read by the press." And what interests the press resonates thunderously, Fitzwater observed, "making bloggers power players."

Concluding euphoria: Your blogmeister a power player? What a rush!

Posted 11/8 10:15 A.M.

Bloggers ethical stumblebums? We shall see.

The panel members, all seemingly genuinely interested in blogging with integrity, are in place. One of them is Greg Miller, the self-described premiere podcaster of rope bondage—a dirty job, but somebody has to do it. Miller does it under the pseudonym Graydancer. He says, "Part of what I do is tell people's stories and talk about how to do it [rope bondage] safely so you don't get hurt and people can lose some of the stigma attached to it."

First thought: Graydancer is right. If you're going to do rope bondage, for God's sake do it safely.

"So I think that in some ways ethics might be more important to bloggers because that's all we have," he says. "We have our reputation as our credentials, and nothing else."

At the dais is moderator Amy Gahran, who blogs for the ethics-minded Poynter website and has a personal blog called contentious.com. Very smart lady.

Posted 11/8 10:20 A.M.

Update: The audience has swelled to 16, including yours truly.

"Are there any universal absolutes for ethics in communications through blogs?" Gahran asks before throwing out some ethical issues that relate to mainstream media as well as blogdom.

Posted 11/8 10:21 A.M.

The new buzzword is *transparency*. "Is it ever okay, in any way, to mislead or deceive your audience, either by commission or omission?" asks Gahran. "Do you clarify how you go about creating your content? Is it ever okay to conceal or disguise the source? Would you allow advertising that is or could be considered misleading on your site?"

Posted 11/8 10:24 A.M.

Garhan also touches on "privacy and identity." She asks, "Would you ever post anonymously or under a pseudonym?" Anonymous blogs and posted comments are an ongoing issue in some circles, regarding whether they're fair play.

First thought: Hiding behind anonymity—unless you're a whistleblower whose public exposure would put you at risk—is cowardice.

Posted 11/8 10:25 A.M.

Another update, another question: "Would you disguise identities of the people you blog about?" Gahran now asks. "Or allow them to comment anonymously or under a pseudonym? Would you limit access to your blog? And then who would you let in and who would you keep out and why? Would you ever post e-mails or conversations or content you received from a third party with or without their permission? Would you ever reveal personal information about people in any way, with or without warning?"

Graydancer ties in (sorry) to this topic: "There was a recent event where three people had participated with me in a rather difficult sort of stunt type of thing. Afterwards I had gotten permission from each of them to post the video of it. They were all fine with it." However, he adds, one of them later insisted he had posted the video without receiving her permission. It turned out that she had forgotten that she gave it. "Now the issue became what would I have done if the damage to her might have already been done, if she had not wished to give permission. But if she had asked me to take it down, then it comes down, no question, no argument. Even though she had given permission. My responsibility as a blogger, I feel, is that to make sure I don't do harm to people. So I took it down, no questions asked. Which I think lends itself to the question, At what point is there a cross between reporting the news or reporting the honest versus not doing damage to people's reputations?"

Comment from a blown-away blogmeister who now regrets not taking Graydancer seriously: This is truly groundbreaking. The potential conflict between reporting news honestly and doing minimum harm has weighed on journalists for ages. It's discussed at length in ethics classes, but usually not associated with rope bondage.

Posted 11/8 10:28 A.M.

As for disguising identities, Gahran mentions that some U.S. troops are blogging anonymously from the Middle East "because their butt is on the line there." She asks, "If you do that in order to get the news out, you need to conceal or skew your identity. Is that wrong?"

Your blogmeister thinks no, that is not wrong.

But now another panelist speaks. He's Josh Lasser, who writes about TV for the online magazine *Blogcritics,* and says his first blog was under the pseudonym TV Film Guy. "I wanted to start writing reviews, looking at television and film from a critical point of view, but I was working in the television industry." Not a conflict? No, he says. "I was certain every time I wrote an article that I never touched on anything related to the show I was working on."

"So," Gahran sums up, "you maintained your personal ethics, in terms of what you should have covered, and you didn't necessarily disclose that to your audience, that you weren't covering these things because you weren't working in it."

Lasser nods.

Not everyone on the panel approves of bloggers using pseudonyms, though. Says Christopher Calicott, a Las Vegas local and former professional poker player who blogs at WhileVegasSleeps.com, "If you're attacking someone, and you're so spineless that you stand behind a pseudonym, that's just weak," says Calicott.

That logic is sound in most cases, given the "ocean of anonymity sweeping over the Internet and blogs and comments on newspapers stories" that Michael Gartner, former newspaper editor and NBC News president, complained about in a pre-BlogWorld chat. He sounded angry: "You know, *feel free to comment.* Some guy in San Francisco saying that Hillary Clinton is a notorious practicer of bestiality. All that gets on the Web with the same authority as the Census Bureau has when it gets on the Web."

Posted 11/8 10:33 A.M.

Heads up: Garhan now moves on to money. "If you're compensated in any way for your blog, including ads, how does that affect what you say or don't say? Will you ever bend the truth or hold your tongue in order to gain or avoid losing access to privileges, money, stuff? And do you hold any positions of influence over other people or personal trust that you could possibly abuse or compromise through your blogging?"

First thought: A journalists' manifesto applies here, one that relates to conflicts of interest. And it's this—any blogger who is beholden to anyone, for any reason, compromises his or her independence. When your independence goes, so does your integrity.

Now Lasser again, this time recalling that he was "flown by Fox" to New Orleans as part of a junket to publicize "K-Ville," the network's short-lived 2007 cop series set in post-Katrina New Orleans. "And there I was sitting with a lot of different bloggers, and the issue of *access* came up. One of the bloggers was talking about how she had been given a lot of videotapes (of programs) in advance by the network and how she had said she had given them a really bad review for a show, and the network had instantly cut her off from everything that she had been getting them. Now this blogger said, 'Well, maybe I did go too far, maybe I did push the bounds of what I was allowed to do.'"

And so? "But I know," Lasser went on, "that if she wasn't a blogger, if she was a journalist, the network never would have cut her off, because you wouldn't do that to a journalist. However, as a blogger she felt that it was okay for her access to be denied. And of course, she was being flown by a different network now, down for this event. And I wondered, is that going to change the way she covers the new event? Is it going to change the way she reviews stuff? Would anyone change the way that they would do anything for any network or book or whatever it is in order to maintain access?"

11/8 10:39 A.M.

Confession: Your blogmeister was slow on the trigger, and should have spoken up and asked Lasser, "Did getting flown to New Orleans by Fox change what *you* wrote, and if Fox did pay the tab, wasn't the flight freebie a form of payment, and thus a conflict of interest?"

11/8 10:40 A.M.

Garhan correctly notes that "access can be considered a kind of compensation. It's a reward you get. There are all kinds of compensations that are meaningful. Money is one, but there are other kinds. You can get gifts, you can get trips. A hot-button issue in the journalism world is travel writers getting free trips." She adds, "There is a reason why at conferences like this they have hospitality suites. Yeah, you're getting free stuff, you're getting free alcohol and food and flash drives, whatever they're giving away. But what they are trying to do is get access."

First thought: There's a hospitality room?

Posted 11/8 10:43 A.M.

Update: attendance is now at 24.

Posted 11/8 10:44 A.M.

Flashback: Heard of Josh Wolf? Young guy, video blogger who spent 226 days in prison for contempt after rejecting a grand jury subpoena to show the FBI his raw footage of a July, 8, 2005, demonstration in San Francisco by the group Anarchist Action. Wolf had planned to post the footage on his website, *The Revolution Will Be Televised*. Although Wolf calls himself a journalist as well as an activist, the court found that he did not meet the legal definition of journalist. And in any case, the California shield law that now covers bloggers as well as journalists does not apply in federal cases. So off Wolf went to the clinker.

"That is a big fear for bloggers," Gahran says. "So be concerned when you're gathering information. You could be expected to become an arm of government or law enforcement whether or not you publish that information."

Posted 11/8 10:47 A.M.

Next buzzword? *Confusion.* Is a blogger a journalist? It's a touchy subject for Calicott. "Not every blogger wants to be treated like a journalist, but for those that do and show a little effort (including him, presumably), it really stinks" that they are not granted the same access as mainstream media to Vegas openings and other events.

Posted 11/8 10:48 A.M.

Heads up: The conversation turns to anonymous sources, and yours truly speaks up and asks how panel members who believe in using them would respond if commanded by a court to reveal the identity of someone they had promised anonymity.

A couple of panelists say they'd go to jail to protect sources; the others don't appear to have thought about it.

Posted 11/8 10:53 A.M.

Two buzzwords: *hot button.*

Posted 11/8 10:54 A.M.

Finally, Gahran brings up accuracy, a hot-button topic directly related to speed. Still memorable is what a blogger once said when asked to assess the perils of haste: "I haven't seen stories go wrong because of the speed we have in the blogosphere."

Question to that blogger: What planet have *you* been living on?

Gahran: "Should you attempt to independently verify or corroborate information? And how do you decide what is a credible source? Should you ever delete or alter notes? And if you do, do you have to note it and explain why? And would you ever knowingly sensationalize or hype or even underplay a story or otherwise skew the content for any reason?

"How hard is it to pick up a phone?" a guy in the audience pipes up.

Very hard, apparently, when you're in a rush. "Bloggers want it both ways," he continues. "They say, 'I'm just a blogger, I have no responsibility, so I'm going to write (negatively) about FedEx . . . and not talk to FedEx and get their side of the story. Or I'm going to write that Staples was charging to do a virus scan, just point blank report it. Well, he [the person who did make that charge in his blog] was too lazy to call Staples."

(Background: The reference is to a 2005 posting by a tipster on BoingBoing.net that turned out to be false.) "It was crap. It's not hard to pick up the phone and talk to somebody," the guy in the audience says. "So the question that bloggers have to ask themselves is, Do you want to be professional, or do you want to have the luxury of saying, 'Hey I'm just writing what I'm thinking'?"

Question: Bloggers engage in thinking? Why has this been kept secret?

Posted 11/8 10:59 A.M.

Panelist Charlotte-Anne Lucas, who teaches journalism at the University of Nevada–Las Vegas, has her students maintain blogs, and she tells them, "No making stuff up. No taking other people's stuff. And always the truth. That's how you get people's respect." She adds that if a mistake is made, always run a correction.

It's crystal clear: If only everyone in media—whether in blogdom or in the netherworld of 24-hour news—were guided by that Bethlehem Star.

Posted 11/8 11 A.M.

Fitzwater has a take on blogger ethics that he expressed in our preconvention conversation. "It's the ruthlessness and the undisciplined aspects of bloggers that makes them so different in the process of communications. Before the bloggers, you generally had a work of journalism where the journalist had a certain set of principles and rules that they played by. These were the rules that they learned in journalism school or on newspaper staffs or magazines and so forth. And those rules went to fairness and balance, accuracy and objectivity. But they also went to ethical behavior, such as partisanship and truthfulness and plagiarism, those kind of issues. And bloggers have ignored all of those."

Not that some in the traditional media haven't ignored them as well. Too many of them, in fact.

But the blogosphere, with its exploding numbers, ups the ante dramatically. So no wonder online communicator Calicott is using this panel discussion to urge that bloggers "come up with a set of tenets" covering ethics. Others have advocated the same thing, and listen, he says, *why not* a code for bloggers?

Posted 11/8 11:06 A.M.

In my mind I'm picturing Jeff Jarvis, who teaches about new media at City University of New York's Graduate School of Journalism. I'm picturing his scowl if he were here now, picturing him sharpening his tongue on a razor strap. Why?

Another flashback: "No code is going to make a difference," he said emphatically when the issue was broached in a chat before the convention. "That's why I oppose the notion of trying to get bloggers to sign up to a code. The Internet is a place more than a medium. I don't move into my neighborhood and sign a code telling my neighbors that I won't be an asshole. They have to trust that I won't be until I prove myself not to be."

A rebuttal: In the case of many bloggers, that proof is already rock solid, placing a heavy burden on blog readers.

Jarvis would still be scowling. But Gartner knows the score. As he said, "Just as you have to learn reading, writing and arithmetic, just as you have to learn civics and geography and physics and chemistry and science and math, the schools now are going to have to teach how to be a good consumer of information."

Which they should have been doing all along, right?

Posted 11/8 11:13 A.M.

Amen! That's what Judy Marlane and Lou Cannon, who are not here, surely would shout if they were here.

You might say that Marlane, former broadcasting department chair at California State University–Northridge, feels rather strongly about blogging: "We have people who are putting stuff on the Internet, things and statements and facts that are at best misleading and at worst absolutely wrong, both intentionally and/or stupidly, and we have no one to give us the kind of judgment and the kind of sane wisdom that permits us to say—that is not good."

Of like mind is Cannon, the Ronald Reagan biographer and former White House reporter for the *Washington Post:* "These rumors, these scandals are grist for the mill. The White House was always pretty good at propaganda and lying and telling you what you wanted, and I think they adopt it to the mode of the times, but I do think scandal involving anybody, it's always hard to undo the negative, it's always hard to say, 'I'm not a Communist. I'm not gay. I didn't have sex with that woman. But it's harder now."

Cannon brought up the Internet's instant lynching of Idaho Senator Larry Craig, after the family-values crusader's 2007 arrest on suspicion of lewd conduct inside a men's room at the Minneapolis-St. Paul International Airport. The way he was strung up by bloggers, you'd have thought the guy was Osama bin Laden.

"I mean, I don't have any grief for him," said Cannon, "but he was destroyed before he even got to say anything about it."

Real big exclamation mark: Such is the ability of the Internet to swiftly launch and sustain lethal whisper campaigns.

Posted 11/8 11:18 A.M.

Another buzzword? *Speed.* It's a seminal issue now, blogs or otherwise. It's surely made a difference in how *Washington Post* media writer Howard Kurtz does both of his jobs. He also hosts the CNN media program *Reliable Sources.*

"It has changed drastically," said Kurtz. "Certainly in the early days of writing the column and doing the show, say, in the early to mid-90s, a lot of stories about journalistic swiftness—which can tied to journalistic mistakes—involved television and particularly cable television. They were the ones that had to throw it up there almost as it was happening. In the last five years, though, I have written and talked much more about the role of blogs and websites in getting out the news, not just more quickly but allegations and opinions that might not otherwise seep into the mainstream media. What we used to call the Drudge effect. . . ."

Posted 11/8 11:20 A.M.

Information alert: Time for a pause to introduce Matt Drudge, whom your blogmeister—not a Drudge fan—once said wore his trademark hat to hide his lobotomy scar. His widely heeded *Drudge Report,* which began as an e-mail newsletter to friends, was described by *Time* magazine as "a ludicrous combination of gossip, political intrigue and extreme weather reports . . . still put together mostly by the guy who started out as a convenience-store clerk."

Giving the man his due: Nonetheless, it was Drudge who in 1998 first reported news that would became the Bill Clinton–Monica Lewinsky scandal, and his highly influential website's home page, the *New York Times* reported, is read avidly by "television producers, radio talk show hosts and newspaper reporters (who) view it as a bulletin board for the latest news and gossip."

A big-time thought: In other words, anyone with an audience has power, a level of influence that this blog has begun to achieve after just four hours and 20 minutes of life. How exhilarating.

Posted 11/8 11:21 A.M.

Oh, yes, Kurtz. As he was saying in a chat that took place before BlogWorld, "What we used to call the Drudge effect—the site's ability to kind of drive a story into the so-called mainstream media—is now replicated by a hundred other sites, many of which have ideological or other agendas. I don't complain about this—this is the world we now all live in—but there's no question that it sometimes erodes the traditional safeguards that journalists like to think they have erected for careful reporting."

Exclusive to this blog: Press, for one, finds Drudge "a valuable resource." Nonetheless, he recounted this story that related to the 2003 recall of California Governor Gray Davis and election of his successor, Arnold Schwarzenegger: "I had heard from a very good source of mine that Schwarzenegger was not going to run and instead was going to endorse (Los Angeles Mayor) Richard Riordan, and he was going to announce that on Leno that evening. I shot an e-mail to Drudge and told him that I had just heard this from L.A., that I didn't know if it was true, but that he ought to check it out because if it was true, it was dynamite. Five minutes later, I just happened to check Drudge's site and the banner headline on the top was 'Schwarzenegger Not Running, to Endorse Riordan.' I knew damn well I was the source. And it was frightening because I knew it wasn't true. And I also knew that he had not checked one thing, which to me was a pretty scary insight into how the blog can work."

As the man at the ethics panel said, "How hard is it to pick up a goddamned phone?"

Posted 11/8 11:24 A.M.

Heads up: If there were an alarm bell here, I'd sound it, for here's the rub, as noted for us by Ron Nessen, who was a print reporter before joining NBC News and later becoming president Gerald Ford's press secretary: "I had a mentor at UPI [United Press International]. I'd be filing a story and he'd cut in on the line and say, with a real gruff voice, 'How d'ya know? How d'ya know?' You can't do that with a blogger. There is no fact-checking. There is nobody saying, 'How d'ya know?'"

Fact-checking? A novel concept, but impractical. No time for fact checking. Besides, say many bloggers, who needs it? When challenged about their sped-up, revved-up methodology they play the self-correction card.

Here was radio talk show host Taylor Marsh when asked about blogger accuracy: "If you get something wrong, that's why comments are so important. They can keep you honest faster than anything. If you get something wrong, they are going to put up a link so fast it's going to make your head spin, and you're going to know you got it wrong. It's very self-correcting. That's not the case with corporate media."

So why worry? Jarvis doesn't. He was a newspaper and magazine journalist before swooning over the Internet, and he finds the "old architectural of news" inferior to the exciting new frontier of blogging. In print, he says, "I had to get it done and put a bow on it before it could go into publication." Yes, so musty, so yesterday. "Now," he says, "a story has a continuing life and I see that as a continuing chance to improve it."

Note to Jarvis: How d'ya know?

Posted 11/8 11:27 A.M.

Ah, yes, the story-has-a-continuing-life theorem.

Your blogmeister first encountered it in Detroit, at the 1980 GOP convention that nominated Ronald Reagan for president. This was back in the days when party nominating conventions still meant something (or at least more than they do today) and were televised live, wall-to-wall, by the big TV networks.

Reagan was a shoo-in, with only the vice presidential nomination seemingly in doubt, and the networks—as always ravenous for scoops—reporting almost as certainty the widely circulating rumor that Reagan had picked former president Gerald Ford to be his running mate and that Ford would serve as a sort of copresident should the GOP ticket be elected. That continued throughout the evening until the very last minute, when it was announced that Reagan had picked George H. W. Bush, not Ford.

When an NBC News executive was confronted about this erroneous reporting that had been driven by competitive pressure, he gave the screw-up his blessing. His positive spin? It benefited viewers by giving them a peek inside the process of TV journalism.

A major insight: That's like saying it was good having Attila the Hun around because it gave us a peek at a ruthless pillager.

And what did it matter anyway, the NBC news executive added, because they had gotten it right in the end.

And there it was, a watershed moment in journalism: the "continuing-life" story, with the process of gathering news—in this case repeatedly getting the story wrong before finally getting it right—sharing a spotlight with the actual facts. And incredibly, as coequals. In other words, getting it right in the end justifies the means.

The most important thought so far: Did this not foreshadow the screw-the-facts philosophy driving much of today's blogosphere?

Posted 11/8 11:35 A.M.

Getting down and dirty: "Let's not forget," Huffington has correctly pointed out that "much of the false information that came out in the run-up to the war was disseminated not by bloggers but on the front pages of the *New York Times*" and other major newspapers.

And not getting it right? Puh-*leeze*! Enough, already, he can't stand it, says Andrew Breitbart, who operates his own Breitbart.com while helping run Drudge's website from Los Angeles. "If you're going to talk about mistakes made because of speed," Brietbart said in advance of BlogWorld, "there are mistakes that were made in the pre-Internet era that are corrected on page 52 that don't undo the damage. The ability of the Internet to correct mistakes is almost immediate. And the people who make those mistakes, if they don't make them front and center to alleviate the damage, other people—other bloggers—will."

Jarvis sees this process as "a chance to get more people involved who know more than I do, who can contribute and we can work collaboratively together."

Bottom line: The blog police are bloggers themselves. But something is wrong with this picture, for who's to know if those other bloggers—rushing to make their own posts—have gotten it any straighter than those they're supposed to be correcting?

Segue to the next posting: Are we to trust in the organic wisdom of the crowd?

Posted 11/8 11:40 A.M.

Heads up: At this point, another pause here to introduce *The Wisdom of Crowds,* a James Surowiecki book that much of blog-dom appears to regard as a manual, if not divine holy scripture. They've virtually memorized it the way characters in Ray Bradbury's cautionary creed *Fahrenheit 451* did the classics in response to book burning by a futuristic visceral society with no tolerance for literature and reading.

For his purposes, Surowiecki defines a crowd as "any group of people who can act collectively to make decisions and solve problems." In other words, he's saying that the collective knowledge of the group is greater than the individual knowledge of each of its members.

Surowiecki says this collective knowledge is not about consensus. He says it emerges from disagreement and conflict within the group, as a sort of a dialectic or Socratic dialogue.

On the other hand, Charles McKay argued in his classic work, *Extraordinary Popular Delusions and the Madness of Crowds,* that only individuals are capable of intelligent decisions and that grand-scale decisions are doomed to failure.

Others equate crowd wisdom with Trivial Pursuit. And "what defines the best minds," blog-bashing Keen insists, "is their ability to go beyond the wisdom of the crowd and mainstream opinion."

Posted 11/8 11:45 A.M.

The newest buzzwords are *eye of the beholder.* In other words, one person's crowd is another's unruly mob.

Sometimes, "you have to wince at it," says even blogger-friendly Klein, "because it lets the mob in. Men are much more praiseworthy beings as individuals than they are as groups. Most of the bad stuff that's ever happened to man has been done in groups."

And what do mobs do? Driven by "groupthink," they drive forward with great speed, blindly, mindlessly. "A mob," says Klein, "is never really a good thing."

Posted 11/8 12:40 P.M.

Research beyond the call of duty: Found Graydancer's blog, then used it to link to the Global Orgasm Blog. Then had lunch.

Posted 11/8 1:30 P.M.

Another room, another panel, this one on the impact of blogs on popular culture. Also, another scantly attended chat room.

But they could fill the place, your blogmeister is certain—just a feeling—if the popular culture under discussion here included global orgasms.

The most rabid champions of the Internet play down the role of expertise and experience in media while pushing a neoliberation theology that worships amateurs as noble, angelic, even godly liberators. Keen, who can hyperbolize with anyone, sees these amateurs as "idiots."

Your blogmeister senses in the room today burning embers of hostility toward traditional media. It's a contemptuous, make-a-bonfire-of books ideology born from an arrogance that the anointed ones and their acolytes, and only they, can divine truth; they regard the rest of us as sightless and clueless. As an AARP grayhead, yours truly wears a scarlet letter here, marking him for consignment to an attic of has-beens, if not assisted living.

Posted 11/8 1:40 P.M.

But heads up, for someone from a newspaper website has these reassuring words: "We all will watch TV, we'll still read the newspaper." Your blogmeister asks him if he thinks the Internet will change the character of news and the way it is reported.

His reply is on the money: "I think it already has. I think you're seeing a lot more, through blogs, especially, a lot more opinionated stuff, more columnizing."

The question, of course, is whether this "columnizing" is necessarily a good thing, and whether the public—with all due respect—can be expected to always distinguish between news and opinion.

"Yes," the website guy says. "I give the public a lot of credit."

Yeah, well, too much credit. Having faith is one thing, but is there any evidence to suggest that today's news consumer is any smarter than his pre-Internet predecessors? None that is visible.

Astute eyeballing: The room is tipsy—drunk on its own optimism, keeling over from it. But—just wondering—do any of the panelists see negatives associated with the Internet's speed culture?

"Of course," answers moderator Eric Olsen, founder and editor in chief of *Blogcritics,* with no hesitation. "There is much to be said for the delay that goes into processing material, assimilating material, thinking about other connections, giving it context. All that takes time. Then the other negative aspect is the whole fact checking side of it. If you're just tossing it out there, there's no time for fact-checking."

Not a problem, says Olsen. "You can couch it this way: 'This is a rumor, and so and so is saying this.' Or this way: 'I've heard this, and this is what's going on.'"

"That's how you get away with it," he says. "You're saying, 'I'm not saying it's true but it may or may not be true,' and you're able to put just about anything out there. There's a lot of negatives to that, no question. It comes down to personal responsibility."

And giving the public more credit than it deserves. Which may or may not be true.

Posted 11/9 10:00 A.M.

Another day, another room, another royal schmoozing, this one considering whether the Right or Left is "winning the battle of the blogosphere."

The very existence of this lefty/righty panel affirms just how important it is for blogdom's armchair commentators to feel they are making a difference in politics, that their ranting manifestos amount to something more than a jackhammering din that drowns out more reasonable voices.

Some do make a difference—witness the 2007 Chicago convention sponsored by *DailyKos,* the popular blog of antiwar activist Markos Moulitsas Zuniga, attended by seven Democratic presidential hopefuls trying to curry favor with bloggers. All the scraping and bowing was pretty pathetic, actually.

Today's Left versus Right theme is also a metaphor for just how much opinion dominates the blogosphere. In fact, moderator Hugh Hewitt, a radio talk show host and fairly influential Internet player based in Los Angeles, suggests that blogging has "destroyed a lot of careers before they ever began because a lot of young people, as writers, have left virtual trails which render them absolutely radioactive for public service."

Crystal ball gazing: That will be the day, right, when a U.S. Supreme Court nominee is rejected because of something he blogged at 2:00 A.M.?

Posted 11/9 1:42 P.M.

Time to pop into a sports blogging panel, and just in time to hear a guy who writes for the *Sports Illustrated* website reflect about trying to keep up with Internet rivals: "We're just shoving things onto (the website) because if they (competitors) are reacting to a game fast, we'd better, too." Speaks for itself, right?

Posted 11/9 2:00 P.M.

Time for lunch.

Posted 11/9 2:30 P.M.

Lunch was bad. Stomach growling (draw self-correcting line through stomach). Update: A blogger is growling.

Posted 11/9 2:40 P.M.

What is this? Why, it's a circle of 14 souls in a workshop put on by Godblog.com. One man says about the Expo, "There's hardly anything here about ideas. It's all about technology." Another man says, "Everyone is interested in the *now*."

The chat turns to Internet speed and bloggers possibly not finding time to edit themselves. Someone else dismisses this, saying that crudeness of blogs "is part of their charm."

A thought: Much like crudeness of graffiti is part of their charm.

Posted 11/9 3:05 P.M.

Some wit from academe: Moderator David Perlmutter, who teaches journalism at the University of Kansas, opens a panel on political blogs by saying that after the Virginia Tech shooting massacre in 2007, his own school decided to initiate a warning system that would be delivered to the campus in a text message. "That means," he says, "all the students will escape and the professors will not."

Posted 11/9 4:15 P.M.

It's like the last day of Boy Scout camp. Hundreds of us are packed into a big hall, standing room only, excitedly awaiting the arrival of the wrap-up keynote speaker.

His royal blogness, Mark Cuban.

Yes, Cuban, the outspoken billionaire owner of the Dallas Mavericks basketball franchise, chairman of the HDNet cable network and an avid blogger.

Scanning the room and seeing this: Attention is focused, camera phones are poised, eyes are forward.

Well, not all eyes. As Cuban approaches the dais, the blogger dude next to your blogmeister, laptop up, is reading the *Drudge Report*. Moments later, as Cuban begins speaking in praise of blogs, the former Drudge reader has moved on and now has something else up on his screen.

What? Oh, c'mon.

Cuban is here with us in the flesh, talking to us, speaking the poetry of fluent *blogese* to us, enthralling us, energizing us, entertaining us with his good-ol'-boyness, making the room roar at his jokes, bending us over with laughter. Yet beside me, just to the right, this other fellow's gaze is locked on something else; he's transfixed, consumed, transported, immersed to his eyeballs in a private, can't-be-bothered infotopia, the reality of the here and now giving way to the brawnier reality of the Internet. Seeing this is a dreamlike, almost surreal and out-of-body experience, for as Cuban delivers his speech, this fellow's mind appears to be elsewhere. Eyes lowered, he's reading Cuban's blog.

Final thought: *Blog on!*

CHAPTER 5

A New Protestant Reformation: Citizen Journalists to the Rescue

I offer nothing more than simple facts, plain arguments, and common sense.
> —Tom Paine, pamphleteer and citizen journalist, in 1776

"Drums and gunfire are the music of the night," I blogged. Neither the reader nor I could know what would happen next.
> —Blogging actress Mia Farrow on filling in her 30,000 readers about violence in the Central African Republic

The Internet makes everybody a journalist. You sit at your computer, you type something that is true, not true, partially true, hit the button and it goes out around the world. You can't stop that.
> —Ron Nessen, former NBC News reporter and press secretary for President Gerald Ford

When asked for his opinion of citizen journalism, *60 Minutes* creator Don Hewitt is said to have replied, "Yeah, I'm for that; and I'm for citizen brain surgery, too."

As that implies, *citizen* in this case is a euphemism for—*uh-oh*—amateur. Not someone-not-paid-for-his-work amateur, necessarily, but wet-behind-the-ears amateur, untested-and-doesn't-know-what-he's-doing amateur, likely-to-screw-up-and-do-damage amateur. If, as the adage goes, having a little knowledge is a dangerous thing, having none at all surely can be catastrophic, especially when those unencumbered by it are moving at warp speed.

"I think people can certainly be great informational sources, and we've all been scrambling for peoples' cell phone video," says online journalist Kevin Sites, "but I'm not one that believes this job can be done by someone with no training."

Training is important? We've seen the TV commercials. So, wouldn't spending the night in a Holiday Inn Express do it?

"A certain amount of training, yes," says Sites, who covered news abroad for CNN and NBC before joining Yahoo as its first news correspondent. "And an ethical code, a responsibility to sources—a huge responsibility that I think most citizen journalists and most bloggers probably wouldn't want to shoulder. Because there's a cost with protecting your sources, with treating them with dignity, with being willing to go to jail for them (if ordered by a judge to reveal them). And I don't think that's something that has been necessarily meditated upon by citizen journalists."

For better and largely for worse, though, the timing seems right at present for citizen journalists, given that newscasters still largely underperform and traditional newspapers continue to slash jobs—creating gaps in coverage—amid declining circulation and advertising.

Think of it as massive change resulting from Internet technology, something like another industrial revolution. Or, even more to the point, it's a modern reformation that preaches a new-media theology, one that elevates amateurs to exalted status with little halos glowing above their golden heads.

Arianna Huffington, the empress of blogging, sees new media and its citizen journalists as "a wakeup call to the newspaper business."

Remember, though, that U.S. consumers were generally well served by newspapers for at least a couple of hundred years before the business was clobbered by a souring economy and fast-rising Internet that offered glitzy new alternatives and made the press, as Russell Baker puts it, seem like "yesterday's thing, a horse-drawn buggy on an eight-lane interstate."

Not that it's easy to wake dead men walking.

The stench of rotting flesh is everywhere across the media landscape, especially in the killing fields of print where casualties mount daily. As the smoke of battle clears, citizen journalists and their friends come down from the hills to shoot the wounded. As a result, these would-be scribes—some call them participatory journalists—are becoming a major factor, rolling in on the Web like a dense fog and increasing their numbers in print and TV news, too.

Scratch the traditional middleman/gatekeeper. "From now on, news can break into public consciousness without the traditional press weighing in," writes Clay Shirky in *Here Comes Everybody: The Power of Organizing without Organizations*. Here they come, indeed. Taking to the streets, the blogging realm's grassroots amateurs say their primary goal is a noble one—to rescue journalism, and news consumers, from the tyranny of expertise and experience. Yes, free at last, free at last! But is something not quite right here?

One metaphor comes vividly to mind: book burning.

"Instead of a dictatorship of experts," predicts Andrew Keen in *Cult of the Amateur*, we'll have a dictatorship of idiots." Keen, a former Silicon Valley insider, sees the Internet darkly, as slaughtering our culture by drooling over media novices instead of professionals. Owning a computer and Internet connection, he says, "doesn't transform one into a serious journalist any more than having access to a kitchen makes one a serious cook." He dismisses this "citizen" phenomenon as "journalism by nonjournalists."

Far more generous are Shayne Bowman and Chris Willis. In *We Media: How Audiences are Shaping the Future of News and Information*, they write that citizen journalists aspire to provide "independent, reliable, accurate, wide-ranging and relevant information that a democracy requires."

So that's what impulsive blogging and online regurgitation of rumor and raw, skewed, or wrong data are about. Democracy—which George Washington, John Adams, Thomas Jefferson and their progeny passed on to us—requires it?

We all know by now that the depressing economics of the news industry requires something, too. Just about anything, in fact, to raise it from the ashes of its deadly sharp decline. For most newspapers, that has meant grabbing and bear-hugging an Internet presence the way someone fallen overboard reaches for a life preserver to avoid sinking. Although the U.S. appetite for news is surely as robust as ever, newspapers generally have not found ways on the Internet to turn a profit that equals the money they pocketed from print in happier times. But with backs against the firing squad wall, they're trying desperately, even as severe cost cutting continues to reshape their futures and those of the communities they serve.

"If a newspaper reduces staff by 20 percent, some portion of that community is going to be operating in the shadows in a way it was not before," Tom Rosenstiel, director of the Washington-based Project for Excellence in Journalism (PEJ), told the *Los Angeles Times*.

So, trumpets sounding, citizen journalists gallop to the rescue? Are they any help at all to a beleaguered traditional news industry now gasping for oxygen while stretched thinner than ever?

Here and there, yes. But don't expect much original reporting or fact-checking from citizen journalists. Instead, they generate mostly unlabeled opinion and commentary, not nuts-and-bolts reporting about the world or the local institutions (city councils, school boards) that affect both urban and rural societies in meaningful ways, according to the PEJ.

But they're read—especially by the young. And what they write is relayed to others by readers, as the young increasingly become conduits of news in addition to consumers. They send out "e-mailed links and videos to friends and their social networks" and receive news back in the same manner, Brian Stelter reported in the *New York Times*. A market researcher told the *Times* of a college student saying, "'If the news is that important, it will find me'"—a process Stelter calls "online word of mouth."

Walter Isaacson, former CNN and *Time* magazine chief, agrees. He's had his eye on this wave of citizen journalism, and is largely skeptical. "Ninety-five percent of [citizen journalism] is people just spouting off opinions without much shoe-leather reporting," he says. Oh, sure, as if mainstream journalists were not overtly opinionated at times, too? And not superficial and lazy? And the public hasn't noticed? "People are in some ways responding to a yawning need that we in the media world at large have left open," says Geneva Overholser, director of journalism for the Annenberg School of Communication at the University of Southern California.

Don't forget, also, the mainstream press debacle of our time— the run-up to the U.S.-led invasion and occupation of Iraq when, as Huffington notes, "media watchdogs acted more like lapdogs" and much of the journalism community was not only gung-ho compliant and complicit with the Bush administration, but stood and cheered with thunderous applause.

Nonetheless, Isaacson sees a continuing critical role "for what is dismissed as mainstream media, such as funding a Baghdad bureau or sending correspondents and photographers around the world, and that costs money. And if citizen journalism undermines the business model for the old-fashioned professional who is paid to go places, we may find ourselves with an excess of opinions but a dearth of actually reported facts. When I listen to *New York Times* or *Time* people tell me how many millions of dollars per year it costs to keep a Baghdad bureau open, I realize that not everything can be done by citizen journalists."

Well, you know what? The *Times* and all of its newspaper and magazine pals can keep Baghdad—and everything else outside the U.S., too, said Taylor Marsh at the 2007 BlogWorld and New Media Expo in Las Vegas. Traditional media should focus on Iraq, Afghanistan, Darfur, the Israeli-Palestinian conflict and all that other stuff across the pond, she said, "and let the bloggers, let *us* do the rest."

Bloggers doing the rest? How would that be possible? Citizen-journalist bloggers contribute mightily now and then, especially when they alone have access. But not with consistency, and with good reason. As Keen notes, they haven't "the resources to bring us reliable news. They lack not only expertise and training, but connections and access to information. After all, a CEO or political figure can stonewall the average citizen, but would be a fool to refuse a call from a reporter or editor at *The Wall Street Journal* seeking a comment on a breaking story."

That didn't stop Brad Friedman from insisting at the same BlogWorld Expo, with a straight face, that even an epic story as tumultuous, deeply layered and complexly draconian as the Watergate scandal would not have been beyond the skills and resources of today's blogdom.

He makes some of the nation's most honored news organizations sound like Journalism 101. "Look, when I have whistle-blowers come to me, it's usually because no one at the *Washington Post* or the *New York Times* or *60 Minutes* or whatever gave a damn about their story," said the Los Angeles–based Friedman, who runs the investigative *BradBlog*. "If those corporate media outlets went back to what they used to do, which was reporting rather than repeating press releases, I think they'd kick our ass." You had the impression from his confident air, however, that he didn't *really* regard his and other blogger asses as all that kickable.

The citizen journalist as savior? Just who are these people who would redeem us from the demon darkness of traditional media?

They've been around for ages, actually, going back at least as far as Tom Paine and other 18th-century pamphleteers who were informational loners and issued their manifestos independently. And much later, a version of citizen journalist surfaced in tiny weekly and community papers that were limited by the miniscule sizes of their staffs. So they made space for local correspondents, usually a column, to report on happenings (birthdays, weddings, anniversaries, graduations) and all manner of oddities in their neighborhoods and adjoining towns. If someone grew a turnip that weighed 25 pounds, you'd read about it and probably see it, too, in a snapshot provided by the correspondent.

What we have today is a sped-up extension of that—with strong messianic leanings. In other words, as much as a reformation, there's a crusade going here: Out with the old, in with the new, and damn the consequences. How widespread are the potential consequences?

The Pew Internet and American Life Project found in 2006 that 34 percent of 12 million bloggers in the U.S. regard their online efforts as a form of journalism. Do the math and you get more than four million of these nimble-fingered crackerjacks on the loose. That's either four million voices or an unruly mob, depending on your point of view. And by now that number has surely increased enormously.

In other words, today's citizen journalist is anyone who calls himself a citizen journalist, whether posting his observations on his own website or blogging election news and views for a larger, umbrella one like the *Huffington Post* website or uploading video for CNN's *I-Report*.

Always of concern when media are rushing so fast on a breaking story that it's tempting for them to cut corners is whether citizen journalists are scam artists or actually who they say they are.

"When we launched *I-Report,* the first of the news network up-your-own-video programs," says Jonathon Klein, president of CNN/U.S., "we added staff to [vet submissions] as best we could, to at least determine what the material was what it purported to be. That may be as far as you are able to go. It's an imperfect system. You can't ultimately know that everyone is telling you the truth."

Which is not very reassuring.

"We take more care in fast-breaking situations," says Klein, citing the April 16, 2007, shooting rampage on the Virginia Tech campus that left 32 people dead. "The most watched video of the massacre was shot by a student who wandered by the engineering hall with his cell phone and heard the shots, knocked out 45 seconds worth of video and uploaded it to CNN. It took us an hour-plus to track him down and verify that what we were seeing was true.

"Now, what did happen was that a rumor spread around campus that it was an Asian-American gun lover who had done this, and people quickly went to MySpace and found an entry for an Asian American gun enthusiast, a Virginia Tech student, in which he's showing off photos of himself with all his guns and everything, and that was sent around the Web—you know, 'We found the guy who did it.' But it was the wrong guy. So that can happen, for sure. But the only part of this Web that I've got any control over is CNN.com, where we try to vet the material. But in a larger sense, all bets are off."

Along with a few other sites, the *Huffington Post* is the upmarket, high end of the spectrum. Huffington says she accommodates some 1,800 bloggers at her hybrid site that features celebrity commentators, professional journalists (some of them full-time staff), and citizen journalists. Many of the latter are part of the site's high-minded presidential election project called "Off the Bus." It was initiated at the start of the 2007–2008 campaign with the help of New York University professor Jay Rosen.

The aim was to "provide an alternative to the horse race press," said Rosen when the project was just getting underway. The reference was to coverage of the 2007–2008 presidential campaign by the traditional media's whinnying Sea Biscuits, which would turn out to be ferociously mediocre. As its name indicates, "Off the Bus" has not been the usual "boys and girls on the bus" one finds covering such campaigns—the traditional media who embed with candidates full-time, staying in the same hotels, traveling on the same planes (and buses) and reporting as a herd from one photo op to another, at times becoming so cozy with their subjects that they see themselves almost as extensions of those campaigns.

The unpaid "Off the Busers" are a mostly younger crowd of amateurs whose age alone was expected to give them a fresher take on politics and the process of running for office than that of their professional counterparts. This is no exclusive club. Just about anyone could have joined, Rosen said. "If your sister wants to contribute to 'Off the Bus,' she can do that. Anybody who has that desire can do that."

Participants were vetted, and in addition, their blogs and news accounts had to adhere to a set of guidelines created by seasoned professional journalists.

However energetic and enterprising, however fresh their perspectives, these citizen journalists are not professional reporters. And they'd appear to be rather green, given the basic nature of some of the guidelines they've been told to follow ("Be sure you have checked for spelling and grammatical errors." "If you quote someone you interviewed, make sure you can back it up").

The blog-tracking Technorati website ranks the *Huffington Post*—which advertises "breaking news and opinion"—as the fourth most popular blog site, one that its creator says attracts more than four million readers a month, a figure that still lags behind monthly totals for major mainstream newspapers and TV newscasts.

But perhaps not for long, if present trends continue. Yet Huffington, an oft-interviewed writer and media celebrity, seems much less absolutist than many of her fellow blogophiles, instead seeing new and old media coexisting, with traditional media surviving as a hybrid of the two.

"I don't see citizen journalists supplanting traditional journalism," she says. "There is more than enough room for the quick 24/7, get-me-the-latest-details tone of the Internet and the longer-to-develop journalism done by magazines and some newspapers."

The conundrum: Few of those magazines and newspapers now have the funds and resources to undertake as many ambitious reporting projects as before, a situation exacerbated by the explosive growth of the Internet as a primary news source, increasing the likelihood of the "24/7, get-me-the-details" crowd prevailing.

○ ○ ○

An absolute of human history is that each generation views the universe through its own distinct prism and that viewing the distant past through today's eyes cannot only give you a migraine but can produce distortion. Will we look back on this generation of citizen journalists some day and remark nostalgically, as some have done about Edward R. Murrow and other journalists of earlier times, "Now that was the golden age of news media?" It is an intriguing scenario that carries its own distortion.

In fact, here's a little history of what citizen journalists are *not*—and likely never will be. It starts in Manhattan, on West 43rd Street.

Entering the tradition-laden structure that housed one of America's premier news organizations in the last half of the 20th century was like going to church with sunlight streaming through lots of stained glass. You could almost hear an organ and choir, and found yourself speaking in a whisper out of respect.

The solemnity in this lobby of the old *New York Times* building had an eerie resemblance to the somber ambience one found crossing the threshold of, say, Saint Patrick's Cathedral or yes, even the Vatican. The newspaper's grand grayness felt sacred, and inhaling it became almost a religious, if gloomy, experience.

Gay Talese acknowledged as much when he chose *The Kingdom and the Power* as the title of his encyclopedic, behind-the-scenes book on the *Times* that captured the newspaper's awesome and singular power. A few other U.S. newspapers have attained greatness through the years, but none carried a brand quite equal to that of the *Times*. Even its enemies have been chastened by its influence and stature as a seemingly indestructible national institution that even in the darkest times stands tall amid the flames.

If there was a television equivalent to the *Times,* especially in the latter years of the previous century, CBS News was it.

Newspapers have their stars, but relatively modest ones that shine less brightly than those in TV's constellation. In contrast to personality-driven TV newscasts, a newspaper's credibility, or lack of it, does not center on a single person or even a few. *The Times'* arrogant front-page boast of having "All the News That's Fit to Print" does indeed imply stone-tablet weightiness not unlike the Ten Commandments that Moses schlepped down the mountain. *Thou shalt not worship false idols,* however. And it's the entire paper, not one individual, that shares the glory as well as the burden of fulfilling its vow to omit nothing of relevance.

Contrast that with the TV lens, which from its inception has conferred celebrity on whomever it framed, from lightweights and middleweights to heavyweights like the legendary Murrow. Parishioners—that is, practitioners of the craft of electronic journalism—came from just about everywhere to worship at the altar of Murrow, the pioneering CBS radio aristocrat whose clipped accounts of ferocious conflict ("This is London . . .") crackled over the airwaves early in World War II, well before he became the first icon of television news in the 1950s. Murrow gathered Americans around the radio as President Franklin Delano Roosevelt had done with his famous "Fireside Chats." And later, Murrow's *See It Now* series and gutsy, pinpoint reproach of right-wing, witch-hunting demagogue Joe McCarthy were high marks for a TV news medium still wobbly on toddler legs.

Yet by the early 1960s, the once-almighty Murrow had been cast aside, to be succeeded on CBS by His Holiness, respected and revered Walter Cronkite, whose reign over U.S. airwaves as anchor of the *CBS Evening News* was to last 20 years, nearly all of that when the news division was headed by the late, great Richard S. Salant.

It was Cronkite who assumed Murrow's mantle as the most admired voice in all of journalism, if not all of the United States.

It was Cronkite who most famously informed Americans that John F. Kennedy had been shot in Dallas, and because it was Walter who reported it, they knew it was true.

It was Cronkite who told the nation that the Vietnam War was lost, causing embattled President Lyndon B. Johnson to remark, "If I've lost Cronkite, I've lost Middle America." Cronkite's pronouncement carried such moral authority that it must have resonated in the Oval Office like the clarion call of some heavenly prophet. If not God himself speaking, this was surely a very close relative.

It was Cronkite whose words on CBS authenticated, for much of the public, the Watergate scandal earlier reported by the *Washington Post* and others.

It was Cronkite, rubbing his hands together with relish and smiling, who became TV impresario for the historic Apollo 11 mission that put humankind on the moon.

It was Cronkite—along with CBS News—who came to symbolize the best of television journalism from the 1960s to at least the start of the 1980s. NBC News, in the era of Huntley and Brinkley, and also John Chancelor, had many admirers. But the pedestal occupied by Cronkite and CBS News loomed above all others.

Most notably, it was also Cronkite whom Americans believed and trusted when he proclaimed each night, in a papal-like encyclical, "And that's the way it is."

He presided over the *CBS Evening News* from 1962 to 1981, his acolytes tuning to him for nonpartisan reporting, confident that he would tell them without bias what they needed to know about their world that day. No news anchor since Cronkite has had anything approaching that much stature and influence or been that sacred to the masses. And when he decided to step down, it was such a big deal that you half expected CBS to signal that his successor (Dan Rather) had been chosen by sending up white puffs of smoke from the roof of its mid-Manhattan headquarters.

If he was to television news what the Pope was to Catholicism—and there is ample evidence that he was—then one can almost imagine High Mass with the much-adored Cronkite delivering a sermon followed by the congregation chanting, in unison, "And that's the way it is! And that's the way it is!"

Say *amen.*

Cronkite and his rivals competed for the souls as well as eyeballs of Nielsen families. Their newscasts were their pulpits and ministries, their audiences to please or anger, to win or lose. Their news programs were the only national ones in the United States. No serious competitors loomed on the horizon, for the cost of news gathering, reporting, filming—does anyone who is not a codger remember news *film?*—and delivering stories on the air was prohibitive.

And no wonder, for the process—involving reporters, field producers, camerapersons and sound technicians focused solely on getting the film to network headquarters in New York, where it was developed in a lab and then shaped into a story by editors—was cumbersome and tortoiselike compared with how things are done now. Live shots? Never heard of them. Stories transmitted by satellite? Only a few of them. Compared with that of today, the technology was rudimentary.

There was, however, at least some time to think.

How could Cronkite or anyone else have known then what was to come a few decades later, that the journalistic liturgy he had helped craft would be in crisis? There was no way for them to anticipate the virtual reformation that would gush up with little warning, its supporters hoping to marginalize and in some cases replace professional journalists (even the best-trained and most skilled of them) with so-called citizen journalists who were thought to have a better handle on sped-up digitized news and information. Nor could they have foreseen that these callow newcomers to journalism would become central to a crusade promising to "democratize" news and information as part of a movement echoing across centuries from when Johannes Gutenberg invented the printing press in 1440.

The operative word was *democratize*—for what Gutenberg did, in greatly increasing the speed and efficiency of producing books, was make the written word accessible to virtually everyone who could read. In other words, ideas would now be spread faster than anytime in history, and directed toward the global multitudes.

Ideas, for example, from the likes of Martin Luther, an Augustinian monk and academic in Saxony who in 1517 managed to break the hold of the Roman Catholic Church. He did it by nailing to a church door his *95 Theses,* which attacked the authority of both the church and the Pope for, among other black deeds, the selling of "indulgences."

Luther's *95 Theses* and other writings were speedily distributed far and wide. Although surely having no idea that his actions would lead to something that would be known later as the Protestant Reformation, Luther clearly grasped the value and potential of the technology that Gutenberg had created 77 years earlier. Plus, he exploited it to the hilt. It was the printing press that enabled Luther's challenges to Catholic doctrine to be disseminated so widely and with a swiftness that would not have been possible earlier. The speed of communications had changed dramatically, and because of it, so had something else—the authority of the Catholic Church. It would never be the same.

Just as advocates of another reformation now believe that mass communications will never be the same, thanks largely to them. And just as they believe that the speed-driven Internet—along with citizen journalism—is this generation's democratizing printing press that will snap the authority of traditional media much as Luther did that of the Catholic Church. Can there be any doubt at all that these true believers see themselves, in effect, as reborn and as liberated from the mother church's forces of repression?

Helping drive this modern journalistic reformation is a belief by most champions and practitioners of citizen journalism that the sprawling media empires that were formed and allowed to grow largely uncontrolled in the 20th century—from Time Warner to News Corp. to Viacom—are akin to informational dictatorships that need to be tightly regulated if not dismantled for the greater good.

On that score, they're acutely on track. Granting greater media power to the few is a scenario every bit as dangerously undemocratic as the "plantation mentality" PBS journalist/commentator Bill Moyers attributed to media owners in a speech in 2007. "Virtually everything the average person sees or hears outside of [his or her] own personal communications," Moyers said, "is determined by the interests of private, unaccountable executives and investors whose primary goal is increasing profits and raising the share prices. More insidiously, this small group of elites determines what ordinary people do not see or hear."

However, it's highly doubtful that the Internet can achieve the holy grail of "democratization" that these reformers so fervently desire because the same corporate behemoths they understandably distrust and fear are themselves widening their influence by extending their empires to the web.

"Go to the top 20 news sites on the Internet," says Federal Communications Commissioner Michael J. Copps. "Do you think they're run by bloggers or independents or Mike Copps out of his home in Alexandria, Virginia? They're owned by the same folks that own all the other properties in cable and broadcast. That's what I'm saying. These ills that were visited by excessive consolidation in the media are now being visited upon the Internet."

The likely results of this spreading inkblot? Many citizen journalists will wind up tap-tap-tapping on their laptops on behalf of the very corporate bad boys whose influence their presence is meant to undermine.

Nonetheless, in many circles these modern-day messiahs are seen, without reservation, as the future, as the coming golden age of mass media.

The ongoing explosion of citizen-journalism websites affirm that this new reformation is rushing ahead at full speed. The Institute for Interactive Journalism at the University of Maryland identified 700 to 800 such sites in early 2007, about 60 percent of them launched since 2005. Many fuse "news and schmooze" while promoting "the kind of civic engagement that the mainstream press in theory aspires to, but in practice has been slower to encourage." In other words, these sites have secured "a valuable place in the media landscape."

Just how valuable to the rest of us is subject to debate.

Cable's 24/7 crowd brings the planet news as it happens (and as it doesn't happen), including live, up-to-the-millisecond coverage of trivia. The Internet and its growing throng of citizen journalists take this several steps beyond mere reporting by providing millions an opportunity to instantly go public about what they've just seen or are seeing on their TV and computer screens at the moment.

The simplicity here is stunning, the process strikingly visceral. No time is wasted on deep—or any other kind of—thought. You see . . . you like or don't like. You see . . . you react, and react instantly. You can watch an event unfold on cable in real time and (if too impatient to wait until it concludes) simultaneously go online and throw down a gauntlet—your opinion about what you're watching and what should be done about it. In doing so you'll be among friends, reaching an audience that likely consists mostly of Internet users who hold the same views as you. In this way, the Web can be as much a cyber–echo chamber as a rich, stimulating interchange of diverse ideas. Or to put it another way, picture a parakeet in a cage, chirping away at its image in a mirror, not realizing it's communicating only with itself.

Equally worrisome is the ever increasing din of this drumbeat as it gathers speed. Take *Blurbgate*.

In late May 2008, charges and counter charges raced through the blogosphere and mainstream traditional media as the Bush administration faced a crossfire of controversy with the publication of a highly critical memoir by the president's former press secretary, Scott McClellan. However, the controversy had been foreshadowed months earlier.

"If It's Fit to Blog, Is It Fit to Print?" asked the headline on ombudsman Clark Hoyt's December 9, 2007, column in the *New York Times*. Beneath that questioning headline, Hoyt's column gave a clear answer: A resounding *not necessarily!*

At issue was what occurred after a provocative excerpt from the book *What Happened: Inside the Bush White House and Washington's Culture of Deception* surfaced on the publisher's website promoting its coming spring releases. The author of the book was Scott McClellan, President George W. Bush's former press secretary. The excerpt, released by PublicAffairs Books, related to the leak of CIA undercover operative Valerie Plame's name that resulted in a felony conviction for Vice President Dick Cheney's chief of staff, Lewis Libby.

And, as Hoyt noted, what occurred was a cable news and Internet "firestorm."

The published excerpt from McClellan's book recalled a series of press briefings he had given:

> The most powerful leader in the world had called upon me to speak on his behalf and help restore credibility he lost amid failure to find weapons of mass destruction in Iraq. So I stood at the White House briefing room podium in front of the glare of the klieg lights for the better part of two weeks and publicly exonerated two of the senior most aides in the White House: Karl Rove (Bush's closest adviser) and Scooter Libby.
>
> There was one problem. It was not true.
>
> I had unknowingly passed along false information. And five of the highest-ranking officials in the administration were involved in my doing so: Rove, Libby, the vice president, the vice president's chief of staff and the president himself.

Talk about a certain something hitting the fan! What happened was more like the contents of a manure storehouse being tossed inside a wind tunnel. Cable's 24-hour news channels and the Internet—citizen journalists, too—instantly ratcheted into high gear, with anti-Bush blogs especially active in pumping out a continuous stream of opinion and speculation about whether the president had ordered his press aide to lie. Because if he *had* . . . because if he *had* . . .

There was one problem. He hadn't.

This didn't stop the destructive buzz from being repeated and amplified with each retelling as it boomeranged from citizen-journalist blogs to mainstream media, including the *Times* website, and then back again to citizen journalists in an orgy of frenetic, wild, bug-eyed reporting. It took only a few hours for the Bush-told-McClellan-to-lie scenario to take hold and assume a life of its own as common wisdom, although few had bothered to call McClellan or the publisher to ask what the vague excerpt actually meant.

While McClellan kept mum, PublicAffairs calmed the waters next day by announcing that McClellan had always believed that

Bush had *not* known that the information he fed the media was false. Which is exactly what McClellan had told CNN's Larry King months earlier.

Oh.

"It's surprising," said PublicAffairs founder Peter Osnos afterward, "that people shoot first and ask later." Surprising only if you're hermetically sealed inside a cave somewhere and don't watch 24-hour news or read blogs.

The kicker was that the *Times* website had run a tiny item about the excerpt, but the newspaper, which publishes "All the News That's Fit to Print," took a pass. Wrote Hoyt, "The case of the exploding book blurb is worth a second look for what it says about today's environment, in which, with no further reporting, an ambiguous snippet from an unpublished book can become a momentary sensation in the deadline-every-minute world of the Internet and cable news."

With more than a little help from citizen journalists.

○ ○ ○

Strike up the choir and envision church bulletins speeding through cyberspace like jet-driven paper planes.

"I'm all for many voices," says NBC News legal affairs correspondent Pete Williams. "People get charmed by the technology of the Internet. But to me it's sort of like a church bulletin at the speed of light. A lot of people put stuff in church bulletins without doing a lot of checking to see if it's true."

Is he saying it's different at NBC News, one of the corporation-owned (General Electric) demons that tee off the citizen-journalism crowd and many others? "We are under some obligation to not just blurt stuff out," said Williams, who was Pentagon spokesman late in the George H. W. Bush administration. "We are expected to check it out. Our organizations [network news divisions] have reputations that they jealously guard, and which they have earned over a period of decades. Yes, we screw up. But there are real consequences. People get fired. Commissions get appointed to investigate. Heads roll. There is a real expectation of accountability, and that's just not so much true on the Web. A lot of these Web folks apparently [think they] can do no wrong. It's almost like they just want to do it first, and they don't really care whether they are right or not."

Dude—chill.

Because bloggers and citizen journalists assure the world that errors they may make in various stages of a story's evolution don't really matter because the process is, as Huffington puts it, "remarkably self-correcting." If it's the blogosphere's role to "hold the mainstream media's feet to the fire," as she has said, who will hold the blogosphere's feet to the fire? The same public that has failed to make the mainstream media accountable?

"A combination of the public and other bloggers," Huffington replied. "Bloggers do a very good job of policing each other. Because of interactivity and interconnectedness, mistakes do not go unchallenged very long."

Like gashes that heal over, in other words, mistakes ultimately get set right by other bloggers and citizen journalists. At the end of the day or the week or whatever news cycle, the public will know the truth. And if that truth also is not the real, absolute, honest-to-God, swear-on-a-stack-of-Bibles truth, other bloggers and citizen journalists will correct it. And if *their* corrections are incorrect, then still more bloggers and citizen journalists will be sure to weigh in. In no time at all, in other words—what, two, three months of this Socratic back-and-forth?—they'll finally get it right. And those forces of repression (professional journalism, corporate journalism, and anyone else who pisses you off) will be defeated.

At least, that's how it works in theory.

But the self-correcting blogosphere is a "myth," argues CNN leader Klein. Not that he doesn't see positives in the blogosphere—he does. And not that some mistakes aren't corrected by other bloggers—some are. "But there's much opinion masquerading as fact, and that's inherently not correctible," he says. "There are assertions made all the time on many of the blogs I read that are just interpretations of a smaller set of facts, and how do you possibly correct that? But the people who read them could mistake those opinions as actual truth."

However, this take on the process may not be entirely fair to citizen journalists and their minions. So let's have a *Crossfire* here, even though it's nothing more than a literary device because the participants gave their opinions separately, with no knowledge of each other or that they'd be participating in a debate.

On one side we'll have Jeff Jarvis, a blogger himself and strong advocate of nontraditional journalism; Greta Van Susteren, host of *On the Record* on the Fox News Channel; and former CNN reporter Charles Bierbauer.

On the other side we'll have former *Los Angeles Times* editor John Carroll and the journalist authors of this book.

A zealous advocate who operates the straight-talking Buzz-Machine blog, Jarvis acknowledges that the blogosphere's frenetic pace has drawbacks. "The speed brings more news more quickly, and as a newsman I think that is a good thing," he says. "The speed also can bring more inaccuracy and more need to let people know about that." But he says bloggers do this, and quickly, by correcting errors almost as they are made.

"Take a look at correction in the blog world, the online world," Jarvis says. "They are just much, much faster than they were in old media where they were often non-existent. How many times have you seen a correction on network news?"

Uh, next question?

"We do corrections in blogs in certain ways," says Jarvis, a former print journalist who heads the graduate interactive journalism program at the City University of New York. "If we mess up, one of the ways we're expected to do this [correct errors] is not erase the mistake, but cross it out, show that it was there, and go on from there."

Very ethical, all would agree. Correcting and taking responsibility for errors is also an admirable facet of most magazines and newspapers, with the larger, most prestigious papers at times setting aside as much as one-fourth of a page daily to prominently identify and rectify their mistakes. In contrast, a vast preponderance of TV newscasts correct serious errors only rarely and minor ones never at all.

One important difference, though. If a print or even a TV journalist continually makes errors, in nearly all cases that person will soon no longer have a job. But no one can fire citizen journalists (can you fire yourself?) who blog independently, however fictitious the writing. They can go on blundering indefinitely, doing great damage, their rising error counts notwithstanding.

Former newspaper editor John Carroll notes another difference separating professional journalists and amateurs who, after all, likely have day jobs unrelated to their dabbling in journalism. "This is a full-time job," Carroll says about the journalism racket.

And then there is a little matter of honing one's skills. Carroll recalls that as a cub reporter learning the trade he had highly trained editors who held his feet to the fire when necessary, editors who insisted he get his facts right, editors who might spike one of his stories if he'd done it badly. "Without that," says Carroll, "I would have been a menace to the truth."

In the topsy-turvy universe of citizen journalism, anything less than lightning speed appears to be the only menace.

"And there's a discipline that comes from working within an organization that has standards of professionalism," Carroll says. "In addition to that, with citizen journalism, you will also get some people who are not acting in good faith—who are trying to mislead the public or trying to promote a particular politician. And there's no editor, really no way to catch that person. I know there's a belief in the wisdom of crowds and that the truth will come out eventually by virtue of other people contributing their knowledge to the Web, but I'm skeptical."

Van Susteren is not. We have her on split screen and, see, she's incredulous and thumbing her nose at Carroll. Her embrace of citizen journalism is predicated largely on the speed it can deliver when covering breaking news. "I love citizen journalists," she says, "because they are right there on the pulse. They can give it to you firsthand without the interpretations."

Is Van Susteren, an attorney who heads a free-swinging, ripped-from-the-headlines brand of news/interview program, endorsing delivery of facts to a ravenous audience before there *are* facts?

"If I'm on the air and there's been, let's say, a mining accident," she explains, "do I want to ask a journalist who has just arrived there four hours after the accident, or do I want to ask a citizen journalist who was there and watched it? Who is the better journalist on it? Not to take away from the one who has been working in the business, but the better journalist is the one who is there and saw it with his or her own eyes."

And eyewitness accounts become especially critical when traditional journalists have little or no access to the scene. That was certainly the case when Tibet was hit by waves of violence as Buddhist monks and others protested Chinese rule, and technology undermined the government's attempts to shape its image (by denying entry to western journalists) in advance of the 2008 Beijing Summer Olympics. Well before state media began beaming its own pictures, vivid blog accounts of the uprising instantly began streaming out of Tibet, along with photos and video that were uploaded and made available to the world, lifting a shade on a region stringently controlled by China.

"Everyone is afraid to speak," began a blogging Dutch tourist.

On a more fundamental level, though, research shows that faulty identifications are the biggest cause of wrongful convictions, and Van Susteren, no stranger to courtrooms, surely knows that lawyers and even many police organizations tend to be skeptical of eyewitness accounts. With good reason.

Flash back, for example, to the night of July 17, 1996, when TWA flight 800, an early model Boeing 747 with 230 passengers and crew aboard, lifted off from John F. Kennedy Airport bound for Paris. Some 12 minutes later it exploded in a giant fireball just off the coast of New York's Long Island.

Mobilizing immediately, reporters did what they always do when responding to pressures of time and competition to deliver instant answers to something even as complex and initially mystifying as the crash of a modern jetliner. They began interviewing eyewitnesses to the explosion, with TV putting on the air with alarming swiftness anyone who claimed to have seen what happened in the sky that evening. And it was highly dramatic, for a fair number of these "eyewitnesses" were sure they'd seen streaks of light heading toward the jet, suggesting that it had been hit by a surface-to-air missile, thus setting the stage for all sorts of conspiracy theories.

But they were wrong.

After a four-year investigation, the National Transportation Safety Board found that the TWA jet had exploded because a spark, likely caused by a short circuit, ignited fuel vapor in the plane's huge center fuel tank.

What of the eyewitness accounts that appeared to point to a missile attack? Investigators concluded that what they had seen were pieces of the flaming wreckage falling from the sky.

So much for the infallibility of eyewitnesses and, by extension, citizen-journalist eyewitnesses.

"Citizen journalism can be very good or it can be blather," says former CNN correspondent Bierbauer, now the dean of the College of Mass Communications and Information Studies at the University of South Carolina. One of his faculty members has been working with a small community paper to create a citizen-journalism program, and Bierbauer says it's "bringing in contributions that would probably not otherwise come to the paper. I think it has to come with the same kind of cautions that any journalism has to have. Is it right? Is it verifiable? Is it attributable to knowledgeable sources?"

That's reasonable. More worrisome is the dual duty—reporting and opinion—embraced by many citizen journalists, with no clear line separating one from the other. "It's important that we categorize and label that this is coming from the citizen side rather than the journalist side," says Bierbauer. "Can we effectively do that? To some degree. But we've muddied the waters so much, blurred the lines, that we don't [even] know whether Larry King is a journalist or not."

King does. He has said repeatedly that he is not a journalist, which is a convenient way of letting his bosses and him off the hook for the frequent banality of his durable but fawning CNN interview show that traffics about equally in Hollywood celebrities and breaking hard news. In most cases, if he were any cozier with guests, he'd be sitting on their laps.

In fact, King is a "talk show host" when CNN sees its best interest in titling him that, choosing to look away when he gets paid for doing commercials and when his laudatory blurbs (he appears to like everything) appear in ads for movies.

But on the many nights that his show responds to hard news, King does, indeed, function as a journalist with his guests, even though he is only playing one on TV.

"Anyone," says Jarvis, "can perform an act of journalism." He makes it sound sexual, as if there were billboards promoting safe newsgathering: *Before you perform an act of journalism, reach for a condom.*

But he's right. And Fox's Van Susteren, herself a hybrid who straddles both worlds, sees no difference between a citizen journalist and others "who work for news organizations. A journalist is someone who collects facts. I don't think you get any particular training by working in a news organization. Some citizens are damn good fact finders. So I am interested in what they have to say."

She recalls a confrontation she once had with a card-carrying professional journalist who was annoying her while she was with CNN. "This is how you become a journalist," Van Susteren snapped back. "You say, 'I'm a journalist!' To be a lawyer, you have a particular education and you take an exam of competency." Lawyers, she added, also have a code of conduct they're expected to follow—"unlike journalists."

Van Susteren is correct about no blanket *official* code of conduct existing for journalists, although institutions that employ them usually have their own. And who is and is not a journalist is often in the eye of the beholder.

"It's important for us to understand in clear English, what exactly, a journalist is, and what a journalist is not," Carroll, who is steeped in the tradition of newspapers and has edited some very good ones, told a Seattle audience in 2006. His words speak for themselves.

Yet, just as there are good doctors and bad doctors, good accountants and bad accounts, good plumbers and lousy ones, journalists come in polar opposites, too. So, dropping the semantics, the debate here is not so much about defining a journalist or a citizen journalist, but which are professional and which clueless amateurs.

"Who is a journalist?" asks Clarence Page, a syndicated columnist and member of the *Chicago Tribune* editorial board. "Anyone who wants to be." Even if naïve, inept, biased, or corrupt.

And yes, citizen journalist Tom Paine turned out rather well, even though his specialty was opinion, not hard news. He's been titled "the Father of the American Revolution" because of his early championing of independence from British rule, set down most famously in his 1776 pamphlet *Common Sense,* a colonial best-seller. He presented complex ideas clearly and concisely, as citizen journalists tapping away in today's chaotic, razzle-dazzle blogosphere surely aspire to do. But how many of them, do you think, are Tom Paines?

CHAPTER 6

"In-Depth Instant Results"

"What would you do, in the eyes of Muslims, to repair America's image? Mayor Giuliani—90 seconds."
   —A question from Anderson Cooper during the
   CNN-YouTube GOP candidate debate on November 29,
   2007

"How do you repair the image of America in the Muslim world?—30 seconds to respond."
   —Cooper asking another candidate to respond to Giuliani

They were juiced, pumped, goosed, buzzed, crazed, revved up, hopped up, bouncing off the walls, hearts thumping like Tom-Toms. They were sizzling, on fire, tongues blazing. They were unbuckled and unstopped, running and gunning, jet-powered zombies roaring faster and faster, blowing over speed bumps and through red lights, rolling, rolling, rolling, wind at their backs, adrenaline in their tanks.

Rarely have so many filled so much time saying so little with so much conviction.

It seems almost a paradox that extreme speed would have colored the coverage of a presidential election season as swollen and tortuously drawn out as the 2007–2008 one in the U.S. As *60 Minutes* grouch Andy Rooney cracked, "It's the earliest we got tired of the next election."

There was speed in reporting primary and caucus results, often before there were results to report. There was speed in candidate debates that undermined their potential to inform the public. There was speed all across the board, none of it contributing to a level of knowledge that would help voters decide which candidate to support for reasons beyond the superficial.

The candidates were visibly exhausted—and voters at once energized by some of the historic choices before them and fed up, grumbling about the exaggerated length of a grueling odyssey that awkwardly straddled 2007 and 2008 like an obese dancer attempting a split. It was the earliest starting presidential campaign in U.S. history, but a toss-up as to what irritated Americans most, its length or the sped-up campaign narratives thrust at them by much of the media coverage.

Nearly every election finds candidates with track records flip-flopping their positions to gain an edge with voters, and getting attacked for it. But the screeching media U-turns between early January's Iowa Caucuses and the New Hampshire Primary were especially amazing, a stunning flip-flop for the ages.

Virtually overnight, Hillary Clinton went from being the media-pronounced Democratic front runner on the eve of the Iowa Caucuses to being the media-pronounced hapless also-ran whose campaign was in collapse. (So why didn't she get out of the race and go back to New York, already, so the media could get on with their early worship of Barack Obama?)

Five days later she had boomeranged, again becoming the media-declared front runner when winning the New Hampshire Primary. During this same period, Obama experienced a media-driven reverse metamorphosis, going from underdog . . . to soaring Zeus . . . then back to underdog, but only after much of the coverage had blown it again.

Wrote Howard Kurtz in the *Washington Post,* "The coverage had been so out of control there was speculation about when Hillary might have to drop out. Polls giving Barack Obama an 8- or 10-point lead were accepted as fact. The news surrounding the former First Lady had been uniformly negative for days. She'd done everything wrong. Obama has done everything right. She got too emotional in the diner. People just didn't like her. She campaigned in boring prose and Obama in soaring poetry (to use her analogy). Bill was hurting her. A campaign shake-up was on the way. An era was ending. Some pundits were predicting a 20-point Obama margin.

"And then the voters actually went to the polls."

○ ○ ○

State caucuses and primaries are elections that send delegates to national Democratic and Republican conventions that, in turn, officially nominate party candidates for president. The 2008 election campaign's early start was caused by states bumping up the dates of their caucuses or primaries, at times chaotically, to protect or expand their influence on the nominating process.

"If the job of scheduling the presidential nominating contests were assigned to an insane asylum this is pretty much what the patients would come up with," said University of Virginia professor Larry Sabato, a long-time follower of politics and the nominating process. "It is a disaster in so many different ways."

Let us count those ways.

Take Nevada. Nice spot, famous for sagebrush, bighorn sheep, mountain bluebirds, cutthroat trout and slot machines. And in 2008 one of the states that gambled by moving up its delegate-selection process (to January 19 from February 15), hoping to grab more limelight and exert a bigger impact on picking party presidential candidates.

The problem for the wider election process? Nevada's rush to move up its caucus dealt it an influence disproportionate to its population (about 2.5 million) and delegate count (25).

Oh, *that*. Pundits couldn't be bothered. In too much of a rush.

Instead they used the Nevada Caucuses results (Mitt Romney was the GOP winner, Clinton the Democratic winner) as a launch pad for a scattershot of predictions regarding where the African American vote or Latino vote or elderly vote or youth vote or (if there had been one) Martian vote would likely go in coming state contests and in the national election as well.

Senseless? Yes. Perhaps the most pernicious effect of this sprint to hold earlier and earlier caucuses and primaries, however, was the enormous financial strain it put on candidates at what was still an early stage of the election process, when the vast majority of voters had not yet had an opportunity to have their voices heard.

Then . . . a chorus, a regular Mormon Tabernacle Choir of voices.

In a 2008 version of the California Gold Rush, 22 hard-charging states held presidential primaries or caucuses on so-called Super Tuesday, February 5. The result of this speed-up? Campaigns for both Democratic and Republican candidates were forced to try reaching as many voters as possible, in as little time as possible, to convince them to vote for a specific candidate. This left voters themselves with little time to contemplate their choices.

All of this came at epic cost. The 2008 campaign spending figures were astonishing even by U.S. political standards. From January 12 through February 3, Obama lavished nearly $11 million on television and radio ads to run in most of the Super Tuesday nominating contests. From January 17 through February 3, Clinton spent some $8 million.

The *New York Times* estimated that between them, these two candidates spent about $1.3 million daily just in the week leading up to Super Tuesday.

These huge expenditures were directly related to speed and the acceleration of the entire election process. In years past there would have been enough time for the two leading candidates to travel to many of the 22 Super Tuesday states to present themselves to the voting public, pressing the flesh *in* the flesh. They certainly would have had time to raise money.

But there was no time to think about that during the 2008 presidential campaign. The only way to reach masses of voters as quickly as possible was through television and radio, and that meant spending obscene amounts of money, and spending it fast.

In other words, high velocity can metastasize dangerously like cancer cells. It's not just television, the Internet and to some extent newspapers that have been afflicted by this scourge of speed. The very foundation of U.S. democracy—the presidential election— has been, too.

○ ○ ○

Some of the campaign reporting featured the usual mindlessness often available in any kind of live coverage from local news to the big boys who go national:

- CNN's Wolf Blitzer to Mike Duncan, chairman of the Republican National Committee: "If you lose the House, if you lose the Senate, if you lose the White House, that's a big setback for your party." No, Wolf; big gain.
- Blitzer doing some deep thinking about former New York Mayor Rudy Giuliani's campaign strategy of sitting back and counting on Florida to boost him toward the GOP nomination: "Either a brilliant strategy or a not-so-brilliant strategy." Once again, Wolf nailed it.
- MSNBC's *Hardball* host Chris Matthews on Hillary Clinton: "Let's not forget—and I'll be brutal—the reason she's a U.S. senator, the reason she's a candidate for president, the reason she may be a front runner, is that her husband messed around." Matthews later apologized . . . sort of.
- As did MSNBC's David Schuster for saying the Clinton campaign was "pimping out" the candidate's daughter, Chelsea, by having her phone Democratic Party superdelegates on her mother's behalf. He apologized, but got suspended for a short period anyway.

Meanwhile, 24-hour news kept shoveling election coverage of caucuses and primaries like coal into a furnace. CNN, not willing to wait for definitive vote counts, took the extra step of having its politics guru, Bill Schneider, contribute online "running commentary on what's going on"—like a simultaneous translation—even though nothing *was* going on.

Not that something "going on" had ever been a standard for coverage, especially when it came to 24-hour news favorite Obama, whom many in the media seemed determined to speed along toward the Democratic nomination early in the campaign. They lapped him up like a cat does milk.

As Jeff Jarvis blogged, "The way Barack Obama is being covered by the media and the blogosphere, he's not a political candidate anymore—he's a celebrity. He doesn't have political followers—he's got fans."

Perhaps this is the kind of coverage he had in mind. On January 28, CNN, the Fox News Channel, and MSNBC carried a 30-minute media event on the campus of American University that was worthy of two or three sound bites and 30 seconds tops. It was an endorsement of Obama by Senator Edward Kennedy; his niece, Caroline Kennedy; and his nephew, Representative Patrick Kennedy; and it was granted an orgy of gratuitous coverage that included speeches by the elder Kennedy and Obama that amounted to nothing more than stump oratory at a carefully staged rally, with strategically placed celebratory students waving banners in the background.

Length and tone are powerful persuaders. And the message here was that this photo op was a pivotal moment in U.S. presidential election history, though it wasn't, for Obama would go on to finish behind Clinton in the subsequent Massachusetts Primary, despite this bear-hug from the state's popular senior senator and some of his family.

"We're covering all the speeches, trying to bring it all to you in real time," said CNN daytime anchor Kyra Phillips. Translation: They were happily consuming time in what the 24-hour news crowd calls feeding the beast. The beast was the seemingly bottomless cavity of round-the-clock news itself, and as always, it was hungry.

In fact, ravenous on February 26, when Clinton and Obama debated in Cleveland on MSNBC, after which the 24/7 channel's pundits appeared to agree that the two candidates had created little if any news. Then, they spent the next 85 minutes talking about it.

○ ○ ○

However, it was earlier coverage of the 2008 Iowa Caucuses and New Hampshire Primary that deserves to be indelibly memorialized as a disaster of historic proportion in the great pantheon of speed-driven media screw-ups. If February 5 was Super Tuesday, the earlier 2008 Iowa and New Hampshire contests turned out to be a Super Toothache—largely one of their own making for most of the press, especially 24-hour news and much of the Internet. And even though the two events together occupied but a small corner of the vast campaign stage, the accompanying media wreckage would become a lasting eyesore.

In 2004, eight days separated the Iowa Caucuses—traditionally the first major electoral event of the presidential nominating process—and the New Hampshire Primary. In earlier years the distance separating these events was even greater, rather like the geographical distance between the two states.

But that gap narrowed to five days in 2008 after Iowa moved up its Caucuses to January 3 and New Hampshire its primary to January 8.

After months of drum-roll crescendo, heightened by a string of much-hyped candidate debates, the curtain rose dramatically in early January, with the Iowa Caucuses and New Hampshire Primary in line to become a spectacular metaphor for media speed freaks digging in their spurs, whipping hard and horse racing as they'd never raced before.

Count some bloggers as offenders, too, along with the Fox News Channel, MSNBC, and "the best political team on television," as CNN had humbly anointed its own gang of reporters, pundits, and staff gonzos. As if buzzed by electronic cattle prods, this 24-hour news herd hurriedly stepped it up, reporting news before it happened and reacting to news that hadn't occurred. In fact, these speedsters got so far ahead of themselves that at times they seemed to be having out-of-body experiences. Some bloggers did, too.

On the morning of the Iowa Caucuses, before a single vote had been cast, here was the well-regarded Politico website's "Political Playbook" blog speculating about Senator Fred Thompson's shrinking bid for the Republican nomination: "Thompson may drop out, back McCain." *Wrong.*

Here that same morning was the popular *Daily Kos* blog operated by Markos Moulitsas Zuniga: "The rumors are flying rampant. For example, I just heard from a rival campaign that Hillary's overnight internals are showing an Edwards, Hillary, Obama 1-2-3 result. This is many people removed from the original source, so likely crap, but indicative of the frenzy for information in Iowa right now." *Not only likely crap, but wrong crap.*

Here was the *Daily Kos* early that evening: "I suspect that whoever finishes third is done. . . . If Clinton finishes third the inevitability thing will have completely exploded and I doubt she would win NH." *Wrong.*

Here was the *Daily Kos* later, with figures based on early entrance polls showing Barack Obama first, John Edwards second, and Hillary Clinton third: "I'm pulling these numbers out of you know where, just like anyone else venturing predictions. This thing is so tight that anyone can win it. But bragging rights are important, so go for it."

Obama, Edwards, and Clinton did, indeed, finish in that order, but "pulling numbers out of you know where" was risky speedway reporting that valued bragging rights over gettingit right.

On CNN, meanwhile, you knew speed was a powerful factor when a timer was displayed in the bottom right corner of the screen, counting down the minutes and seconds to the start of the evening-long Iowa Caucuses. "A very exciting night unfolding," gushed CNN's Blitzer in front of a panoramic wall of graphics lit up like Times Square. You could almost hear his pulse pounding.

Blitzer said entrance polls (in contrast to the exit polls used in primaries) boded a "tight race" between Obama and Clinton. Actually, the closer race would turn out to be between Edwards and Clinton, with Clinton finishing a disappointing third.

Wiser CNN voices were ignored that evening. David Gergen's was—as if he were a hologram or speaking Latin—when he soberly counseled "patience" as his fellow "best political team" members jumped the gun and went giddy over Obama early in the Iowa vote before there was a reason to do that (even though Obama would go on to win).

Patience? Had Gergen really uttered the obscene "P word" on television? You half expected Blitzer to press a button and send Gergen through a trap door reserved for heretics.

That surely would have happened on MSNBC, where the excitable Matthews was as comfortable with measured reporting and analysis as he would have been face down on a bed of nails. As the returns began favoring Obama, he announced, "This election will be as big as [Ronald] Reagan beating [Jimmy] Carter." He said, "Obama is a man with a third world view and with his election the whole world will be happy." He added, "The big story out of tonight will be if two-thirds of the population says no to Hillary."

But did yes to Obama necessarily mean "no to Hillary"? Wasn't it possible also that voters liked them both, but Obama better?

Political blogger Larry Johnson had it right about Iowa coverage when singling out MSNBC's revelers: "They danced around like crack addicts celebrating the demise of the Clintons."

By evening's end, with Obama's victory now a certainty and Clinton vanquished to a has-been Siberia, former *Boston Globe* columnist Mike Barnacle and Joe Scarborough, both MSNBC regulars, hammered the last nails into her coffin:

> *Barnacle:* There is a sea change in this country. People want to get away from the last 8, 12, 16 years.
> *Scarborough:* Is that why Hillary's campaign is in third?
> *Barnacle:* That's part of it.
> *Scarborough:* Stopping Barack Obama's momentum in the next five days will be like stopping a hurricane in Pensacola Beach.

Wrong. But stopping Matthews' mouth would be.

"Obama's appeal is heroic," he gushed.

Get a grip, already.

There was certainly nothing heroic, five days later, about media coverage of the New Hampshire Primary. You could have cut them some slack, just a little. After all, pollsters from A to Z had Obama whipping Clinton handily in New Hampshire. But fault these media sheep for lack of circumspection in gleefully following pollsters off the cliff.

As media scholar Jay Rosen wrote later for the *Salon* website, "The narrative had gotten needlessly—one could say mindlessly—ahead of itself, as when stories about anticipated outcomes in the

New Hampshire vote reverberated into campaigns said to be preparing for those outcomes even before New Hampshire voted." It's no wonder that Rosen found the coverage "spectacular wreckage in the reality-making machinery of political journalism. The top players," he wrote, "had begun to report on the Obama wave of victories before there was any Obama wave of victories."

Matthews saw more than a wave; he saw a tsunami. For sheer futurist nonsense, no one topped him on the night of the New Hampshire Primary (which Hillary Clinton would win) when he joined fellow wiseass Keith Olbermann and MSNBC's other mad prophets in virtually endorsing Obama under the guise of reporting news. At one point, Matthews called Obama a "latter-day Lawrence [of Arabia]." Why stop there? Why not a latter-day Moses?

That was bad enough. Yet the lengthy monologue that erupted breathlessly from Matthews that night, before the polls had closed, was volcanic even for him:

> *Let me talk about the phenomenon of Barack Obama. You know what politics has become in this country? It's people voting automatically, for the familiar name, usually that of the incumbent for the same party, probably the same party their parents voted for, usually for the names from their same ethnic group. It's called pattern voting. It's members of Congress running again and again in districts designed and regularly groomed and gerrymandered to ensure that they are reelected again and again. It's senators and congressman voting the way their party whips steer them to vote, obeying and avoiding trouble from the usual interest groups, the usual suspects of Washington influence, saying and being careful not to say, every word according to the prescribed culture of the political system they have joined, a political system that gores more and more Americans to death and drives young people to any other interest, grand or trivial, that offers at least some moments of surprise. This is why the arrival of Barack Obama is so stunning, so phenomenal. In a world packed with professionals of various calibers of ability, too many of them schooled in how to speak without saying anything new, much less interesting of provocative, this guy stirs the air and, yes, elevates the spirit. It's not our job in the news business to pick candidates. That's for the people who get out there and vote. It is part of our job to report the excitement and, yes, the phenomenon now daring to*

challenge the political way things are. The young and the young at heart are, for the first time I can remember, being talked to, being called into action, being told, "Don't be afraid to hope." My fellow Americans, as a president used to say, this is politics at its best.

Not that he was in the business of picking candidates.

When Matthews "talks, at some point do oxygen masks drop from the ceiling?" *Daily Show* host Jon Stewart asked his guest, Tom Brokaw, a few weeks later. "When it comes to politics," Brokaw replied, "Chris has a form of Tourette's syndrome."

Less than an hour before the polls closed, meanwhile, Barnacle expanded on MSNBC's Obama/oceanic theme: "The acceleration of this thing, the pace of it. The wave of it. The building. The cresting of the wave." In addition, he foresaw "basically, potentially, the end of two dynasties—the Bush dynasty and the Clinton dynasty," even though Clinton would remain a U.S. senator regardless of how the Democratic race would turn out.

"After tonight, Barack Obama is going to be the front runner," prophesied NBC News political director Chuck Todd. The celebration, like much of the reporting, though, was premature, and not only by U.S. media. Three prominent British newspapers, the *Telegraph*, the *Independent,* and the *Times,* miscalled the New Hampshire Primary for Obama.

At evening's end, NBC senior statesman Brokaw went on camera for an egg-on-the-face sitdown with Matthews about excessive speed and impatience having caused the media debacle that had transpired, and what could be done to avoid a repetition in the future:

> *Brokaw:* You know what I think we're going to have to do?
> *Matthews:* Yes sir?
> *Brokaw:* Wait for the voters to make their judgment.

It was a novel concept for election coverage in the report-and-think-later age of new media, one that appeared to make Matthews uneasy.

> *Matthews:* Well what do we do, then, in the days before the ballot? We must stay home, I guess.

Amen to that, and to NBC News anchor Brian Williams. "We the media will beat ourselves (and deservedly so) for reaching conclusions before the voters have spoken," Williams blogged after the New Hampshire Primary. "Give us a few weeks—we will promptly forget the lessons of this debacle in polling, predictions and primary politics." The media's dismal New Hampshire performance will be hard to top, Williams added, but "we will all live to screw up another day. . . ."

He was right; some of them did.

Although Super Tuesday coverage went more smoothly, and featured less cheerleading for Obama, the Associated Press and even the usually measured National Public Radio, as well as the Public Broadcast System's *NewsHour with Jim Lehrer,* all goofed on the same call. Late in the evening, with Obama and Clinton running neck and neck in Missouri, all three jumped the gun and projected Clinton as that primary's winner. Later they corrected themselves, projecting it for the actual winner, Obama.

In addition, one major pollster erred badly in another Super Tuesday state. The Reuters/C-SPAN/Zogby poll had Obama trouncing Clinton 49 percent to 36 percent in California. The reverse was true; she trounced him. And on the Republican side, the same poll forecast Mitt Romney whipping McCain 40 percent to 33 percent; the percentages were fairly close, but the winner was McCain.

"We blew it," pollster John Zogby acknowledged. "This is not one of our happier moments." But will anyone, especially the media, remember long after the dust from this mad dash has settled?

If they do, is it possible that the 2008 presidential contest will finally lead to a much-deserved devaluation of public opinion polls in trying to predict an election's outcome even before anyone has actually voted? About as possible, to borrow from Adlai Stevenson, as hell freezing over.

Media tradition is not easily reversed. The reporting of opinion polls on the eve of elections, even if they turn out to be grossly inaccurate, is so much a part of political coverage in the United States that few bother to ask why we pay attention to them in the first place.

Our worship of speed, once again, is an answer.

Another is that polls are a vital element of that age-old media malady, horse race coverage—the who's winning/who's losing today syndrome that at some point in every election campaign resonates loudest and eclipses all else.

Still another answer is that news organizations that have their own polling operations, or utilize them in partnership with others, see them as ways to establish or extend their brands in high-profile stories like elections.

Finally, parroting polls that predict an election's likely outcome is far sexier and attention-getting than reporting in depth on the global and nation-shaping issues that define candidates.

The Reuters/C-SPAN/Zogby poll was not the only poll to publicize data that conflicted with reality in advance of Super Tuesday results in California. In the days leading up to February 5, when nearly half the nation went to polls or caucuses in more than 22 states to help pick Democratic and Republican Party presidential nominees, other published polls indicated strongly that not only had Obama closed a considerable lead by Clinton in California, he might actually win the state and its treasure trove of delegates that could pave the way for the nomination.

Once again, predicting the news had become far more compelling to many in the media than simply waiting to report it.

And then facts got in the way.

Not only was the race between Clinton and Obama in California not close, it was not even really much of a contest in the end. She clobbered him in the popular vote in addition to taking away more delegates.

Nonetheless, the race was on, and everyone rushed to quote the polls. In fact, the early-bird syndrome was visible everywhere in much of this election season.

There was a time, for example, when "absentee ballots"—that's what they were called—were reserved for those unable to vote in person either because of illness or because they were away on election day. However, 31 states now permit early voting with essentially no reason required, and increasing numbers of voters cast their ballots by mail in advance of various election days. In fact, they are encouraged to do so.

The chairwoman of the Florida Democratic Party, in fact, sent an e-mail reminder that "absentee ballots will save valuable time and money in the final weeks of the campaign and help busy people to remember to cast their ballots."

"Save time"? *Los Angeles Times* columnist Patt Morrison asked incredulously the day before the February 5 California Primary, more than half of whose voters opted for mail-in ballots. "The country asks its citizens to sit up and pay a little attention to politics every four years, rather than choosing a president by the venerable 'one potato, two potato' method, and you can't spare the time to check the headlines for a few more days?"

Voting early also can be self-defeating, Morrison noted. "If you marked John Edwards or Rudy Giuliani's name that political eternity ago, you blew your vote," she wrote. "They've dropped out. So have Bill Richardson and Fred Thompson. Ditto Dennis Kucinich." She added, "The world's tanking stock markets, the flop-sweat in home sales, the deepening, darkening sub-prime chaos and the candidate's dueling recovery proposals—forget about it. You voted already."

There was another downside to the vote-early surge. "As more ballots are cast early, campaigns scramble to keep up," said the *New York Times*. And early voting, the paper said, tends to favor wealthier candidates with better-financed campaigns that "are in better position to take advantage of this dynamic by having more time to spend on phone banks, mailings and other tactics" aimed at mail-in voters.

O O O

The race among states eager to host the first primaries was matched by the race among 24-hour news networks to stage the first debates in 2007–2008, leading to a slew of these nationally televised events before and after the first votes were cast in the Iowa Caucuses and New Hampshire Primary. Why? Because CNN, the Fox News Channel, and MSNBC coveted the opportunity to stamp their brands on this dominant story and woo new viewers while again filling the basic need to feed the hungry beast. In fact, call these occasions feeding frenzies, from the deluge of advance stories on the debate to the actual debate to the same-night instant review of the debate to the inevitable days of debate analysis.

Political debates have a storied tradition in this nation, going back at least as far as the 1858 series of clashes between Republican Abraham Lincoln and incumbent Democrat Stephen A. Douglas with an Illinois seat in the U.S. Senate at stake. They faced off in seven different cities, focusing mostly on slavery, the format calling for one candidate to speak for an hour, the other candidate to speak for 90 minutes, with the first man then receiving a half hour to wrap up. Historians say the process worked fine, but Lincoln and Douglas didn't have Wolf Blitzer snapping his fingers in their faces.

What a difference a little more than a century has made.

Journalist Emmet John Hughes wrote in the *New York Times* in 1960, just prior to the historic series of televised presidential debates with Richard Nixon and John F. Kennedy, that something historic was about to happen. He predicted, correctly, that the voter's image of candidates would thereafter be formed on that little screen inside the home.

"So stunning are the factors of size of audience and speed of communication on the grand scale," he said, "that the very rhythm of political life does seem revolutionized."

Mostly for the worse.

Can there be anything more tailored to speed, as well as attention deficit disorder, than these televised so-called debates—what were there, a couple of hundred?—that threaded the marathon run-up to the 2008 presidential election?

There were some exceptions this political season as the fields of candidates from both major parties were each ultimately winnowed to something less than a platoon, allowing more time for more carefully calibrated political schmoozery. In the main, however, emphasis placed on these TV-choreographed events is greatly at odds with their actual worth, for most of them stress the exact qualities no thinking voter would desire in a president. They celebrate hair-trigger ad-libs and quick, agile wit—the stuff of good TV but not necessarily good governance. Along with flashy TV skills, they reward that familiar bugaboo, speed, and place a premium on hurry-up replies to questions.

Consider this: The candidate who weighs an answer thoughtfully before responding—a trait we should value in a president—most often appears indecisive, flustered, out of touch, a musty old soul worthier of assisted living than the Oval Office. At least that's the word afterward by reporters and commentators given the task of instantly choosing winners and losers. No one dares publicly criticize sound thinking, of course. It's a nice bonus if you have the rest of the package. But brevity and crisp sound bites resonate much louder with most of the media.

Flash back to June 3, 2007, when the election season was still young. The state was New Hampshire, in advance of the state's primary, the occasion a YouTube/CNN–staged "debate"—the quote marks are necessary—with eight Democratic candidates, all of them prodded to communicate in *fastspeak* by moderator Blitzer. The stopwatch format gave candidates barely enough time even for sound bites, with Blitzer speeding them up by muttering, "All right, all right, thank you" even before they had finished their brief answers.

The entire evening was an exercise in racetrack journalese, for immediately afterward came instant analysis from CNN's usual cadre of chin strokers. And five minutes after that, CNN had a focus group in front of the camera judging Obama the winner.

Now, flash forward to a January 21, 2008, CNN debate with Democratic candidates in advance of the South Carolina Primary, after which Candy Crowley, a veteran CNN political reporter who surely knows better than to report news before it happens, predicted, "This [the just-ended debate] will not move the polls." How did she know?

To CNN, a more critical question was how the debate had moved the fingers of 17 independent voters from South Carolina who had been equipped with hand clickers to measure their instant responses to what the candidates were saying in real time. Really now, just how goofy was that?

This goofy. After the debate, CNN's Erica Hill reviewed the results, interpreting the meaning of the multicolored lines squiggling across the screen:

"Passion paid off when Hillary Clinton . . ."

"What didn't pay off were attacks . . ."

"And when they started attacking each other . . ."

"That left our voters cold . . ."

"Hillary got the biggest jump. . . ."

"Obama got the biggest spike."

How much value was this gimmicky exercise? Well, it filled time. Which, surely, was why—other than farce, what other possible reason?—CNN deployed the same technological nonsense in other candidate face-offs.

Take the Obama/Clinton debate that CNN and Univision cosponsored in Austin, Texas, less than two weeks before the March 4 Texas and Ohio Primaries that were widely assumed to be essential for Clinton to win in order to sustain her candidacy. In a scenario echoing the aftermath of her defeat in the Iowa Caucuses, Clinton's campaign again was said to be gasping for breath, as Obama, after running off an impressive string of primary and caucus wins that gave him the delegate lead, looked ahead toward a match-up with McCain, then the presumptive GOP nominee.

The 45-minute debate was another small blip on the election landscape and largely forgettable, as was CNN's postdebate drool, except for what it said so clearly about a 24-hour news network's zeal to pass off an hour of absurdity as constructive analysis.

In other words, it was beast-feeding time again.

"We're going to be talking to our political analysts all about what happened tonight, what they saw happen tonight, what you all saw happen tonight," announced Anderson Cooper. Translation: They'll tell you what you watched, because you weren't swift enough to get it on your own.

A sampling included Gloria Borger, Donna Brazile, David Gergen, and Jeffrey Toobin—at one point each allotted a fourth of the screen like celebrity players on *Hollywood Squares*—ticking off the candidates' "best moments" and "worst moments" even though the debate had yielded no moments worth mentioning.

Noted Borger, a veteran political reporter, "What we've seen tonight are two candidates who don't have very many differences. We've seen this in debate after debate." Then why had it been necessary to *have* debate after debate?

Yet Toobin, a legal specialist who usually makes good sense when he appears on CNN, did see something in Clinton, a certain wistfulness perhaps, even a sense of the inevitable, and he wanted to pass on to America what he'd seen. Watching her that night, he felt that she recognized that her campaign wasn't going well, that this could be her final major campaign riff, and "she's going to leave . . . on the high ground, not the low ground."

Well . . . not quite. Clinton and her campaign lived to riff another day. And two days later, she was getting down and dirty when stridently, even angrily charging in front of cameras that Obama had misrepresented her views in his speeches.

Meanwhile, Brazile, a highly placed Democratic activist, felt Clinton "scored better on several issues, but he (Obama) is connecting better." Come again? She scored but didn't connect? He connected but didn't score?

How do these people do this with a straight face?

Later, it was time for "CNN gives candidates strategy advice," with Gergen saying Clinton needed to "open up on the trail and be more personal and be more connecting," and Brazile saying she "needs a message firewall."

And finally, it was time again to laser in on the handful of randomly independent voters that CNN had wired up so they could dial in their instant responses to what the candidates were saying as the debate was occurring. As if an instant response was somehow more meaningful than a thoughtful one.

Again, the squiggly lines, superimposed against videotape of the debate. "Always remarkable to see that dial testing," said Cooper. Almost as remarkable as disingenuous commentary by members of the media.

Just what will the media's deep-thinking technophiles think of next to speed up the process of thought and deliberation?

Possibly this. In 2007, the *New York Times* asked seven people with media experience to propose ideas for a candidate debate in the age of new media.

Matt Bai, author of *The Argument: Billionaires, Bloggers and the Battle to Remake Democratic Politics*, foresaw candidates having laptops at their lecterns in front of a giant screen. "Then, as one candidate is talking, the others will use instant messaging to create a kind of scrolling commentary and critique, and all the comments will appear overhead."

The 24-hour news networks are likely working on it now, just as they and others have sought to enhance their election coverage by merging technology with "gotcha" journalism, the kind of thing tabloid TV shows and some local newscasts have been doing for years.

It has come to putting candidates under the "videoscope," with 24-hour news outfits and the news divisions of ABC, CBS, and NBC hoping to widen their panorama of coverage, cheaply, by equipping young, mostly nonunion "off-air" reporters with lightweight portable cameras to enable them to record candidates' most "candid"—think embarrassing, think revealing—moments. These mostly very green and youngish "campaign embeds," as NBC News has titled them, have shadowed candidates, filing video and blog posts along the way.

This candid-camera approach to election coverage is hardly new; the camera-phone-at-rallies-and-campaign-stops surge had been unstoppable for some time, making candidates' every unguarded, unscripted moment a potential Internet blockbuster. What's more, TV news organizations have employed "off-air" reporters in past election campaigns.

But never to this extent, their sheer numbers raising questions about their value and validity.

As Brian Stelter wrote about "off-air" reporters in the *New York Times*, "Their relative inexperience, combined with the constant deadline pressure, has raised some concerns about this increasingly digital type of election coverage."

Of course, it's been much harder to sneak up on someone these days, with candidates now acutely aware of the perils of off-the-cuff stumbles that show up on YouTube within minutes if not seconds. So they've been much less likely to babble off the tops of their heads than to pose and put on an act for any lens within range of their bombast.

There's a larger point than staging to consider here, however. Even if candidates were not performing for the camera, even if they were getting caught in untidy moments, would showing Americans these "gotcha" spectacles be a productive way to educate them about the policies of presidential aspirants and their abilities to govern?

The answer is no. But education is not what much of this generation's new media are about, as evidenced by an oxymoronic primary election night "crawl" that ran at one point on CNN, promising "In-depth instant results."

It's a speed thing, you see. They don't call it *instantainment* for nothing.

CHAPTER 7

Desperate Newspapers
Play Catch-Up

I wonder, "What the hell is the New York Times *doing putting out a news bulletin on its website at 10:30 in the morning?"*
—Jim Lehrer of *The NewsHour with Jim Lehrer* on PBS

It just makes so much sense that this is what we should be doing.
—John Moore, managing editor of the *Ventura County Star*

It's much easier to maintain the status quo, even as we sink.
—Joe R. Howry, editor and vice president of the *Ventura County Star*

Tuesday, February 12, 2008, began the way most days do for 23-year-old Adam Foxman.

He awoke before sunrise, at 5:00 A.M., in his parents' home in the West San Fernando Valley area of Los Angeles. He showered, shaved, and dressed, ran a hand through his mop of thick auburn curls, had his customary green tea and bagel and was off, heading northwest on the #101 Freeway toward Camarillo in his creaky 1997 green Ford Taurus. Soon he was cresting the Conejo Grade and swooping down into the flatlands, traveling in the opposite direction of a serpentine trail of headlights from rush-hour traffic that was already starting to build in the darkness.

By 6:00 A.M., after a commute of more than 30 miles, the UCLA grad was at his desk in the vast, brightly lit newsroom of the Ventura County Star, *a reputable, small-to-medium Scripps Howard daily headquartered on the fringe of metropolitan Los Angeles.*

It was just another morning, as routine as his bagel for young Foxman, who had worked for the UCLA Daily Bruin *and then briefly for the English-language* Tico Times *in Costa Rica before joining the* Star *in its modern new building behind the sprawling Factory Outlet Mall. He made his usual round of calls to local agencies to catch up on what had happened overnight, compiling a "morning report" of police, fire, weather, and traffic news that yielded a pair of "briefs." Then he began work on a story about a web-based tip system employed by Ventura County Crime Stoppers, a privately funded citizen's group that works closely with local law enforcement.*

It was calm, pleasantly tranquil, a good time to concentrate and chart out a worthwhile story without interruption. Yet experienced journalists know that newsrooms can be deceptively quiet, and then kaboom, like a volcano blowing without warning, major news suddenly erupts: A space shuttle explodes. A foreign leader is assassinated. Britney Spears escapes her handlers or Paris Hilton is hauled away—again.

The excitement began for Foxman at 8:30 when an editor asked him to check out a reported shooting at E. O. Green School in neighboring Oxnard, a city of some 200,000 that leads Ventura County in violent crimes. Not that school shootings are that unusual in a nation that tops the Western Hemisphere in shootings of all kinds, thanks to just about every American with a trigger finger being a candidate to own or gain control of a gun. But breaking crime news, however tragic for victims and their families, is adrenaline time for most reporters.

So Foxman responded quickly, phoning the Oxnard Police watch commander to get confirmation of the shooting and the address of the school. Then he went to a yellow filing cabinet near his desk and did something that only a few years ago would have been alien to any newspaper reporter.

He opened a drawer and reached for his SONY DVCAM video camera, complete with a 12× zoom.

O O O

A question from Jim Lehrer, anchor of *The NewsHour with Jim Lehrer,* a thoughtful PBS program that stubbornly adheres to gold-standard traditions that some regard as several laps behind today's media dragsters: "How do you use technology without destroying your standards?"

Perhaps you don't. With that prospect looming, it's time for a brief detour down memory lane with Lou Cannon, a former esteemed White House correspondent for the *Washington Post* who has written a slew of nonfiction books, including five about Ronald Reagan. Someone as prolific as Cannon doesn't spend his time euphemizing the good old days of newspapering; nor, on the other hand, does he hold back when contrasting their upside with what he sees as drawbacks of new media.

"At the better papers you had time to be a little bit thoughtful," says Cannon, who also worked for the *San Jose Mercury* and the *Los Angeles Times.* "You could go and talk it over with other reporters, talk it over with your editors, go back to sources. There were a lot of stories that were slow to develop, and I think a lot of that is gone now."

Today's reconfiguration of media, along with the accelerated news cycle, is taking its toll, he says: "The problem with this cycle, even compared to four years ago, is that reporters have to spend so much time doing other stuff like filling in for the online version . . . that there really isn't time to think about the story. At a time when we are making huge reductions in the number of journalists at major papers, the impact on the reporter is enormous. Huge demands, extra demands. It makes wire service reporters of just about every journalist who is out there. The result tends to be less-reflective and more hurried journalism."

It happens in the UK, too, where research from Cardiff University purports to show that cost cutting and newspaper expansion into the Internet has the average Fleet Street reporter tripling output since 1985. Is it possible that today's Fleet Streeters are three times better than 23 years ago? More likely just three times as stressed.

So let's give this metamorphosis a name.

In the United States it's usually called *multimedia*—a strong, irreversible movement toward split personalities in the news business. But journalism schools across the country have another name for the transformative process redefining much of today's print and electronic news industry. They call it *convergence,* as in divergent elements of media coalescing into a single androgynous globule. There are no newspaper reporters, television news reporters, radio news reporters, Internet news reporters per se, students are informed. There are just reporters . . . who do it all.

Yes, multimedia reporters, the designated caped superheroes of a new journalistic age.

They're seen increasingly as the future for a cratering newspaper industry pummeled by repeated budgetary calamities that have led to drastic cutbacks, and by news consumers who play media musical chairs. As a consequence of these hard times, newspapers are transferring more and more of their resources to their Web incarnations while having staff members do double duty and more, including encouraging them to write blogs. Television news operations are doing much the same—cost-cutting CBS laid off 160 news personnel from its stations in 2008 amid rumblings that network anchor Katie Couric's early exit was also on the table—as the rapidly growing Internet pushes everyone to sleek down, rev up, put down some rubber and roar out at a faster pace.

Multimedia mean speed is in, time to think is out!

It's a condition of the age, right? Newspapers we have known and cherished—enjoying the tactile touch of them, holding, folding, and wrapping fish in them—are wheezing, gasping for breath and, pessimists say, clearly en route to becoming an endangered species in their present form. The days when families would spread out the Sunday paper and spend an hour or two leisurely reading it are long gone. That scene is available today only in private memories and old Warner Brothers movies.

The decline that began some time ago as a drippy faucet has become a steady stream moving seemingly toward a full-on flood. Change has been ongoing for years, as renowned newspaper families like the Binghams, Chandlers, and McCormicks have withdrawn and transferred ownership of their properties and legacies to corporations and faceless financial institutions that often become absentee owners with no emotional ties to the cities where their acquisitions publish.

In a sense, one wonders why it took so long. Newspapers have generally carried the aura of anachronism since midway through the last century, never having been able to match the speed of radio and especially television, whose everything-live, this-just-in, caught-on-tape, breaking-news-all-the-time mania is delivered and promoted so effectively with theater-marquee graphics.

The Gannett Company proved it knew the score when launching *USA Today* in 1982 as the nation's first general-interest, daily paper to impersonate—*oh, the horror!*—TV news. It was a jolt for some, beginning life as a national newspaper featuring generally thinner, easy-to-read fare packaged in short, punchy articles enhanced by brightly colored graphics, diagrams, charts, and back-page weather maps. No wonder it helped to wear shades while reading it. And in case you didn't see the intended connection, the paper's TV-look-alike vending machines sharpened your vision. Talk about surrendering to the enemy.

Or, in effect, becoming the enemy, for six years later, in a touch of the surreal, a *USA Today on TV* series surfaced on the small screen, a short-lived case of TV imitating the newspaper that imitated TV.

The striking success of *USA Today*—which would endure into the 21st century—persuaded some newspapers to rethink their own formats and content, for better or for worse. And as TV continued chipping away at newspaper circulation, afternoon publications—increasingly vulnerable in reporting breaking news long after it broke—began dropping in droves. In addition, morning newspapers also began scrambling to keep up with the timeliness of their TV rivals, stressing their strengths—in-depth reporting and thoughtful interpretation and analysis—instead of instant news.

However, the basic template remained largely unchanged through the years.

Then . . . a stake through the heart. The unfortunate, already-drained-and-embattled poundee was conventional journalism, the pounder a fast-burgeoning Internet that had made obsolete the traditional once-a-day production schedule of newspapers. Along with that, meanwhile, came an opportunity for news hybrids like Adam Foxman, notebook in one hand, video camera in the other.

Are journalists—a generally skeptical, rebellious lot that tends to bitch about most things—taking this in stride? Or instead are they taking to the streets, waving banners and burning their top bosses in effigy?

Hardly, concludes the Project for Excellence in Journalism (PEJ) in its 2008 *State of the News Media* report.

"Those who straddle technologies tend to see it as a good thing," write the PEJ's Amy Mitchell and Tom Rosenstiel. "About half say it has improved their work, twice the number that has doubts." Of course, some of the doubters may have already been history when the survey was conducted in late 2007, having taken buyouts, been cut loose, or fled the multiple-hat onslaught by some other means. "But one way or the other, the profession is becoming more accepting," Mitchell and Rosenstiel comment.

Tell it to "#32," the irate reporter who related the following account on angryjournalist.com, a website that lets newspaper types post anonymous comments about the state of the industry: "I wrote a story that was unique, took a lot of work and wasn't from a press release and wasn't from the wires and wasn't stolen from a comic book. I spelled all the words correctly and used proper punctuation."

The kicker as described by "#32:" The story "did not run because it did not have a video and audio component for the web."

Sounds a lot like your local *Eyewitness News,* except "#32" is referring to a newspaper.

Of course, "#32" may represent just a small minority of malcontents. For example, the PEJ study found that most journalists, though generally pessimistic about the future of what they do for a living, approved of how their news organizations were making a transition to the Internet. About half of those who saw the Internet weakening journalistic values, by the way, were older than 55, a clear indication that age was a factor in rejection of new ways imposed by this technology.

Also, perhaps "#32's" story was spiked because he couldn't write a cogent sentence. Look, it happens. Nor can newspapers as a group be that much holier than thou about this. Is there one anywhere, even among the elite, that more than once has not linked the value of a news story to its "art" or pictorial possibilities?

Nonetheless, more than a fourth of national print journalists spend at least half their time producing Web content, according to the PEJ study. And the shotgun marriage of newspapers and the Internet does present inherent conflicts—including a dissatisfaction of a different kind now simmering at the newspaper where Cannon used to work.

The problem at the *Washington Post* concerns speed, not video, says Howard Kurtz, who scrutinizes media for that paper while—call it multitasking—also observing his own newsroom.

The *Post* remains one of the nation's premier newspapers—witness its six Pulitzer Prizes in 2008. Yet, "The pace has gotten dizzying for me and my colleagues just in the past few years," says Kurtz about the impact of adapting to today's sped-up media universe. "In the last year, the pendulum has swung in our newsroom to putting things on the Web almost immediately, with the exception of some big exclusive story or long investigative piece. You know, everybody wants it now-now-now. And that's understandable in a wired world. But the sacrifice clearly is in the extra phone calls and the chance to briefly reflect on the story that you're slapping together."

As for *Post* reporters doubling, tripling, and even quadrupling up? It's now routine "to be asked to post a story online minutes after an event has happened," Kurtz says, "and while you're trying to finish the longer version for the next day's paper to be asked to talk about it on the radio or in a TV interview or maybe in an online chat, which many of us do regularly."

Of course, it's only reporters at bigger papers who generally are invited to share their wisdom with radio and TV. But Kurtz is right when saying the "compression factor" has never been greater.

Equally so across the pond. That's the word from Nik Gowing, who counts his own experience with the "environment of real-time news" as unpleasantly memorable. "I live with that tyranny every hour," the BBC World Service anchor told a Harvard University gathering of journalists not long ago. "We have a constant deadline. How do you measure truth and accuracy in that?"

Perhaps you don't even try. Nor is it productive to ignore reality and swim upstream against the powerful currents of new media that by now appear to have gained wide acceptance, even at the nation's premier newspaper, the *New York Times,* which in early 2008 instituted radical changes that made itself look more like its own website. These included a couple of pages of paragraph-long summaries of the paper's stories and another page devoted in part to summarizing its website. As a rather astonishing editor's note reported, the changes were intended to "help readers navigate and mine the paper and . . . nytimes.com."

Or perhaps not so astonishing, given the general freefall of newspapers compared with the Internet's ever-increasing stature. Nielsen ratings for average home Internet usage during January 2008 put the active worldwide digital universe at nearly 354 million. A recent Zogby International poll, moreover, found that nearly half of Americans—and 55 percent of those age 18 to 29—make the Internet their primary news source. And about two-thirds of Americans see traditional media as "out of touch" with what they want from news.

The designated "out-of-touch" bunch includes TV news, which just 29 percent of Americans now say is their primary news source, radio (11 percent) and newspapers (10 percent), according to Zogby. In other words, even the most zealous traditional-media diehards can see this glass as less than half full, and for newspapers (dismissed by 90 percent of Americans as largely irrelevant), the glass is all but empty.

Any wonder that newspapers and their Sancho Panzas are frantically hurling themselves onto this speeding Internet bandwagon and hoping for the best, even as its wheels remain wobbly and out of line?

Although the profitability and economic impact of their efforts remain to be seen, early signs are anything but rosy. To date only one major newspaper, the *Wall Street Journal,* has persuaded consumers to pay for access to its online product as they do for the newspaper they buy on the street or have delivered to their homes.

The specter of falling circulation is an even gloomier facet of this increasingly wired culture, however, for just how long can subscribers be expected to pay for something they're getting online at no cost, and with a surfeit of up-to-the second news and chatter? This is hardly a promising business model.

Just as larger papers continue to expand online, so are the industry's small and medium fry turning to the Internet as a way to survive and do it profitably, as Web services such as Craig's List siphon off classified-ads revenue that has long been their lifeblood.

One of them is the *Ventura County Star,* whose strategy for survival is pretty much a microcosm of newspapers nationally. "We're trying to find our way," said Joe R. Howry, the newspaper's friendly vice president and managing editor—a journalist for 35 years—about chopping through the uncharted thick underbrush of multimedia journalism. He's doing it with a full-time editorial staff of 83 (more than a third with multimedia training) and nearly as many lesser-paid freelancers. This proliferation of freelancers would seem to mirror economic times that are tenuous even for a newspaper like the *Star,* which is owned by media behemoth Scripps Howard, even though stories assigned to some of them don't extend beyond the local strawberry festival.

Fully embracing the online universe was pretty much a no-brainer for the *Star.* It had little choice given doomsday national trends and its shrinking circulation in an area whose population of about 800,000 extends across a generally affluent, suburban sprawl of communities, a 362-square-mile region that also takes in a narrow fringe of Los Angeles County.

The handwriting was not only on the wall for the *Star,* it was on the ceiling, floor, computer terminals, and everywhere. Howry sees its new mission as "a big, grand experiment," and his multimedia staff as "modern-day" journalists.

"What does upset me is that the stuff that gets on the Web is lighter, initially," says one of Howry's modern-day reporters. He's veteran John Scheibe. "So I would just as soon not have my byline with it," he says. "The newspaper's appetite tends to be insatiable;

they are hungry for content because they know the ground under their feet [the newspaper industry] is changing."

So, as Howry says, you either change or join the worms beneath that ground. But change or survive at what cost?

That question—predicated on the impact of new media speed—was posed to *Star* managing editor John Moore in a large, white, bare-walled conference room where he and eight other editors had concluded their regular 9:00 A.M. editorial meeting to plot the day's "news budget," which would likely include substantial coverage of the E. O. Green shooting, though details about what happened were sketchy at the time.

A big board at the front of the room provided marching orders for the staff:

Our Priorities
Local, Local, Local
Use Freelancers Tactfully
Use Staff Strategically

Unmentioned was the priority of speed.

"The decisions you make now, both in print and online, are quicker," as is the frequency of making "instant decisions," said Moore, a ruddy-faced man whose large brush mustache gives him the look of someone sent from central casting to appear in a movie about newspapers.

As for changes in philosophy, *online* is synonymous with *breaking news*, after all. So expect *big* changes.

But get out! Traffic reports? From a newspaper? They are one small facet of the breaking-news-as-it-breaks mantra—a redefining of what constitutes printworthy news—that separates the older, slower, traditional *Star* from the new speedier online *Star* whose webpage gets about 17,000 hits a day, according to Moore's boss, Howry.

"In the past, we wouldn't report a traffic accident that slowed down traffic on the 101," says Moore, whose easy manner has him smiling a lot. "It happens every day. Now if you get it, and it's slowing down traffic and backing up, we'll give you three lines online. The information has always been there, but (in the past) we've chosen to say it's not a news story. Now we're saying that online this information has value to somebody out there."

However soft-soaped, changing long-established rules of operation is a prerequisite for newspapers extending operations to the Internet. For example, Howry says that in years past, the *Star* would post a story online only "when it was completely done and completely edited. We would not go online until it had gone through the whole process." And now? "At the first blush of information, we get it up [on the website], then fill it out," says Howry.

Posting instant information and *then* filling it out? That equals shooting first and asking questions later. And wearing a bulls-eye here is the time-honored journalistic tradition of not reporting until there is something *to* report.

Equally striking are the print page/webpage double standards now in place at the *Star,* one involving the correction of mistakes, historically an admirable trait of most newspapers compared with a general reluctance to admit error by mistake-ridden radio and TV news operations.

Although mistakes are inevitable, slowpoke newspapers catch most of theirs before they creep into print. In contrast, the online practice is to highlight the *process* of reporting—the equivalent of exposing news consumers to a reporter's preliminary raw notes and initial impressions that may contain numerous distortions and inaccuracies.

Mirroring live TV, online operations infrequently make corrections in the classic sense, preferring instead to make continuous updates. In this netherworld of semantics, there are mistakes and, to quote Moore's euphemistic definition, there is this: *"At that time, this was the best information we had."* And if that information was flat-out wrong, bogus? That is different from "an error in reporting," Moore says.

And does *"At that time, this was the best information we had"* occur with greater frequency in the online *Star* than in the print-newspaper *Star?* Yes, according to Scheibe. And the harm? None, he answered, if online readers understand that "the cycle of the Web is so short that we're bound to make errors and that they'll be corrected." Scheibe paused before continuing. "And I'm not so sure they do, by the way."

So eager are some papers to adapt to and embrace the Internet, meanwhile, that they readily ease or lower traditional journalistic standards to make them better conform to those online. For example, the layer after layer of editing that newspaper writers face provide the kind of multiple safety nets that have long been touted as a strength of print in contrast with say-it-live-and-it's-gone TV news.

"But it's time to put that net away," *Washington Post* managing editor Phil Bennett said when announcing a pilot editing plan for the paper's "A" section that would include "fewer touches" on some stories by editors to better parallel the online model. Bennett vowed that quality wouldn't suffer.

In the case of the *Ventura County Star*, there are gaping holes—large enough to drive a double standard through—in the safety net afforded veteran columnist Timm Herdt, the paper's Sacramento bureau chief who's been covering California, says Moore, "since voting machines were invented."

In addition to his newspaper column, Herdt writes a blog about the state's politics for the *Star's* website. It's the paper's only present blog, which, like print columns, usually reflects the opinions of those who write them, often in a free-associating, let-it-all-hang-out way.

Herdt's regular column does not go into the newspaper before it's seen by editors. And his blog?

The following dialogue about Herdt's column and blog with the paper's two top editors (abbreviated for space reasons and edited slightly for clarity) illustrates just how much of a work in progress the paper's online incarnation remains, and that like other newspapers facing this challenge, a consistent policy governing both print and online formats remains illusive.

Q: Is Herdt's blog edited?

Moore: No, not at all.

Q: So, whatever he puts out, goes out?

Moore: Yes.

Q: Does that concern you?

Moore: No.

Q: Why not?

Moore: He's a veteran journalist; he is a great writer. He also writes a column for us, so we know he will express opinion, and we don't mind. I just trust him.

Q: But the column he writes in the newspaper is edited?

Moore: Yes, the column is edited.

Q: So why not the blog?

Moore: Well, because I think that he needs to be able to feel like he can connect directly to his readers.

Q: He's connecting with his readers in his column, so why—?

Moore: Then why edit his column?

Q: Yes, because obviously you don't feel the editorial process gets in the way of his communicating with readers in his column. Why would it get in the way with the blog?

Moore: Well, that's a good question. I don't know that I have an answer to that.

[At this point, Howry took a crack at the question.]

Howry: I don't mind a veteran reporter like Timm Herdt blogging, because I know what he will provide will be the information he provides on his blog, and will be based on information gathered in a responsible way. And he has his standards, and I know what those standards are. I don't want every reporter out there doing it. I don't think that's a good idea.

Q: But doesn't everybody need a good editor?

[Howry did not answer that question directly.]

Q: But [help us] understand better the distinction that you're making between why an editing process would be interference with his ability to communicate with the public in a blog when it's not viewed as interference in a column.

Moore: Interference is an interesting way to look at it. I'm not sure I perceive it as interference.

Q: Intervention?

Moore: I would say that it's a matter of the timeliness of it. You know, any editing process obviously slows things down, and the blog world is supposedly immediate.

Boy, is it ever! Although you'd think that this immediacy factor would make careful scrutiny of it especially critical.

Related to that, readers of the *Star's* website can easily circumvent its editorial process—and oddly, with the paper's acquiescence. Allowing the public to post instant comments is one of the practices that distinguishes online media from newspapers and, it's said, lets it take advantage of the "wisdom of the crowds." Wisdom is in the eye of the beholder, however. And because of this policy, the *Star* at times has found itself in the strange position of giving exposure on its website to material vetoed by the paper's editors.

That includes "situations where our readers and their comments have beaten us on an ongoing story," says Moore. "And we've had discussions about whether to use the information."

One of those times involved the paper's decision to omit the name of a suspect from its online breaking story about a shooting because of uncertainty about whether this person was the actual suspect. "We wanted to get it right," Moore says; which is basic journalism, but still admirable.

However, he notes, "a reader went out and did searches online and came up, based on the information we reported, with who it was and posted the name."

Come again? A reader posted a name that editors, for good reason, had decided to withhold? Moore blames the Internet's speed, which he said didn't give editors time to vet the posted comment.

Yet something appears terribly wrong with this picture; after discovering the comment in question, editors could have immediately deleted it from the website, but chose not to do so. Why?

Because it's the Internet, stupid.

The *Star*'s website, explains Moore, was designed to allow comment on stories. "And so we allowed it to go up." And stay up.

Later, the paper did manage to confirm the suspect's name and add it to its online story, but only after a reader had forced the *Star*'s hand.

Howry is candid about the decision to open the website to comments in the first place. "We didn't have to, we just stupidly did it," he said. And along with that, the *Star* vowed not to block or edit online comments the way newspapers have always reserved the right to not publish letters and to edit those they do publish. Newspapers also insist that letters to the editor be accompanied by full names, addresses, and phone numbers, for verification purposes. But online comments can be anonymous.

Howry said he naively assumed that those posting comments would "play by the same rules" as those submitting letters to the newspapers. But that hasn't always turned out to be the case. The newspaper does reserves the right to take down a comment it finds inappropriate—but, of course, that can happen only after the comment is out there for everyone to see. And as for editing comments, no way.

"It's a conundrum," says Howry. "We have opened the door for our community to interact for the first time." And now, he adds, "there's no way to close it." That's not quite the case, however. The paper could close the door if it wished, but it won't, choosing instead to throw up its hands and surrender to the unofficial rules of new technology.

Because—all together, now—it's the Internet.

The same Internet that has remade young Adam Foxman as Multimedia Man.

"Our expectation of Adam at the scene," said Moore, "is to go out and give an initial reporting, have the cell phone, call in and say, 'Here is what I see, I found, I can report.' It will go to his editor here—dictation—who will then take that story that I hope has already been online, and we're able to post it up.

"It really isn't double duty," Moore adds. "It is really part of telling the story. Adam Foxman is out covering the breaking news story. Part of covering the breaking news story is doing video, and so, he will do video."

And, of course, he did.

○ ○ ○

Violent crime scenes often present dual realities, each moving at different speeds, each almost dreamlike. In one, police go about their business routinely and methodically, at normal speed, unhurried, facing no deadlines. In the other, media members are on fast forward as they scurry to gather information in advance of their individual deadlines. Unlike police investigating a crime, reporters are expected by their bosses to produce results immediately. As in . . . now!

Hence, the mingling of excitement and stress when Adam Foxman slid his Ford Taurus up to the curb by E. O. Green School on South C Street, where it would be confirmed later that eighth grader Larry King, 15, had been shot in the head at close range by a another student, 14-year-old Brandon McInerney.

Foxman and a radio reporter had beaten the inevitable crush of other media—including four TV vans—that would soon be streaming into the largely Hispanic neighborhood where the school was located and already cordoned off by police. He'd be joined soon by Scheibe and Ana Bakalis, a Star *reporter who covers the city of Simi Valley to the northeast.*

In another era, Foxman the newspaper reporter would have pulled out his notebook and immediately begun recording what he saw, from the low clouds to the apprehensive faces of the thickening crowd. And there in his notebook the story would stay for the time being. But this was Foxman the multimedia reporter, expected not only to gather facts as quickly as possible and relay them to the Star *for its print editions, but also to call in updates for posting on the paper's website and scout for good pictures (known in the trade as "B-roll" footage, silent film that TV news uses to accompany narration and help tell a story visually).*

No one was talking when he arrived, and Foxman felt a little overwhelmed. But he knew what to do; he'd done it before. So he pointed his camera at the customary symbols.

He shot B-roll footage of an Oxnard Police cruiser. He shot a street sign. He shot yellow crime-scene tape. He shot the school site, which was situated behind a chain-link fence. He shot worried parents waiting in line there for information about the shooting and when their children would be released from the school, which was in lockdown. Scores of them had lined up on the sidewalk much like travelers about to remove their shoes before passing through airport security. Many more parents would later join the queue, waiting for police to give school officials approval to allow them on campus one by one to pick up their children.

Foxman also shot A-roll (sound) footage of a police spokesman giving him and another reporter a brief rundown of what had happened: The shooting had occurred inside a computer lab where 24 students had been working on projects for their English class. Motive unknown. Status of the victim? Still undetermined.

Foxman then interviewed some parents, using his fluency in Spanish to question those who spoke no English, putting down his camera as they spoke because he didn't believe in thrusting it at his subjects. Then he called the paper on his cell phone (one of many calls he would make to the office that morning) and gave education reporter Cheri Carlson what he had. Then he interviewed some more people and shot some more B-roll footage, and some more, and some more, before again doing some interviewing. Then he called the paper again and spoke to an editor, who had news.

What was that? The victim had died? "Jump on it," the editor commanded. A TV cameraman later strode by, telling a colleague, "CNN was reporting he was dead. Did you know that?"

Not true, the police spokesman soon told Foxman, who relayed that back to the paper.

But the erroneous news of the teenager dying, which was later retracted, already was having a powerful impact—"instant information in space," Scheibe called it—evidenced by a crossfire of text messages about young King's "death" passing back and forth between students still inside the school and parents and others waiting behind the fence to hear word of their children's fate.

As that played out, Foxman shot video of a statement by a school administrator that Scheibe had already interviewed, and that became the paper's second online video update of the morning, the first of which had drawn 6,000 hits.

Later, he and Scheibe secured eyewitness accounts of children who were in the lab when King was shot, confirming for the first time the names of the victim and the boy alleged to have pulled the trigger. Then Foxman shot some more B-roll footage of the crowd before putting down his camera and looking around. He felt he had everything he needed.

Foxman spent most of the evening writing his story at the newspaper before checking out just before 9:00 P.M. Then it was into the Taurus for the long commute back home. Tomorrow would surely bring more multimedia coverage, and for him, another bagel.

In addition to its coverage online, the Star *featured Foxman's 40-point main story on the front page of the next morning's edition with two sidebars written by others. There would be more stories about the case by Foxman and other* Star *staffers in subsequent days, as the shooting story endured for some time and became national news when there was speculation that the shooter's motive may have been related to the flamboyant King being openly gay.*

The announcement of his death before he died was yet another case of rushed reporting having potentially bad consequences, and media speed gone awry. It turned out that King had been "brain dead" and comatose, but it wasn't until two days after the shooting that he was pronounced dead.

But no problem. As they say in new-media circles, "They got it right eventually."

CHAPTER 8

Mr. Inside and Mr. Outside: A Conversation

Charles S. Feldman spent nearly 20 years as a reporter for CNN in New York and Los Angeles and has also freelanced for several other news organizations. Howard Rosenberg spent 25 years covering the coverage—including Charles—as TV critic for the Los Angeles Times.

Howard Rosenberg: Let's talk about speed and blogs for a minute. And I know you have a blog—which makes you the maven—but there was something that happened in the thick of the presidential campaign that I just have to mention. When [Hillary] Clinton and [Barack] Obama were still fighting it out, this newspaper headline was circulated saying "Former Clinton Pastor Arrested for Child Abuse" or something close to that. And talk about instant Internet! Right away, fast as that, some left-wing blogs jumped on it and some Obama supporters called talk shows saying how dare Hillary criticize Obama for having ties to Jeremiah Wright (a Chicago clergyman known for making incendiary speeches) and all that.

Charles S. Feldman: The headline was phony?

Howard: No, no, it was real. But it turned out it had nothing to do with Hillary. It was a story about a guy from Clinton, New York.

Charles: But it made the rounds anyway. Well, something just as nutty happened with my own blog—also a speed thing. You know I don't do any original reporting there.

Howard: Just your musings.

Charles: Right, and short items. And I make it clear—I very clearly label it on the top—that some of it is satire. All right, so there was this big hurricane—Dean, I think it was—headed toward Texas and the Gold Coast, but it missed.

Howard: That was 2007, right?

Charles: Uh huh, So I decided to do a riff on what Jerry Falwell said after 9/11. You know, when he blamed 9/11 on gays, lesbians, feminists, and everyone else he didn't like—God's wrath, that sort of thing.

Howard: And I remember Pat Robertson was there and he agreed.

Charles: Well, he didn't *disagree*. So I wrote that if the hurricane devastated Texas, it was God's wrath on Texas for giving us George Bush. Mean-spirited, I know, but totally tongue-in-cheek.

Howard: I know what's coming.

Charles: Right. It was incredible. Within a half hour, a *half hour*, hundreds of hits on my website, 500 within an hour, which is not typical for me. And all the comments criticizing me for everything from not knowing meteorology to not knowing the Bible to being a left-wing nut job. I could tell a lot of it was orchestrated. And when I wrote another blog saying it was satire, that I didn't mean it, people wrote back saying I was trying to cover my ass because I got caught. Even Rush Limbaugh picked up on it in his blog, attacking what I wrote, taking off on the whole God's wrath thing.

Howard: I've always said Rush's wrath is worse than God's.

Charles: It was sort of funny. But think about it: something like this could have serious implications. There was a lot of back-and-forth among blogs about what should be done about me, how to end my career, that sort of thing. No death threats, but it could have happened. I wasn't starting out wanting this to prove the point we make in the book about speed and how things can get out of hand really fast, but it did.

Howard: It nails it.

Charles: Everything that TV and radio covers is about speed, too, because of the nature of the deadline.

Howard: It's not just TV and radio, Charles. Newspapers are slaves to speed, too.

Charles: It's getting that way, you're right. More and more, they're trying to clone themselves online. But the *New York Times* took it one step farther. They made the paper itself—some of it anyway—look like the Internet.

Howard: Oh, yes, your precious *New York Times*. When did you start reading it, in preschool?

Charles: Almost. So you can imagine my reaction—

Howard: I don't have to. You told me. I remember you went into mourning for like, what, a week?

Charles: So I picked it up [on March 25, 2008] and . . . remember that sci-fi movie, *The Invasion of the Body Snatchers*? When these big pea pods from outer space show up and become clones of these people in a little town? So I pick up what I think is the *Times*—

Howard: And it's a pea pod.

Charles: Sort of. That's my point, yes.

Howard: Instead of the *Times* you've always known, it's different, they've made it into a copy of the Internet. *Invasion of the Newspaper Snatchers.*

Charles: Exactly. Almost like a hard copy of the paper's website. Several pages, anyway. Pages 2 and 3, quickie summaries, little paragraphs, boiled-down versions of stories inside for people who want a fast read and don't want to bother going through the rest of the paper. And then another half page or so with summaries of its website stories. You know, for short attention spans.

Howard: The Internet generation. Well, it worked for *USA Today*, right?

Charles: That's different. This is the *Times*.

Howard: Well, don't take it personally.

Charles: I know. It's still not like CNN or all-news radio stations, where the deadline is yesterday for whatever story is happening. I remember the time—it was right after the first Gulf War (in 1991). CNN wanted me to do a story on the rise of Islamic fundamentalism in the Middle East. They wanted 60 seconds. I pointed out to them that it takes 30 seconds just to say "the rise of Islamic fundamentalism in the Middle East."

Howard: That left you 30 seconds for the story. Quit complaining.

Charles: Yeah, right. And people ask why Americans have such a lack of understanding about Islamic fundamentalism. How can you have an understanding of anything if you've had only one minute of explanation?

Howard: There's a reason why Americans are such an ethnocentric society. And that will continue with fewer and fewer people reading newspapers.

Charles: But talking about speed—more than anything, more than being intrinsic, it was a general condition, a frame of mind. It was all about rushing there, rushing things on the air, not having a lot of time to think about what you want to write or to check things too thoroughly. And that was applied to just about every story.

Howard: Did anyone ever worry about speed, I mean, worry about making mistakes because of going so fast?

Charles: There were a lot of discussions about it over the years, usually in reaction to a story that went bad. About slowing the process down, I mean. Let's not rush it too much. Let's make sure we've got more sourcing on it. That would usually hold for about maybe a week, if that. Or until another major story came along. And certainly once the Fox News Channel and MSNBC got into the mix—and it got much worse with the Internet—once that got into the equation, it was all but impossible to slow anything down. I mean, the thinking was, you know, we've got to beat the other guy. First it was beating MSNBC, then it was beating Drudge.

Howard: That's pretty general. Can you single anything out? Didn't you cover O. J.?

Charles: Yeah, both the criminal and the civil trials. The thing about the criminal trial is that one way that speed worked against the coverage—and this applied to newspapers, too, although more so for TV—was there was an enormous amount of leaking of alleged evidence and information. The overwhelming majority of it came from different factions of the LAPD, and in some cases from members of the prosecutor's office.

Howard: But that kind of leaking happens all the time in trials, so how does it relate to speed?

Charles: Well, because there was this real effort, before the trial even got underway, to get information out—test results, forensic results—even if the results were either inaccurate or not yet concluded. And the purpose of that, especially in public trials of celebrities, is to, in effect, bias a jury before the jury is even picked by making sure that all this negative information is out there. Some of it will never even get into trial because it doesn't rise to the level of evidence that a court would recognize. So, for example, there was a story that was leaked about bloodstains, I believe, on his socks.

Howard: O. J's socks, I remember that. Nicole Simpson's or Ron Goldman's bloodstains, you mean.

Charles: Yeah. And the problem was that some of the results came out, it turned out, before the tests were even done. And this caused all that soul-searching in news companies. It wasn't my story, but I remember there was quite a bit of discussion at the time at CNN about how it was that we had this information when the test hadn't really been completed yet, and yet we had already been reporting it because we had gotten it from so-called reliable sources.

Howard: You got the results before there *were* results? How did that happen?

Charles: They were leaked to CNN by sources in the LAPD. There's no doubt that our reporter in question got accurate information and, you know, didn't make it up. But there was such a rush to get out all this information because Simpson was a celebrity and was given the benefit of the doubt probably more so than the average person. And remember, when this first went down, he wasn't the O. J. Simpson that we now think of. He was still the O. J. Simpson of football lore.

Howard: And Hertz TV commercials.

Charles: Exactly. So he wasn't this sort of notorious figure that we now think of. And so there was this effort—the public wanted to really extend to him more than the benefit of the doubt. The police and prosecutors, on the other hand, wanted to make public as quickly as possible anything that they felt was evidence that showed, in their view, that he committed the crime. So there was a case where the information comes out, and there's not a lot of time to check on that.

Howard: Where does speed enter into the equation?

Charles: First impressions really do count and are hard to overcome. Whichever side in the legal battle gets his or her point of view or evidence out to the public first has a tactical advantage in many cases. So the whole idea was to get out this information really fast once you got it.

Howard: And what about the competition?

Charles: In CNN's case, the competition was really with local TV channels. There really wasn't any national competition on an hour-by-hour basis.

Howard: When I was a very young reporter at the *Louisville Times*, one of my beats was a government body—I can't recall which—that met in the morning. It was a long time ago, but I think the meetings generally ended at 11:00 A.M. or something like that, and I had to phone in a story by 11:30, which was ridiculous, but that was the deadline.

And then again, years and years later as *L.A. Times* TV critic, one of the things I had to do—and I hated it—was write reviews of the Oscar and Emmy telecasts, which would end after my deadline. The pressure was huge because I had to be writing copy as the damn things were going on. And I recall so vividly that I had no hopes of writing anything meaningful—if I did that, it was a bonus. No, my goal was to not make a major mistake. Small ones I could live with, just nothing major.

Charles: Did you?

Howard: Make a major mistake? No, I don't think so—I had plenty of editors backing me up—but plenty of small ones, I'm sure. But the point I'm making is that I knew as I was doing this, that it was risky, and I was walking a slippery tightrope and constantly scared that I'd screw up because of the speed issue. Did you have that same feeling when you're rushing to report, that you were going too fast, or were too caught up in the fervor of the moment?

Charles: Both. It depends. I mean, nobody deliberately wants to put something on the air that's false. But to say that there isn't a lot of emphasis placed on trying to get something out before the competition is just not true. So you are aware to some degree that it would be nice to have another day or two, to look into something. But the reality of the situation is that you can't, because if you wait a day or two there's a good possibility that the competition will have the story and then you get beaten on it.

Howard: But that's so dangerous, right?

Charles: You have to rely on the quality of your sources. I know there was for a time a CNN mandate which was this two-source thing—which, by the way, is an urban myth. It came from Watergate coverage and the movie about it, *All the President's Men*. They (Bob Woodward and Carl Bernstein) always had two sources. But in point of fact, you know, that isn't really the case. If you get information from the police chief of a major city, you don't really wait for a second source. That's considered good enough and you go with it. So the two-source thing is kind of silly, although CNN did nonetheless have it as a policy. But it sort of wasted away in the Simpson case because if you waited to get two sources it would just take too long to put the story on the air. So if you had one pretty good source that was enough.

Howard: Do you recall any kind of marching orders you got from any editors or anybody else to go faster or, you know, don't worry about getting it right. Anything like that?

Charles: Marching to go faster were standards. But no one would actually be crazy enough to tell a reporter not to worry about getting the story right. But everyone in the process knew what the pitfalls of speed were. It's just part of the equation. I covered a lot of court cases—civil, criminal, federal, state, you name it. And when you get a judicial decision in most criminal cases, the jury verdicts are easy because the viewer or listener only wants to know if it's guilty or not guilty. And you get out there and report it. Civil cases tend to be more complex, with lots of shades of gray, and it's hard, if not impossible, to grasp all of that in just a few minutes before going on the air.

Howard: That reminds me—let me stop you for a minute. There's something I have to ask you. I remember watching all these old movies about trials, big trials, and when something happens in the courtroom, all the reporters rush out to get on pay phones. I mean they almost run out, total chaos. Does that ever really happen?

Charles: Yeah, it did before cell phones were ubiquitous, which is only fairly recently. And even now there are some courts where you can't bring your phone into the courtroom. Like, for example, with Michael Jackson [his 2005 California trial on charges—of which he was acquitted—that he sexually molested a 13-year-old boy], you couldn't bring your cell phone, even if it was off, into the courtroom. You had to leave it outside with the security guard. So if you wanted to get information out, you had to run and sort of jockey into position with all the other reporters to get your cell phone.

But yeah, especially in New York, where the courthouses tend to be older than the ones in Los Angeles, I remember banks of pay phones, and sure, as soon as there was a verdict, you would run out and compete for five telephones and hope that you had change. And I remember a number of times, there was a number to call collect at CNN in case you didn't have money, and I remember having four or five occasions where there were interns at the desk who didn't have any idea who I was. I would call up with the verdict or with some decision, and I would say, "This is Charles Feldman calling collect," and they would turn it down. That happened a number of times. And I would have an absolute fit.

Howard: Were they any times when you would rush out of any kind of story and have to go to a live shot when you really weren't sure of your command of the story? I mean, when you were forced to go to an immediate live shot?

Charles: Yeah, sure. But there are tricks around that.

Howard: What tricks?

Charles: The tricks of the trade that you pick up over the years. I mean, the one thing you can't do is have dead air.

Howard: That's a sin. I bet it's a firing offense.

Charles: Not quite, but it's the cardinal rule. Whether it's radio or TV, when an anchor throws to you live, you can't not say anything; you have to say something. But the beauty of television and radio, of course, is that the live shots tend to be fairly short, a minute and a half, two if it's a really nice day. And that actually works to your advantage because you can bullshit in a minute and a half quite easily, and make it sound like you're really saying something when you're really not. So, for example, if you didn't really have time to grasp the nuances of a judge's ruling, here's the first trick of the trade. If it's a 150-page decision, you look at the very last graph or two, which is the summary graph, and so you now know what the judge has decided, even if you don't understand the meaning. So because you only have a minute and a half, what you do is basically talk about, you say what the decision is and then you just skirt the issue of why the decision was made because you don't really know. And you don't have to.

Howard: You don't have to?

Charles: Right, because there's not a lot of time anyway. So by the time you finish your minute and a half, it sounds like you really knew a lot, even though you really didn't.

Howard: Have you ever been thrown a question by an anchor—that anchor-involvement charade that all newscasts do—that really threw you for a loop or took you by surprise?

Charles: Ah, well, first of all, for the most part, these live Q&A's on TV in particular, radio less so, but TV in particular—

Howard: They're scripted?

Charles: Well, scripted to the extent, yeah, that usually the reporter suggests the question. The producer will say to the reporter: "Okay, do you have a suggested question for the anchor?" And then you give it to them and the anchor asks the question, maybe with a couple of word changes but basically the question that you set up. And you, if you like the anchor, when the anchor gives you the question, you say, "That's a really good question." That makes the anchor come off as looking really smart. If you don't particularly like the anchor, you don't say that or you frown or you go, "Well, let me think about that." And then it looks like they threw something at you. So there are all kinds of ways you can do that.

There are some anchors who bristle at the idea of having questions suggested to them, and I applaud that. But they are

few and far between, and those anchors were considered dangerous by reporters because you could get thrown a question that
you had no idea about. I didn't care about that so much, I have
to admit. I rarely got flustered on the air; some people do, but I
never did. I got a lot of questions over the years that I wasn't
prepared for or I thought were stupid, or had nothing to really
do with what I was covering, but I managed to sort of dance
around it or say something amusing or entertaining, so that the
anchor wouldn't look particularly stupid and I wouldn't look
stupid. And then at the end of the live shot, you call up the
producer and yell at him or her about why that question was
even asked. But that happened all the time. I mean, they would
ask you, like the judicial thing, they'll ask you two minutes after
you've walked out of the courtroom, "What was the reason
behind this decision?" Well, you don't know yet, because it's a
100-page decision, it's going to take some time to read it and
digest it, you can't possibly know the answer to that. So you kind of
dance around that and you hope that you don't look too stupid.

Howard: For example? Don't hold back, Charles.

Charles: Well, I once had an anchor who had in his contract, as
   some anchors did, that he always had to open every hour, he had
   to be the first person, even if it was dual anchors, he had to do
   it, and he had to do a sort of set up to the story that was just
   more than a quick question. That was part of his ego trip and
   part of his contract. So I was covering this one particular trial
   and he had this habit of putting too much into his lead-in and
   taking away from what I needed to say. There were a number of
   days where that would happen. And I would complain to my
   producer on site, and she would complain to her counterpart in
   Atlanta that the anchor was putting too much information in
   the lead and then throwing it to me without me having anything
   left to say.

   We did this over and over, and complained day after day after
   day, and we thought he was finally getting it. And then one day, I
   had a very early morning live shot, it was for 6:00 A.M. Eastern
   time, and I was just in a pissed-off mood. I had already spent four
   months already at this point in Providence, which is like
   20 years in some other places, and there happened to be a lot of

development the previous day at the trial and a lot to talk about. So we made it a point of saying to this anchor before we went on the air—my producer did, anyway—"Do not get into this, that, and the other thing, because otherwise you're not going to leave him anything to talk about."

Howard: Leave *you* nothing.

Charles: That's right. Well, it comes to the top of the hour, the theme music plays, the anchor says, "Good morning, here's the latest from this particular trial," and he goes into about a two-minute introduction that includes everything that I was going to talk about. I was so annoyed that he did this long preamble and then threw it to me that—and I never did this before or since—that I said, "Well, you just about said it all; back to you."

Howard: There was a reason I asked you about this. I played for my USC class recently a Lou Dobbs newscast [on CNN] in which somebody did a report in the field—it was on tape with some kind of a voice-over—and then the reporter came into the studio to talk to Lou, who drew his own conclusions about the story. He went into some kind of monologue, criticizing the government or something, and then said to the reporter, "Don't you think that's the case?" Or something like that, and the reporter just froze, the old deer-in-the-headlights thing; he didn't know what to say. And he mumbled something like, "We'll have to wait and see, Lou."

Charles: Lou is a special case at CNN, and always has been. I mean, Lou, the business news department had always been somewhat—although I'm not there anymore, my guess is it still is—autonomous of the rest of the operation. He runs it, and it's independent of the rest of the network. You know, years ago there were reporters who were there who had a lot of experience, who came from CBS, and they'd stand up to Lou and would not toe the party line. There are some very smart people in the business unit, but the problem is that they historically have been petrified of Lou. He's very mercurial and if he decides he doesn't want you, then you're gone. So they were very careful to, not necessarily bend the news, but they knew what Lou liked and didn't like, and there were stories that you did or didn't do, because you knew that either he would or wouldn't approve of them.

And in that sense, he had a big impact editorially on what the business department was covering.

Howard: He's unique, I'll give him that.

Charles: Let's switch tracks to something a lot bigger than Lou.

Howard: Is that possible?

Charles: I think this qualifies—Iraq.

Howard: Oh, right. Well, it's where media speed had a huge impact. I'm talking about the early coverage of the war, the invasion and occupation of Iraq. First of all, let's give credit where it's due. Some of the instant reporting from embedded media was really dramatic, really breaking ground for combat coverage. On-the-spot reporting, pictures, the works. I remember one CNN guy, I think it was Walt Rodgers, a real veteran, and he was interviewing a solder when fear came over his face—and you could see it because this was live—as there was incoming fire, and both of them ran for cover. Some if this stuff was really memorable, nothing like it. You'd agree with that, right?

Charles: Sure.

Howard: And to me, the TV technology was more under control then than it was during the Gulf War in 1991, when it seemed like all we heard day after day were those wailing sirens. Live coverage of those damned sirens, always false alarms, and CNN reporters ducking for cover. It was something that you and I have talked about a lot—narrowing the gap separating news and the reporting of news, where the reporting of news becomes the story when there is no news. Reporters in jeopardy who weren't really in jeopardy, that was the story.

But otherwise, coverage of this one, the second Iraq war? Give me a break. The run-up to the war was bad enough, with hardly anyone asking tough questions. Sure, we'd kick the shit out of Saddam, but then what? I don't remember anyone asking. What I do remember is Dan Rather telling someone that it begins with self-censorship because you have this feeling—and he was talking about himself—that you're patriotic, that you should be patriotic and that you know the right questions to ask but you tell yourself this is not the right time to ask 'em. For a journalist, that's lethal. And there was fear there, too, because you were afraid of not being patriotic.

Charles: And don't forget, most of the stories were originating in the government. The old nonstop news cycle again. Speed again.

Howard: Right, the news cycle. And that left reporters—and I'm talking about just about everybody—less time to dig. So the news cycle and turning stories over quickly encouraged them to rely on official news sources because they could provide stuff—information, I mean—quickly and succinctly.

Charles: And the tendency to rely on official sources was deadly.

Howard: Yeah, and when the invasion actually started, the traditional pause to reflect was out the window there, too, because most of the media I saw on TV—and I know there were exceptions—but most of them were as gung-ho as Bush. They were all rushing to Baghdad.

Charles: With our troops, you mean.

Howard: Yeah, they were embedded with U.S. forces. All together, like one team. I remember having this image of the media in my mind, you know all these reporters, sitting on top of tanks singing "On the Road to Mandalay." And another thing, after Baghdad fell, I can't begin to count the number of stories I saw that began, "Unconfirmed reports. . . ." The operative question, in my mind at least, was, What don't they know and when will they report it? Because, as I recall, most of these reports never were confirmed. Nothing more than rumors. Just throw them out.

Charles: Anything in particular you remember?

Howard: Well, sure. How could I forget it? There was one weekend—had to be in 2003—before Saddam was captured, and the cable news channels were dwelling obsessively on whether he was alive and whether some suspicious-looking white powder—*they* called it suspicious—was conclusive proof, at last proof, that he'd been hiding weapons of mass destruction. They were all abuzz, really excited, doing everything but joining hands and singing "Kumbaya." This was it, WMD at last. Well, of course, the coverage turned out to be more suspicious than the powder.

Charles: Of course.

Howard: You remember, too, right? And if a single paragraph could illustrate the utter folly of some of this minute-by-minute reporting shit, the utter stupidity, it would go like this, which is something I wrote down at the time:

> *Dramatic developments in Iraq today as sources say U.S. troops have found thousands and thousands of boxes of suspicious-looking white powder at an industrial site south of Baghdad with documents in Arabic saying how to engage in chemical warfare that proves that Saddam Hussein has weapons of mass destructions that he may no longer have because we're now being told this is not a nuclear, biological training center and the boxes of white powder are explosives and not chemical agents although we're now being told that the boxes do not contain explosives but talcum powder that we're now being told is related to a plan to infect the United States with itchy rashes of mass destruction.*

Charles: Talcum powder—you know that really happened.

Howard: I know it really happened. I'm not making this up, Charles. And now bonus Saddam, the "Is he alive?" story. Remember this is still when he was on the loose. All right, so there he is on the screen, videotape of him wearing his beret, his uniform, the whole business, and he's making a speech somewhere to a bunch of Iraqis who were euphoric or pretending to be euphoric—who knows? And he's walking among them, touchy-feely, they're kissing his hand, a real media event, a Saddam photo op.

But was it Saddam? That's what all those deep thinkers at Fox were debating. No, they said, it had to be a body double instead of Saddam because the real Saddam feared being touched by ordinary Iraqis. But, someone else wondered, were they really ordinary Iraqis? Couldn't they have been loyalists disguised as ordinary Iraqis? But even if they *were* ordinary Iraqis, maybe they were pretending to kiss his hand. Even more insidious, Charles—and I don't remember if someone actually said this or I was thinking it—but did we even know that was really his hand? If not a fake Saddam, in other words, maybe a fake hand.

Charles: *That* you are making up.

Howard: No, I'm not, I swear it. All they had to do was wait for some military experts to weigh in on this, you know make a couple of calls and get one of their retired generals on the horn. But the clock was ticking—you know what that's like—so they went ahead with this comedic bullshit. And now it's coming back to me even stronger. I remember very distinctly that it reminded me of an old Bob and Ray routine, when they spend five minutes analyzing a bologna sandwich—does the bread go outside or inside the bologna, that sort of thing.

Charles: You mentioning talcum powder reminds me of the anthrax thing.

Howard: The big scare—before Iraq, you mean.

Charles: I remember exactly. It was 2001, and every time somebody got an envelope that had powder in it, you know, "breaking news." And to some degree it was justified because if a big office building with 3,000 people in it—this I'm making up but it's a good example—if a big office building in a major city is evacuated, that's a real news story. And you really have no choice but to report it. But you can report it less breathlessly, I think, than it's reported. I mean, I think although the reporters and the anchors are usually really careful to emphasize, you know, we don't know yet what it is, you would never guess that from the tone of the coverage.

Howard: The tone conveys its own message, though.

Charles: Right. You know, the music and the breaking news and all of that would suggest to a viewer that there was a much more significant development than it would often turn out to be.

Howard: Speaking of breaking news, it always struck me, watching all this kind of thing, that you can be a really good reporter, but that does not necessarily translate to being good at doing stuff live.

Charles: That's right. Like at USC [where Charles has taught], I've always suggested that they should have classes for their undergrads in acting so they can learn stagecraft. Here is a really good, quick story that was told to me by Jim Polk, who you may recall was an old-time NBC network news investigative reporter before he became head of the investigative unit for CNN for quite some time. A real old-fashioned newspaper reporter before that, really solid, good reporter. And we were talking once a few years ago about assignments that really sucked, and how reporters don't want to go on stakeouts. And he said that he had this one friend, a colleague of his, another reporter who was getting paid a lot of money, who was complaining to him endlessly about some story that he thought was silly to cover, and he didn't like that he was standing outside for hours and hours and hours. And Jim said that he said to him, "You know, that big salary you're getting every year? Well, about 10 percent of that is for your reporting ability, 90 percent of that is for your entertainment ability."

And that's actually true. For live television, the key to success is your ability to be *entertaining*. They don't like to use that word, but it's true.

Howard: But some people just have that facility to report live.

Charles: Well, there are tricks to that, too. There are some reporters, less so now than there used to be, who would record beforehand. We used to have a reporter who by reputation would record his live stuff beforehand into a recorder, and keep the earplug in his ear. And then when he would do live, he would play it so he would basically mimic what he heard himself report with the tape recorder.

Howard: How could he do that?

Charles: Well, some people are very good at doing it. But then, of course, the danger to that is that if the tape recorder breaks, you're screwed. The other thing is to write everything in advance. And I've told students this, if they ever decide to go into the industry, that's the kiss of death. Because if you write it in advance, that means you're trying to memorize your lines, like an actor would memorize a script. And the difference is, actors spend weeks if not months memorizing those lines, so that by the time they go on and they do their scene that you watch in the movie and it seems so natural, that's because they've said those lines nine billion times before the camera started rolling. To try to re-create that in five minutes before a live shot is impossible, unless you have a photographic memory. And I've never met anybody who really does. So that's the kiss of death, too. So what is the solution? The solution is, you don't write the script beforehand for a live shot. Live shots are not about conveying a lot of information. The best way TV and radio do information is in scripted, taped pieces or recorded pieces nowadays, where you can think about what you want to say, you can compress your thoughts and put it into neat form.

Howard: Is that really about reporting news?

Charles: You have to understand that live is really about presence. It's 90 percent, if not more, about establishing that the reporter is at the scene of a particular story, and if you can get some information out, that's terrific.

Howard: It's a bonus?

Charles: It's a bonus.

Howard: Was there ever a time after a live shot, after you're off air and you thought, "Oh, my God, I screwed up," or that you shouldn't have said something?

Charles: Oh yeah, sure. I mean, once or twice I convicted people on the air. You know, every reporter has done that. I mean, where I've said, "And the jury found him guilty. Oh wait a minute, no. Did I say guilty? No, it's *not guilty*."

Howard: The perils of live TV, Charles. Look, people who work for newspapers are backed up by layers and layers of editors, and still—and I include myself in this—still they make mistakes. It's human nature. But on live TV, there are no editors to back you up. There are no safety nets. You say it, and it goes. You can't yank it back like a bungee cord. Oh listen, remember the Rodney King riots?

Charles: In the early 90s, wasn't it?

Howard: It was 1992, I think. After a jury acquitted four white L.A. cops of beating Rodney King, who was black—

Charles: They beat the shit out of him, and somebody videotaped it, right?

Howard: Yeah. They just clobbered the guy—King, I mean—after they hauled him in after a car chase. And when the verdict went the other way, all hell broke loose for a bunch of days—arson, looting, the works. Mainly blacks and Hispanics. And local TV is out there covering it all live, a tough job, but that's what they do, and it's all knee-jerk stuff. I remember so clearly, an anchor is talking to one of the reporters who was there when some people were looting a store, and he asks her if they were illegal aliens, and she says yes. Doesn't hesitate. Really stupid. And I'm thinking as I'm watching it, how in the hell does she know? Did they have "Illegal" stamped on their foreheads? Which is something a producer at the station might have asked her if the story had been on tape. But it wasn't, and out it went. Just inane, totally.

Charles: I remember reading critics, criticisms of different things— not of me necessarily, but of coverage—and sometimes I would think, Well, that's fair. And sometimes I would think, Well, that person really doesn't know what the reporter or the anchor is up against, and if they did, they would have a whole different take on it.

Howard: I'm sure I was guilty of that many times.

Charles: Sometimes when you're out in the field, you go, Well, if that person was not in the office, they would see what's really happening.

Howard: Yes, yes, I've heard that before, lots of times. And it's been directed at me. But here's the thing, I'm up against lots of problems when I write, too. It's hard work, big obstacles and all that. But so what? It's what I'm paid to do. If I screw up, I should be held accountable. So don't tell me about the problems you have. Not you, personally—all TV reporters. You're paid to be able to report live, so do it. Don't whine about your problems.

Charles: That's right. And it's not really an excuse for doing sloppy journalism or anything like that. But the key thing to remember is that whenever there's criticism by anybody about sloppy journalism in live shots, my response is, "That's because they're comparing apples and oranges." Live shots are not about journalism, they have nothing to do with journalism.

It is a performance; you're paid for your performance. You're paid and rewarded based on your ability to keep an audience glued to the set for your two minutes or three minutes or whatever time you're on.

Howard: And I would add that what you're describing is flat-out deception. I mean, it's theater, and theater really shouldn't be a part of journalism.

Charles: But it isn't journalism, that's the thing.

Howard: Of course, but it's being advertised as journalism. That's my point.

Charles: Right, of course. It is really theater, that's all. It sounds cynical but it's the fact. The purpose of television, and that's whether it's news or movies or game shows—and you know this, Howard—the purpose of television is not to entertain, not to educate, not to enlighten. If it does any of those things, that's terrific. Its main purpose, though, is to keep you glued to the screen from one commercial to the next. That's what it's about.

Howard: Sure, of course.

Charles: And a lot of people don't get that. They think that the commercials are sort of thrown in there.

Howard: It's a reverse emphasis. I mean, the programming is what comes between the commercials. And you're supposed to be in the right frame of mind—not only be there in front of the screen—but also be in the right frame of mind to accept whatever is told to you in the commercials.

Charles: Yeah, look at local newscasts, the teases (the titillating what's-coming-up promos within newscasts). You know, the people who write teases are valued a lot, and often paid separately. They used to be paid as much as the people who did the news. The reason was because the teases kept you glued to the newscast, through the commercials. Not so much so you would watch the next section of the news, but so you would stay put and watch the commercials. That's what it's all about, and people who don't get that are being naïve or stupid, or they don't understand the way this system works.

Howard: Remember Richard Jewell, that poor schlub of a security guard in Atlanta, who turned out to be innocent?

Charles: The [1996] Olympics bombing in Atlanta, sure.

Howard: Well, he didn't understand the way the system worked either. The media system, I mean. Overnight, he went from hero—he found a knapsack containing a bomb—to accused bomber after the FBI leaked it to the Atlanta papers that they were looking at him closely. A "person of interest," I think they called him. So the papers wrote this huge story, and everyone followed up—I think CNN was reading the story on the air half an hour after the paper hit the streets. Everyone was just hounding this poor guy, hordes of media psychoanalyzing him from afar, stalking him and tailing him to his mother's apartment when local authorities went to search the place. Just wild, scattershot reporting of rumor and innuendo, journalism at its worst, building all these expectations that he'd be arrested. Remember Bonnie Anderson at CNN?

Charles: Yes.

Howard: I just remember her reporting from that apartment, where there was a big media stakeout, like bees at a hive. And she's saying something like, "We'll keep you updated on everything they're taking out of Jewell's condo." And on NBC, *The Today Show,* I think it was Matt Lauer, asking their reporters on the scene if they knew anything about what was being removed. Everybody was being swept up in this thing, and it was all live, of course, taking on a life of its own. It was like a lynch mob. And I remember thinking at the time, Well, maybe he's guilty. On the other hand, what if he's not? I mean, wasn't that possible? What if he's not guilty? But nobody out there was asking that question because they were too caught up in the rush. It was the O. J. story all over again, with the technology becoming an end in itself and goosing everyone to go faster and faster.

Charles: For CNN, you have to remember that there was probably an ulterior motive for being so gung-ho on the Jewell reporting. That was in Jane and Ted's backyard [Jane Fonda and Ted Turner, who were married at the time and living in Atlanta]. At least at the time, CNN was an Atlanta-based organization and was very fast on the draw to cover things in Atlanta. It was right there, and it gave them sort of a sense of self-importance; they had to justify the fact that they were in, of all places, Atlanta, instead of in New York or Washington, where other large national news organizations were based.

Howard: I know. But this Richard Jewell fever spread all across the country. I remember KCBS here [in Los Angeles], really going in depth on it, obsessing on it, exploring his background and past job as a security guard at some small college, and why did he lose his job there? There were suggestions that this was all part of some hero complex, you know that he created the crime, planted the bomb so he could be a hero and find it it, and save everybody. And actually, the only people with hero complexes were the media who perpetuated this stuff.

Charles: Well, it happened again with that guy [Dr. Steven Hatfill] in the [2001] anthrax scare. That was another case of the feds calling someone a "person of interest"—like Jewell, which, if you think about it, doesn't mean anything.

Howard: But I don't think he was ever—

Charles: Charged? No, but the person-of-interest thing was the excuse that news organizations used to cover this story the way they did and to, you know, stake out this guy at his house and go through his garbage. They were picking apart everything in his history dating back to practically when he was born and probably even when he was a fetus.

Howard: A fetus of interest.

Charles: Speed and competition are behind it. I mean, news organizations have always competed, and even in the days when major cities had many more newspapers. New York City, I think, at one time had 11 or 12 daily newspapers with multiple editions per day, and there was certainly competition there and the desire to beat the other guy. But what's changed, I think, is the sheer number of news organizations and the pressure on them and the fact that they amplify these stories way beyond their importance. It's one thing for a local newspaper, say in 1954 in New York, to come up with an afternoon edition that says something inaccurate, only to be countered by the competition's paper that comes out an hour later. It only has resonance within that one city and even there, only within the small population reading the paper. But when you get to a universe where you've got 24-hour news and the Internet—

Howard: The news is instantaneous and goes everywhere.

Charles: So what happens is it becomes a worldwide error instead of just a city one. And now everybody in all corners of the earth is exposed to the same inaccurate information, and that's the real difference.

Howard: And it can do great harm to individuals, as in the case of Jewell and the anthrax guy.

Charles: I mean there are obviously some news organizations that are like the *Wall Street Journal*, which was famous for taking a lot of time to do its stories. Some of its front page stories they would work on for months and months, and they would report it and craft it and hone them, and do all kinds of things, and they would go through multiple editing processes before they got to page 1. That's unfortunately, I think, a relic of the past.

Howard: It certainly pretty much is on TV. Now it's speed, speed, speed and throw everything you find on the air, whether it's news or not.

Charles: This goes to the heart of the problem with 24-hour news organizations, which is that there isn't really, on any given day, 24 hours of real news. So you're left with the dilemma, if you run one of these organizations, and that is, How do you fill up airtime? And so the way you fill it up is you fill it up with opinions and rumor and conjecture, and things that never used to be reported years ago, and would have probably gotten the reporter or an editor fired from a major newspaper had they reported it. But that stuff is now routinely reported because the presumption, as it is now with the Internet, is that if we get it wrong, we'll just correct it an hour later. But that doesn't take into account the damage that sometimes is done.

Not every story causes damage if there's an error in fact. Sometimes it just doesn't make that much of a difference. But every now and then, like the Richard Jewell story, it could really ruin a life and it could also create panic.

Howard: A good point. Panic is something we haven't discussed.

Charles: You know, look at the financial markets. And I know we've talked about how some dispute it or they question it, but I still think that what we're seeing, especially just recently because of the subprime mortgage issue, is that the markets have always been based on rumor and perception more than reality. So I think a real case can be made that it's more so now than before, because we wake up in the morning and, I mean, I knew the night before the stock took a real big drop recently—the U.S. stock market, I mean—that it was going to happen because I was told it was going to happen by all these news reports the night before based on what was happening in European and Asian markets. So even before anything happened, I was told it was going to happen. And there is a psychology that I think goes into play when that happens. There's a sort of panic atmosphere that takes place, or a panic reaction. People are like sheep sometimes, they follow the herd, and in the case of finances you're talking sometimes about billions of dollars that can be wiped out in a matter of 24 hours. Most people don't think of it in those terms because people don't have any concept of what a billion dollars is. But when you consider that in the space of a day, a day's cycle, news cycle, these rumors and other things that drive market forces can lead to a dramatic decline in stock markets. And what that means and what it translates into is a dramatic siphoning off of billions of dollars in assets.

Howard: And your point is . . . ?

Charles: It's not a benign phenomenon. It actually has an impact and it has immeasurable impact, and I think a pernicious impact.

Howard: A lot of this goes back to what we were also talking about, and that is, much of what is advertised as news is not news, it's opinion, speculation. And they broadcast so many things that turn out to be not true. Getting back to Iraq for a minute, Jessica Lynch was another example.

Charles: The hero who turned out not to be a hero.

Howard: It wasn't her fault. Blame the Pentagon for manufacturing the story and the media for buying it and getting it out fast, no questions asked. Army private. Convoy—maintenance, I think— ambushed in 2003. Wounded or injured. Then she's captured by the Iraqis. The Pentagon's story was that she defended herself, guns blazing, and they got her only after she ran out of ammo.

Charles: Which was bullshit.

Howard: Utter and complete bullshit. They needed an instantaneous hero to bolster the war effort, and she was elected. She told some congressional committee later that she never fired her weapon because it jammed. Said she was unconscious and didn't remember anything about being captured. Then U.S. troops went and got her from an Iraqi hospital, and there's a lot of disinformation about what happened there, too. The point is that most of the media, the Western media, went for the entire story without a whimper. Moving too fast and asking no questions.

Charles: They became the Pentagon's echo chamber.

Howard: Yes, but it filled a lot of space and a lot of airtime, so, mission accomplished, right?

Charles: And speaking of that, don't forget the now notorious photo op of President Bush in full flight gear landing on the top of that carrier.

Howard: With the "Mission Accomplished" banner behind him as he gave a speech saying major combat in Iraq had ended. I was watching CNN that day. I think Miles O'Brien and Kyra Philips were on duty, and they were positively swooning. And another one of CNN's people called Bush "commander in chief of the world." Which must have been news to the rest of the world, right?

Charles: That's another example of what happens with live coverage. Everybody bought it. CNN had Frank Buckley—he worked out of the L.A. bureau—on the ship as well. We used to share an office, and I remember when he came back from that story, saying to him in a good-natured way, "How do you know the mission has been accomplished?" Because I thought his reporting was echoing what the administration was saying.

Howard: You actually asked him that? This will make you look like a prophet.

Charles: Well, no, it wasn't being a prophet. I wasn't clairvoyant. I certainly had no reason not to believe Bush's message either. It was just—

Howard: A logical question to ask?

Charles: Yes. And it wasn't just Frank. It was the entire organization, and actually the entire press.

Howard: I don't remember anybody in the media asking that question publicly. Another example of inaccurate reporting—or inaccuracy by nonreporting.

Charles: Well, if you want to talk about inaccurate reporting, here's something else. Airplane crashes are notorious for inaccurate reporting, for a couple reasons. One, because most people in the press have very little knowledge—aviation, like medicine, or even like law, is a very specific industry, it's a technical industry, and if you don't know certain things, things that may be impressive to the lay public are not impressive to somebody who really knows something about the subject.

Howard: I should pause here to note that you fly yourself—you're a pilot.

Charles: Uh-huh. And the other thing is that airplane accidents are almost never caused by a single factor, they tend to be snowball effects, a chain of things that go wrong, from human error to mechanical error, and it's all these things in aggregate that almost always are responsible for an airplane crash. It's never just the bad weather, it's the bad weather and the pilot, and the fact that there was a problem getting the flaps down on time. You know, it's usually a whole bunch of things. But the press needs a very fast answer to these things. And as soon as there's an accident, whether it's a commercial airliner or even a small private plane, you will invariably hear, whether it's radio or TV, within minutes of the reporting, "What went wrong? How did it happen?" And there are usually these man-in-the-street interviews, which are worthless because it's been proven over and over again in court studies that eyewitnesses, so-called eyewitnesses to crimes, are the least reliable witnesses.

Howard: But can you recall any particular crashes when this happened, anything that we can tie it to?

Charles: I mean, there was one that happened here in L.A. recently, the two small planes that collided, and they [KNX radio] called me to give sort of an expert opinion on how it could have happened. And I already heard, even before I went on the air, all this speculation about, well, you know, "it must have been because the sun was in the eyes of one of the pilots and it blinded him to the other aircraft." And when I went on the air, I said, "Well, you know I fly all the time and I have the sun in my eyes all the time, and I don't hit another plane." So that is too simplistic of an answer, to say that that was the single cause of two airplanes colliding with one another. Pilots get the sun in their eyes all the time, it's not a big deal. So I said, "Other things must have happened, which we still don't know about. The pilots may have been distracted. Maybe one of them had a mechanical issue and his attention was diverted and didn't notice the other plane coming. There are all kinds of things that could have been the actual cause, but the heartbeat of news now is such that it demands an answer that's quick, that demands instantaneous analysis and conclusions. And some things just defy instantaneous explanation.

Howard: Defy quick answers.

Charles: Sure. It takes a very long time, it takes usually many months and sometimes years to find out what caused a particular aircraft accident. You know, the TWA 800 thing is a classic example. [On July 17, 1996, a Paris-bound Boeing 747-100 jet exploded in midair and crashed in the Atlantic Ocean shortly after leaving JFK Airport in New York, killing all 230 aboard.]

I was in California and CNN flew me back to New York to cover it. And within minutes, and certainly within hours, there was all this garbage about how—

Howard: Missiles brought it down or something like that. I remember.

Charles: Missiles brought it down, it was terrorism, it was somebody on board the plane with a bomb, all kinds of theories. And none of it was true. And there were all these eyewitnesses, I mean literally hundreds in the course of months of reporting, you know, "I saw a missile going from the ocean up and hitting the plane." So-called reliable witness; by that, they usually mean law enforcement officials, physicians, people that you tend to think of as not being crackpots. And all of that was not true, I mean, none of it was true. It ended up being not a simple explanation but it ended up being one not nearly as sexy. It turned out to be the 747 has full tanks in both wings and also one in the belly of the aircraft and the middle tank is often not kept full of fuel because it makes the plane too heavy and you don't really need it, and it was a hot day that day and the plane was delayed, it was a 747 TWA Flight 800, and the flight was delayed that day taking off and was sitting in the sun and it was a freak occurrence, the heat caused fumes because of the tank not being full and all of that.

Howard: But nobody, at least damned few, waited for that. They didn't want to wait to find out what really happened, the official cause.

Charles: There was an enormous amount of pressure for competitive reasons, and everybody, every news organization wants to look like it's the smartest and has the inside track on what's actually going on. And the result was a lot of misinformation, and it wasn't a harmless thing. It caused a lot of angst for family members of people who were on the plane, and it sent people on wild goose chases. I remember the guy in charge of the FBI said he felt pressured. He talked about that quite openly. He said that he knew fairly quickly that they didn't know what the cause was.

Howard: The only thing he knew fast was that he didn't know.

Charles: Yes, but he said he also knew fairly quickly that it wasn't a missile and it wasn't anything sinister. But there was so much media pressure to check out all of these bizarre theories, and in order to satisfy family members of those who were on the plane, he really went all out, and then some, with the investigation. And you can argue it's good that he did that, but on the other hand, it was an enormous waste of taxpayer dollars and most of it was fanned by media reports that were unsubstantiated, that were ludicrous on the face of it, and reported by people who didn't know a thing about aviation or anything else. And that's bad.

Howard: Speaking of ludicrous, we should talk about election coverage. Wait, that's a little strong. How about moderately ludicrous?

Charles: Ludicrous worked for me. Look, there's been a real crush to get things on the air and form premature opinions. When it comes to analysis, they all jump the gun. And this takes us back to speed again, because we're talking about a combination of speed of transmission and the number of outlets that can serve as an echo chamber. When you put those two together, you end up with a very volatile mixture. What I mean is, everyone wants to get it before the next person.

Howard: What they're doing is frequently guesswork.

Charles: It's always guesswork. And everything is presented in this hyper game show–type atmosphere that lends itself more to the superficial response than more thoughtful responses. You know, I think this is clearly the most media-influenced presidential election campaign we've had.

Howard: I was going to ask what you mean by that, but I can think of examples myself. One example, during candidate debates, when CNN in particular positioned candidates on the stage in a way to create maximum conflict. Especially early on. Like bunching Hillary, Obama, and Edwards together with the others on the outside. The did it to fit their own preconceived notion of how the debate should go. That's stage-managing the news, isn't it?

Charles: It goes back to this desire they have not to wait. They want to create the issues.

Howard: Not waiting—a perfect segue, Charles, to Eliot Spitzer [the New York governor who announced his resignation two days after the *New York Times* reported online that he'd been linked to a prostitution ring—and two days after the Fox News Channel's

Shephard Smith erroneously reported that he'd already resigned and also, erroneously, that he'd been indicted for a possible criminal violation]. So here was another example of media getting into trouble because they couldn't wait. And besides that, you know what my first thought was? This country is becoming so sanctimonious.

Charles: I don't think Americans are any more sanctimonious than they were, say, in the 30s or 40s, even the 50s and 60s.

Howard: What do you mean, that the media are spreading, the prevalence of media makes it seem like—

Charles: And the speed at which it happens. Look, the *New York Times* breaks the story with very little detail on its website and within an hour—

Howard: Much less than that—

Charles: It was on the cable news networks. And the crescendo for his resignation began even before the news organization [the *Times*] that was breaking the story had an opportunity to say what the story really was. I remember looking at the initial report, and it was extremely vague. Spitzer had some alleged connection to a prostitution ring. All right, well, that could have meant a lot of things, that he was running the prostitution ring; it could have meant all sorts of things.

Howard: Or that he frequented it, which turned out to be the case.

Charles: And first of all, the thing that went right out the window was presumption of innocence, which even high officials should have. And you had this growing chorus of news organizations going on and on, like an echo chamber.

Howard: Right, going too fast to be fair. But I'm still not sure about the speed connection—I mean, compared to the past.

Charles: What you didn't have then was this instantaneous cascading effect, this gnawing appetite for constant news, however salacious it might be.

Howard: Oh, I don't know. I think it was probably there.

Charles: But it would have taken some time to get the story out to the public.

Howard: So, what we've been talking about here—not in every case but mostly—are slam dunks, right?

Charles: By slam dunks, you mean the media—

Howard: Jumping to conclusions because they're rushing, moving so fast that they leave their brains behind. They make assumptions, based on incomplete information—

Charles: Or noninformation that turns out be false.

Howard: Uh-huh. O. J. did it, he's going down. Slam dunk. Richard Jewell did it. Slam dunk. The U.S. wins in Iraq, whatever winning means. Slam dunk. And oh, yeah, something we haven't talked about, the Duke lacrosse case. [In 2007, an African American woman claimed she'd been raped by three white lacrosse players at Duke University. But her story collapsed, and the charges were dropped.]

Charles: Spoiled rich white boys victimizing a poor black woman at an elitist school. Of course, they did it. The coverage was quick to react, and pretty one-sided. Another slam dunk.

Howard: And Spitzer definitely had resigned, another one. We don't learn our lessons, do we?

Charles: It's amnesia. That's what we have, amnesia.

CHAPTER 9

What If? Scenarios, Dark and Darker

Well, boys, I reckon this is it . . . nuclear combat toe to toe with the Russkis.
—Major T. J. "King" Kong in *Dr. Strangelove, Or, How I Learned to Stop Worrying and Love the Bomb*

Moses took his time making sure the Ten Commandments reached the right people, and Abe Lincoln did a pretty nice job as president. But they didn't have to worry about getting run over by the new media's Indy 500 or facing strident verbal assaults from the likes of Rush Limbaugh and Sean Hannity.

Does the lightning speed of new media affect decision making in high places, as well as down on the pavement with the rest of us? Does going faster and faster tighten the vise and ratchet up pressure on government leaders to rush critical decisions they should weigh slowly and thoughtfully to preclude blowing it in haste?

Faulting media pressure for poor decisions is "like the artist blaming the tools," says online guru Jeff Jarvis. If that's the case, he suggests that we choose leaders who have more backbone: "If you have no spine and no principles, then, yes, you may find it hard to stand up and make a good decision. We are paying you to, and we are electing you and choosing you to make the tough decisions. So you should do what is necessary to do."

He's correct, of course. But is it that simple?

Several former presidential press secretaries have concerns about the media speed issue and its impact on the way government conducts business.

"We have to figure out how to go more slowly," says Mike McCurry, who faced the media regularly as President Bill Clinton's official spokesperson. "Everything about the technology and the structure of the media today is designed to accelerate the flow of information. We have to understand that policy making and decision making can only go as fast as humans can make it go, and we are artificially imposing deadlines that don't make sense."

And this from one of McCurry's predecessors: "I think the world is operating at least three times faster than it did when I left office in 1992," says Marlin Fitzwater, press secretary for Presidents Ronald Reagan and George H. W. Bush. This acceleration "demands a new kind of decision making" in government, he says. "The people who are hired now, political appointees as well as career civil servants, and by extension, presidents as well, have to be much quicker on their feet and quicker at the process of thinking about ideas. And you have to be more articulate, because the speed of journalism puts a premium on that. And another thing is it requires that you change the decision making process to reflect the speed. Everybody has to be quicker and better and smarter. They've got to deliver good decisions and still do it in a quicker way. But it often doesn't work that way because we don't have that quality of people."

Jody Powell believes today's frenzied media climate would have dramatically affected how he did his job as press secretary to President Jimmy Carter. "Oh, absolutely," he says. "There would have been a considerable amount of pressure, which I hope we could have resisted, but I'm sure we could have only up to a point."

Some administrations would fare better than others in resisting that pressure, he says. "If you're going to do three messages of the day and send a spokesman out to repeat those things ad nauseam and then do a rope-a-dope, this is a great time in which to do that, because the reporters on the whole have less time, fewer resources, and less experience to challenge it. But if you get an administration that really does have a commitment to being straightforward and honest with the public and trying to win informed public support, it's going to be hugely difficult for them do that in this environment."

Former NBC News anchor Tom Brokaw recalls hearing Lloyd Cutler, White House counsel in the Carter administration, tell an audience, "We are under tremendous pressure every night to make decisions in time for the 6:30 news, and we just feel that freight train bearing down on us." Brokaw didn't think much of it at the time, but says he'd be more sympathetic to Cutler today, knowing that media freight train is racing even faster.

As Jay Rosen says, "there are gains, there are losses" with accelerated information. Rosen, an academic whose specialty is media, offers this historical perspective:"When you have a rapid speed-up, a period where barriers are broken or a new technology comes on board, or a sudden increase in scale—like the telegraph for example—you find not only are decision makers affected, but new conditions flood in, too." He offers as an example the oft-criticized 1919 Paris Peace Conference that capped World War I: "For the first time you had real-time news reports of what was being discussed telegraphed through the wire services back to newspapers in the home countries, and reactions from the home countries telegraphed back to Paris within what we would call, today, one news cycle. And the simple fact that word of what might be settled at these talks could flood into the political sphere, and reactions flood back, profoundly affected the negotiations themselves. A lot of historians believe that reactions back home, in the United States and England especially, were factors in some of the problems in the settlement. So when you say, does it [sped-up communication] affect decision making, it always has and, I would assume, it is now."

The question is, how dangerously?

Hypotheticals and *what ifs* are constrained by the crystal balls that enclose them. They resolve nothing; they prove nothing. Instead of reflecting actual knowledge, they are little more than guesswork.

In some cases, though, highly educated guesswork.

Take Watergate, says Brokaw, who covered that story as a reporter. Or, as the late comic Henny Youngman might say, "Take Watergate—*please!*"

Watergate was a White House scandal that traumatized the nation. It began with a 1972 break-in of Democratic Party offices that led to a Republican cover-up and extraordinary revelations that toppled the Richard Nixon presidency in 1974 and disillusioned many Americans.

Had it happened today, "the country wouldn't have come through it in the same fashion that it did," Brokaw believes. "I always thought of Watergate as a great constitutional crisis, and the press was measured, temperate in how it covered it. There was very little that got out that wasn't true because we knew what the consequence was.

"Now the pressure would be to be pumping this stuff out every nanosecond. And there wouldn't be a chance for the country to absorb it at a measured pace or for reporters to deal with it in a larger, conceptual fashion. It would be fragment and rumor; everything would be labeled 'exclusive,' however insignificant it may have been. And it would be bouncing off the Internet and cable all day long."

If anyone is equipped to judge how Watergate coverage might have been different if time capsuled to the current media universe it's Ben Bradlee, the famed former editor of the *Washington Post* during that national crisis and the man to whom Bob Woodward and Carl Bernstein reported.

Bradlee is grounded in a different age, he acknowledges—one before blogs, social networking sites, and so-called citizen journalism. For much of the time during which he guided the *Post,* 24-hour news was the exclusive turf of traditional wire services, not CNN and its offspring.

Contemporary newspapers, and their reporters and editors, have always been organically different from such wire services as the Associated Press, Reuters, and United Press International. Speed was prominent on their list of things to achieve, but rarely at the top of that list.

Not that there wasn't intense competition among newspapers to be the first with a story, from small-towners to the loftiest of the majors. It took years, for example, for the *New York Times* to live down being beaten to Watergate by the *Post*. For the most part, though, newspaper reporters of that day had more time—the *luxury* of time to think about how they wanted to present the facts they gathered. And their editors had relatively ample time to contemplate their reporters' stories and even to decide whether to publish them.

Thanks (or no thanks) to the Internet, however, today's *Post,* like a growing number of newspapers both large and small, has priorities that are greatly expanded from those of its earlier incarnation. Think split personality, for the *Post* now requires much of its staff to write not only for the traditional newspaper but to contribute also to its online version, in effect transforming these people into wire service journalists.

Would its Watergate coverage have been different had Woodward and Bernstein been commanded to write not only for the main newspaper but also for its online editions?

"Yes," says Bradlee. "It was quite a while before we had any sense of the real importance of it [Watergate]. And if these guys [Woodward and Bernstein] had been writing three times a day, and therefore trying to write new leads and get new information, they would start to guess and start to hype. I think that could have driven us into a lot of trouble."

Speaking of trouble, less than a decade after Watergate sank Nixon, the Iran Hostage Crisis—and U.S. failure to resolve it—helped undermine the reelection bid of President Carter.

The excruciating odyssey began on November 4, 1979, when Iranian militants supporting an Islamic revolution seized 66 U.S. hostages at the nation's embassy in Tehran, holding 52 of them for more than a year in an act that would wreck relations between the two nations for decades to come.

"CNN was just being born, and there was no Internet and all of that," says Carter's former press secretary Powell. "But you got a preview of what this world might be like. The mainstream media, insofar of its coverage of Washington and the government, was totally seized with this one issue, and they couldn't find a way to cover hardly anything else. We had a bunch of pretty significant legislative proposals—a good portion of which were actually enacted—on the Hill, but other than doing a prime-time speech sort of thing, it was virtually impossible to get any sort of in-depth coverage of those proposals."

Even then, media pressure on the Carter administration was crushing, not the least of which was millions of Americans witnessing the nightly specter of CBS News anchor Walter Cronkite somberly noting the number of the days that the hostages had been held captive.

The ongoing crisis ate at Carter, who wanted desperately to free the hostages, and he made one stab at it. But an attempt to rescue them five months after they were taken had to be aborted in the desert southeast of Tehran, a chopper crash there leaving eight U.S. casualties.

It could have been even worse, says Hodding Carter, a familiar face on TV as U.S. State Department spokesman during the hostage crisis. It could have happened in a supertech media climate as frenzied as today's.

"That would have revised everything," says Carter, who now teaches at the University of North Carolina. "In the current media world, I don't think we could have bought as much time as we bought. Faced with the drumbeat of war, the political side of the House would have pushed for meaningful military action pronto."

That strategy would have won the day, he believes, even though "the U.S. did not have good intelligence about what was happening on the ground in Iran nor adequate operatives on the ground to locate and extract the hostages."

Is he saying that that famously stubborn Jimmy Carter would have caved to that pressure? "Now, Jimmy is not a man who is easily taken that way," Hodding Carter says. "His certainties are such, for better or for worse, that he is able to withstand that kind of pressure more than some. But even so, I have a feeling the action would have come sooner."

Military action?

"Yes."

With what result?

"The death of the hostages."

An even scarier scenario is offered by Ted Sorensen, who was special counsel and intimate adviser to President John F. Kennedy. So intimate, that he was known as the "alter ego" of Kennedy, who once called him his "intellectual blood bank." So intimate that he was Kennedy's speechwriter and wrote a biography of him, and is thought by many to have been the actual author of JFK's Pulitzer Prize–winning book *Profiles in Courage*.

Sorensen's responsibility had been solely for JFK's domestic agenda until the Bay of Pigs debacle—the failed invasion of Cuba by anti–Fidel Castro Cubans trained and backed by the CIA just a few months into Kennedy's presidency. And it was in this capacity that he was to play an important advisory role in resolving the Cuban Missile Crisis, those 13 days in October 1962, during the height of Cold War tensions, when the planet appeared on the brink of nuclear holocaust.

So we asked Sorensen what he believes would have happened had this epic crisis—that began when a U-2 surveillance flight photographed evidence that the Soviets were building offensive missile bases in Cuba—occurred in today's revved-up media climate.

There had been earlier reports in the U.S. press of Cuba receiving weapons shipments from the Soviet Union. But Kennedy told the public that Soviet Premier Nikita Khrushchev had assured him those weapons were defensive, not offensive. It was a lie. And Soviet construction of offensive missile sites in Cuba was clearly a threat that required a response; these missiles were capable of reaching almost every part of the United States and Latin America.

Kennedy gathered key members of his administration, an inner circle that would later be known as the Executive Committee of the Security Council (ExComm). Seated around the table at this first meeting were about a dozen of the president's most trusted advisers, including Sorensen, described in one historical account as a "constant presence" during the Missile Crisis.

Sorensen says everyone's first choice, as a response, was to "knock out the missiles." Some in ExComm also favored invading Cuba and deposing Castro.

"No decision was made at the first meeting," Sorensen says. "But if a vote had been taken there . . . an air strike was probably number one on everybody's list. That was our [Kennedy's and those closest to him] response, too, the first day. Everybody [favored] the so-called surgical strike; swoop down and bomb the missile sites and fly away—problem solved. They hadn't had time to think through the alternatives, the consequences."

Ultimately, following tense, private back-and-forth notes with Khrushchev, JFK opted for a naval quarantine of Cuba that blockaded Soviet ships, a risky action in itself, but not as much so as an air strike.

Says Sorensen, "Had the first sign of the missile crisis being stalled been communicated to the public, the 24-hour news cycle would have produced enormous pressure on the president to make a decision immediately: "You just can't let that lie there. What are you gonna do right now?" And if we had to make a decision immediately, it would have been the wrong decision."

Was Sorensen saying that if the "wrong decision" had been made, we wouldn't be around to have the conversation we were having at that moment?

He didn't hesitate. "Exactly."

Later, after reviewing what Sorensen said, we wondered if we had understood him correctly about the doomsday scenario he appeared to present. He was known as someone who did not engage in hyperbole or black-and-white theorizing. "Ted does not see things darkly," said Hodding Carter. "He is constantly trying to figure out the upside."

So had he really said what we thought he had said? We sent him an e-mail asking him for clarification. Here was his crisp e-mail reply:

> In all likelihood, today's media pressure would have made it impossible for the Kennedy team to keep confidential for one week the fact that we knew Soviet missiles were in Cuba.
>
> In all likelihood that would have meant public panic, and congressional pressure would have required the President and ExCOMM to decide on its response a week earlier.

In all likelihood that would have meant our selecting everyone's initial first choice, an air strike against the missiles and related targets which, in all likelihood, would have required, according to the Pentagon, a follow-up invasion and occupation of Cuba.

And in all likelihood—in as much as we discovered that Soviet troops in Cuba were equipped with both tactical nuclear missiles and the authority to use them against any USA attack—the result would have been a nuclear war and the destruction of the world.

CHAPTER 10

Five Grams News, Ten Grams Speculation

I'm lovin' it.
—advertising slogan for McDonald's

The kid said he was going fast because he was in the high-speed lane.
—A Massachusetts State Patrolman commenting about a motorist driving 100 miles per hour

Each generation is confronted and tested by new, life-transforming technologies, from the first automobiles rolling off assembly lines in the late 19th century to the introduction of dial-everything, see-everything, do-everything cell phones that are now such a part of our culture that they attach to us like another body part. In our era, the newest thing is the Internet.

The Internet on the interstate—doing 100 mph in a 65-mph zone.

So now what? How do we stop these racing new media from careening off into a cornfield somewhere? How do we make the Internet—and ever-faster 24-hour news—safer for everyone?

Speed bumps? Get real.

And surely not (groan) through more government regulation. There is still a First Amendment, you know. And even the relatively new Internet is already fairly heavily regulated, as University of Chicago law professor Cas Sunstein points out: "The equivalent of trespass is forbidden. You can't libel people on the Internet. You can't commit fraud over the Internet."

Besides, complains former NBC News chief and newspaper editor Michael Gartner, hardly a softie on the perils of extreme Internet speed and other online foibles, "Every time there's a new technology, the government tries to reel it in. Whether it's the print press, whether it's radio, whether it's pictures or television. The worst thing that could come out of this is attempts to regulate."

In defense of the Internet, let's not forget that historic Campaign 2007–2008 will go down as the election run-up when online's ugly graffiti sprawl—though still a blight—was finally eclipsed at times by the big, bold, looping signatures of its fast-moving brighter lights. In one striking example of that, the *Huffington Post* website, not television or a major newspaper's op-ed page, was where Barack Obama chose to post a midcampaign column attempting to distance himself from the sometimes incendiary sermons of his former longtime Chicago pastor, the Rev. Jeremiah Wright. And several weeks later it was a fast-on-the-trigger website, The Smoking Gun, not traditional media that blew the whistle on a prominent *Los Angeles Times* story that had erroneously connected Sean "Diddy" Combs to the 1994 shooting of rapper Tupac Shakur.

Good show, all agree.

So . . . doesn't this prove that much of the concern over new media speed expressed throughout this book is unfair blog bashing and the wild, incoherent ramblings of neo-Luddites or outright abolitionists? Or perhaps just another generational twitch, the groans and squeals one always hears from arthritic geezers and antique Chicken Littles who loathe newness, retreat in panic from major change, and attribute everything fresh and innovative to another chunk of sky falling?

The answer is no. Concern about the Internet's extreme speed is genuine and well founded.

Oh, there is something highly seductive, romantic and even aromatic about nostalgia, especially when the times we live in seem so chaotic. Our selective memories have many of us glorifying and hankering for the good old days, which, truth be told, were rarely as rosy then as when viewed now from a distance.

A good example is the emergence of television just after its umbilical cord was snipped in the early 1950s. Those years are recalled fondly by many from that era as the "golden age of television," even though, as Nicholas Lemann has noted in the *New Yorker*, "There was hardly any news; the appeal of sports broadcasts was not fully apparent, so Sunday afternoons were a dead zone filled with public-service programming, [and] shows were usually sponsored by a single advertiser, who exercised a high degree of control over the content."

That content, by the way, rarely accommodated controversy (which was deemed bad for business) . . . or the unsightly real consequences of the violence that TV sanitized . . . or African Americans who did not conform to demeaning stereotype . . . or women who did not cling to their aprons and dust mops as fiercely as some Muslim women do their burkhas.

That bumpy first encounter with Philcos and 13-inch screens showed that ground breaking for the future was exhilarating in some ways but also not necessarily for sissies, something that Tom Brokaw and his parents learned from their first brush with television.

Picture young Tom sitting rapt before the magic box during one of those frozen South Dakota winters, eyes locked on the flickering black-and-white images. "And my parents were there to say, you don't have to sit in front of the television set 24 hours a day," he remembers. "They were regulators. And when I learned to drive, it didn't mean [just because] the car could go 110 miles an hour that I got to go 110 miles an hour wherever I went. The very facile line about this being the first time that a younger generation is teaching an older generation how to drive is a clever line, but there still is, it seems to me, a real obligation on the part of everyone to try to develop an appropriate culture for the use of this stuff."

That approach is unassailable, its implementation no easy thing.

The challenge, naturally, is defining what that culture should be and how best to attain it by channeling technology in a smart, liberating, and visionary way instead of trying—pointlessly, it seems—to fight it off. As former NBC journalist and presidential spokesman Ron Nessen says, "You can't get the genie back into the bottle."

Nor should we want to. It's the genie's speed that's extremely worrisome.

Slaves to Internet dogma say its critics are the ones who should slow down . . . and instead be cheered by the 360-degree panorama of its acceptance by the multitudes virtually right out of the cradle, rattle in one hand, iPhone in the other.

So what's to worry? Please look around, these guardians of online urge. Look everywhere at youthful enchantment and oneness with the fruits of science and engineering. Are we not, they ask, witnessing something truly remarkable? Are these junior technophiles not aglow with it and doing just fine with it, thank you? Do we not see them, at times barely waist high, with state-of-the-art thingamajigs in their hands, see them push their tiny fingertips against tiny keyboards, watch them with awe as they exclude the extraneous and focus eyeballs intently on blinking, digitalized miniatures that would probably baffle many of their parents and surely much of the U.S. population older than 40 or 50? Do we not take in this scene and marvel at it, thinking how proud Mr. Rogers would be to know that his neighborhood of munchkins has gone high-tech? Should we not see, as evidence that everything will turn out all right, that these precocious mighty mites have it all—the size of it, the volume of it, and yes, the speed of it—under control? As their parents did? As their grandparents did?

They do, don't they, have it all under control? Perhaps not. We'll see about that a bit later.

Meanwhile, how should their elders respond to the boom, the *zoom* of 24-hour news and the Internet? What about those of us who are swept up in this media revolution that we cultivate and sustain by watching from our homes and offices, and from our airports, rapid transit, and street corners where we stand, eyes fixed on palm-sized TVs while waiting for the light to turn green?

As our pulses speed along with the media's quickening metronome, how do we respond to their urgent call, to demands that we *do* respond and not just sit there, but do something—and, for God's sake, do it at once?

One answer comes from the unflustered pipe-and-slippers bunch.

"Whether by Internet, telegraph, radio, television, carrier pigeon or passenger ship, the mode and speed of delivery of information should be met by a pause, reflect, study, discuss—and then respond—approach," says former U.S. State Department spokesman Hodding Carter. "*Responsibility* is a word with many definitions and nuances, but one of them is not quick response. *Responsible* response is."

In other words, Carter suggests responding to the extreme speed of new media this way: "Don't just do something, sit there."

Jim Lehrer is not sitting with thumbs twiddling, nor is he sure the problem is as large as many make it out to be.

What some view as seismic change, the anchor and boss of PBS's *The NewsHour with Jim Lehrer* sees as little more than "pendulums swinging backward and forward." A card-carrying member of the glass-half-full, this-too-shall-pass club, Lehrer believes that the reckless speed and crush of news in all its distortions and deceptive guises—"the conversation about news, the reaction to news, jokes about news, screaming about news"—repels more of the available audience than it attracts. "Most people are working, they're going to school, they're doing other things," says Lehrer. "They don't have time to sit in front of their computer screens, much less listen to their radios or watch television all day to see this stuff. So the need for the old-fashioned kind of trusted gatekeeper is making a return."

In fact, Lehrer would like a writing credit on some of TV's entertainment shows. Without traditional news programs like his giving them their cues, he argues, would Jay Leno and David Letterman have monologues, would Jon Stewart and Stephen Colbert have anyone or anything to satirize?

"Nobody is going to laugh at a Letterman joke about Valerie Plame if they don't know who in the hell Valerie Plame is," Lehrer says. As for boisterous 24-hour news and the shrillest of talk radio, he adds, "If people are going to yell and scream on these television cable shows or these radio talk shows, they've got to know what's going on. I mean, they've got to know what to yell about."

Having little or no knowledge has not impeded this branch of media and their vocal chords in the past, however.

Mike McCurry is no fan of the new media speed, but prefers waiting and seeing to yelling. "I'll hold my powder until we get the most reliable and most trustworthy source giving us the information," says McCurry, who was press secretary for President Bill Clinton. He sees "reliable and trustworthy," not the journalism of cranks and crackpots, as the media model of the future. "We will get to a place where we will reestablish what the gold standard is for reality," he says, "but it will have to be something based on something other than speed of delivery, because we just can't go faster than we go right now. We've already seen the consequences of speed. We get stories that are inaccurate; we get information that's wrong; we get urban legends that propound when they're not accurate."

McCurry wonders if religious denominations, large civic institutions like Kiwanis International, or influential special interest groups like the 38-million-member-strong American Association of Retired Persons someday will create their own media vehicles in hopes of filling a deepening trust-in-news void. Whatever the case, he sees media desperados being overthrown by a marketplace that inevitably will lose patience with today's speed-at-all-costs philosophy and turn instead to news sources whose first priority is to get it right.

Even as audiences appear to shrink for appointment programs like the PBS *NewsHour* and the flagship evening newscasts of ABC, CBS and NBC, Lehrer continues to argue on their behalf and against some of the most accessible alternatives. "Bloggers don't report, they react," he notes. "Talk show people don't report, they react. Comedians don't report, they react."

The eye of the beholder comes into play here, however. A glimpse of today's media palette through the public's speed-twitched eyes shows news and faux news as runny watercolors that merge and become indistinguishable from one another. And perception is the reality that matters most in this realignment of gatekeepers.

"Well, if the blogs and the new revolution and all that stuff caused this to happen," says Lehrer, "then everybody better get used to it. New presidents better get used to it. This is the environment in which they're going to have to govern. Is that good or is that bad? I don't know." You have the impression he does know, however. "But it doesn't really make a damn, it's just the way it's going to be."

In the face of "all that stuff," how *will* presidents be able to govern effectively?

By changing the decision-making process "to reflect the speed," suggests Marlin Fitzwater, boss of the White House Press Office under presidents Ronald Reagan and George H. W. Bush. "One of the ways to produce speed in decision making is to put together a group of people whose job is to sit there and be the responders."

Well, why not? Presidential candidates and those who are elected have closetsful of advisers for every other purpose; why not speedy-answers advisers or a fast-responders-in-waiting team? Those who can't match media speed on their own must "put together a group of the people which [James] Carvel famously called the War Room [when he headed Bill Clinton's 1992 presidential campaign]," Fitzwater says. "Their whole job would be to just sit there and be ready with quick responses. When a question or an issue comes down, you've got six guys in that War Room, and they think it through and immediately come up with a clever answer, write it down, give it to the candidate, and then he goes out within an hour or so and makes a hit."

Of course, don't expect to hear presidents and White House aspirants publicly credit their "fast responders" any more than they praise speechwriters for giving them instant responses and an aura of quick-thinking credibility. So Fitzwater's media speed solution, though possibly workable and perhaps already in place somewhere, comes with a measure of deception.

News*makers* notwithstanding, much of new news *media* have a lot to answer for when it comes to snowing the public vs. serving the public good.

"At the end of the day it is going to be left to individual news organizations, bloggers, online journalists and citizens [as to] how they want to gather, convey and consume information," says former CNN Correspondent Frank Sesno. "There are fewer gate-keepers and more outlets—dangerous situation, I say."

Like the *Titanic*'s encounter with an iceberg was a dangerous situation.

With news now coming in hailstorms, Sesno wants new media to speak the "language of live" that he says rolled of off the silvery tongue of former New York Mayor Rudy Giuliani in the immediate aftermath of 9/11. "This conveys information in the incremental bits and bites in which it comes but clearly conveys that this *is* incremental information. It acknowledges emotion without being emotional. It plainly advertises that information is changing and that the person conveying it will be back with updated, alternate information. It's explicit about information that is not yet known. It is deliberate, concise language that can reflect this 24/7 instant information war, especially in the time of crisis."

This concept boldly travels far beyond familiar news labeling—which media have done for ages—to *truth* in labeling, a postapocalyptic *Star Trek*ian galaxy where relatively few media have gone before.

Today's new media regularly claim to be careful and reliable when reporting news, for example. But as a bonus, it would be helpful if they actually were careful and reliable.

"That doesn't mean they [should not] put out information quickly," says Sesno. "It means in the transparent word in which we live, they should convey to the audience that all the facts aren't in, all the information isn't known. Maybe you create a place called 'story in progress' so you can clearly convey the information is incremental and developing. News organizations simply have to be more public and transparent about how they do business, about how they make their decisions and about what they want their voices to be, because that helps the news consumers."

Even the smartest of those consumers, those who feel they're sophisticated about media, need help quickly. Take TV news, where that old saw about the camera never lying *is* a lie. Nor is perceiving truth an easy matter in any case. "Subjects asked to distinguish truth from lies answer correctly, on average, 54 percent of the time," Margaret Talbot wrote in the *New Yorker,* quoting studies published by deception researchers. Moreover, that percentage would likely drop if speed were factored into the decision making.

It doesn't take an MRI to detect a major need here. Sesno helps us with this grocery store analogy: "When you go into a supermarket and look around, at the end of the day you know what kind of peanut butter you want. If you buy a bad jar, you toss it out or it sits in the cabinet. But you're not less informed for it."

That makes good sense. After all, the U.S. Food and Drug Administration has since 1994 required nutritional labeling for prepared foods such as breads, cereals, canned and frozen foods, snacks, desserts, and drinks. The requirement makes for a much healthier and more informed consumer, just as the public is informed and empowered by ratings attached to most theatrical movies and some television programs.

Making only a small jump, it's logical to assume, as well, that news consumers armed with awareness are better equipped to assume responsibility for their intake of news. So dream along here, for a moment. In a best-case scenario, a label for a typical eight-hour slab of cable's 24-hour news, minus commercials, might look like this:

NEWSTRITIONAL FACTS

Serving Size.................... 8 hours
News .... 26 minutes (6%)
News Analysis .... 18 minutes (4%)
Opinion........................ 128 minutes (30%)
Rumor and Innuendo .... 28 minutes (7%)
Speculation.................... 84 minutes (20%)
Idle Chatter .... 16 minutes (4%)
Self-Flattery .... 20 minutes (5%)
Complete Bullshit.......... 100 minutes (24%)

○ ○ ○

The notion of news labels is pie in the sky, of course, and back on earth, news-transparency prospects are much gloomier. Former

CNN executive Keith McAllister, for one, does see a "new awareness" coming and "human beings adapting to this" neonews universe over the long haul. Just how long, though, is an open question, as is how long we can remain teetering on this high wire before it snaps. Adapting "will take awhile, and there's going to be a lot of manipulation in the meantime," McAlister predicts. "There's going to be a lot of issues and problems and mistakes in the meantime, and the question is what the wreckage will be until we reach a new stage." And also, what will be the impact of that wreckage?

"We're so far from a good place on this," Sesno says. "Nearly all the pressures out there appear to be pushing away from a more informed public, from a more deliberate journalism. Time and ratings pressure, circulation pressures and technology and the (audience) fracturing—it's like, good luck!"

Luck will have little to do with it. Nor will relying on new media to reform and slow themselves to the speed of thought. Ultimately, consumers must prepare themselves to assume control of their own media destinies.

Which returns us to the question about those cute little high-tech toddlers who seem to have it all under control. Do they?

Some of it, surely—most notably, the levers of technology, the means of turning it on so they can play video games, and the means of turning it off. But they haven't full command of the technology's power and potential, both negative and positive, any more than their elders like Tom Brokaw did when flipping on their TVs as children while having scant knowledge of the full panoply of influences before them.

Also, there's the speed.

A flying analogy works here: When pilots first earn their wings and step up to faster aircraft, they generally require additional training and a checkout from a flight instructor. Why? The faster the plane moves through the skies, the faster the pilot's decision making, increasing the probability of error if the pilot is not trained to handle that increased speed.

In other words, what's needed today is Internet flight training. What's needed is a clear blueprint, programs that educate children—starting with the very young—on how to critically assess all media, but especially today's speedier new media that place additional demands on them as consumers. Getting that training—acquiring the right tools and mental discipline—is a prerequisite for handling technology's speed and the pressures it imposes on decision making.

As the National Council of Teachers in English says, "It's not the technology that's the revolution, it's the use of the technology." Or to use a Helen Keller metaphor, it wasn't only deaf, sightless Helen learning to read in five languages but what she did with her gift that made her so amazing.

"We have to think bigger," Sesno agrees. "One of the things we have to teach in our schools is news literacy. And I don't mean waiting until they go to journalism school. We've got kids out there who do not know the difference between a newspaper and toilet paper, just as there are a lot of kids out there who don't know the difference between a credit card and a debit card, and there's a lot of talk about teaching credit card finance literacy so they'll be prepared to deal with this. I'm talking about teaching them how to recognize news and how to use news. How news gathering is done, what sourcing is all about, what is the difference between speculation and analysis. You could take an individual newscast and dissect it. You can talk about how a newspaper does a job, and how people get hold of information that you're prepared to tell the public about. You can explain news aggregating spots online or blogs on line or Drudge online and explain the difference between those things."

Essentially, that parallels Appleseed, an ambitious news literacy project that Alan Miller, formerly with the *Los Angeles Times* Washington Bureau, began plotting in 2008 with a mind toward organizing a volunteer network of journalists who would visit middle and high school classrooms and turn the business inside out for students. It's a highly worthy concept and welcome approach to have precollege students get the word from those who have actually walked the walk. Good idea, *great* idea.

But even middle school is too late.

"You don't wait until kids are 16 to teach them the alphabet so they can read Shakespeare," says Liz Thoman, a founder of the Los Angeles–based Center for Media Literacy. "Technology is driving information at an exponential rate," says Thoman, a self-titled "ambassador at large" for media literacy. "And education is responding to that. The problem is that it takes a long time and there is a lot of inertia."

Tell it to Jeff Share, faculty adviser for teacher education at the University of Southern California–Los Angeles (UCLA). Count him as frustrated by how infrequently media literacy is taught in a meaningful way in U.S. public schools, although nearly all states call for it in their educational standards. It's one thing to allow or even command it, another to educate teachers—who are shaped largely by the same mass media influences that influence their students—to teach it. And, in fact, they're not being taught; many don't even want to be taught.

A large number may be intimidated not only by new technology but also the speed at which it comes at us. Every day, something new; it's a lot to assimilate. Others "are just stuck in this old way, and don't want to change," says Share, a media literacy specialist who wrote his PhD dissertation on the subject. "I do a lot of presentations with teachers, and it's weird because, it's like, 'Oh, yeah, that's so cool.' And the next aspect is, 'I don't have time to do this.'" Others insist on excluding the Internet from class. "They say it's terrible, but it's not terrible," says Share. "It does have some serious problems that we need to address, and the best way to address that is to bring it into the class, to teach the kids tools to critically question it."

There are no flaws in that argument, and what Share says on the subject makes good sense, but apparently to no avail. Even his own UCLA department does not include media literacy as a curriculum item, and he works it into his teaching because of his passion for it.

"The media literacy movement has had very little impact in the United States," Share says. "We're basically in the Middle Ages on this. Canada, Australia, England—they've been doing it for decades now."

In Canada, for three decades to be precise. Every province in Canada, for example, requires that literacy in mass communications—including the Internet—be taught in kindergarten through 12th grade. "There are standards and concepts that teachers are required to teach," says Share. And not only are they required to teach it, here is the kicker: they are *trained* to teach it.

Share says he's asked Canadians, some of them media literacy pioneers, why they believe their country far exceeds the United

States in this field. He's told that protection is one reason—that teaching their children to analyze the character and influence of media—much of it flowing from south of the border—is Canadians' way of resisting the U.S. culture that they feel is imposed on them. For years there's been simmering Canadian resentment over so many in the United States thinking of their northern neighbor as an extension of the U.S. or, as someone once put it, "as Canadian as apple pie." And Canadians told Share that when they observed "our culture being trashed and homogenized by the big U.S. media" they decided media literacy was a way to combat it.

And why has the United States been generally resistant to media literacy for kids? "I think it's because we are the dominant media creators in the world," says Share. "People in the dominant position don't see as much of the negative effects."

The media literacy movement may have hatched abroad (some say in Great Britain in the 1930s) as a blame-the-messenger-for-everything operation, but its significance has expanded far beyond that narrow antagonism, and with good reason given the communications avalanche at our heels. So with that in mind it's especially important to sharpen the critical skills of preschoolers on up, and have them apply those skills to the analysis of popular culture. In fact, TV and the Internet *are* popular culture, as well as the language and literature of this generation.

What is it, precisely, that children should be taught?

"Core concept number one is that all media are constructed," says Share. Which means? "That everything has been created, that nothing is natural. Kids must start to understand that everything has been constructed, from their textbook, from the encyclopedia, from the map on the wall. Everything you see is dependent on a lot of people making choices. So every choice that was made could have been made differently. And just understanding that it doesn't have to be that way is a huge empowering concept for kids when they really get it."

Now, the specifics. Is there a single metaphor that can effectively convey this to young kids? A new twist on something familiar, perhaps, that will really turn them on to media literacy? Absolutely.

None other than a traditional, heavily advertised profit center of McDonald's golden arches, one designed for children, one allowing them to choose a hamburger, cheeseburger, or four-piece order of Chicken McNuggets along with fries or precut apples and a soft drink, milk, chocolate milk, or apple juice. We give you, yes . . .

THE HAPPY MEAL!

That's how respected Canadian teacher and media literacy specialist Vivian Vasquez famously begins her pitch to kiddies up north. As described by Share, "She charts it up on the wall and does a big *M* in the middle and says, 'Okay, tell me everything that's in a Happy Meal.' And the kids say, 'Okay, there's the paper bag it comes in, there's a hamburger, the bun, and maybe the french fries, right?' And she says, 'Okay, that's great. Now what is in each one of those? What's inside the meat, the hamburger? What's inside the bun? What did it take to make that paper bag?' And then she draws a web that starts to shoot out. So from the paper bag, she says, 'Well, there are trees and a factory, and from the hamburger there were some cows,' and she starts to build on this. 'Okay, great, now what's from that? What was involved in getting the tree?' So the whole thing is just growing out. And basically what she is doing is building the blocks for these little kids to understand the social construction of ideas and knowledge, and that how the next time they look at that Happy Meal, it's not just this cool thing that's fun; they start to see it's all connected."

The same concept—there is no such thing as a truly objective message, so beware—can be applied equally to diverse media McNuggets, whether MoveOn.org or Wikipedia or the *Des Moines Register* or CNN or the *Drudge Report* or a myriad of other information sources, regardless of political stripe. And if this is conveyed to preschoolers and continually reinforced in classrooms through the years, everyone ultimately will be equipped to better assess information zooming toward them at warp speed.

"It's not about simply trying to determine accuracy," Share says. "It's looking at everything and demystifying the idea that there could be objectivity. There are things that are more correct than others, but everything . . . passes through filters and has biases and different values. This is important because any information that's out there is benefiting someone and hurting someone else in some way. Bias is inherent in all communication, and power is always tied to it. Teaching media literacy is teaching kids to look at the connections and see who is benefiting from this and who is not. And how many different versions do I need to look at to try to find what for me is the closest to the truth?"

Share believes it's in the doing as well as the observing, including teaching young children how to keep a blog. "It's not just that we teach kids all these new cool tools, but that they use [them] in ways where they are also learning how to critically analyze," he says. He's done it himself. With teacher permission, for example, he showed his son's first grade class how to create PowerPoint presentations, one of which—a bloody, rather gruesome sequence of a whale being slaughtered and cut up—the students showed to a kindergarten class, which found the images gross.

Share was wowed by how his son's class responded to that. "It was a shining moment to hear these first graders—you know, five and six—discuss it. They all talked about how the kindergartners were so disturbed by the picture. A couple of kids said, 'We should remove it because we don't want to upset anyone, that's not our goal.' And then a couple of other kids said, 'No, wait a second. We've been talking about really serious things and these animals are dying, and this picture showed something that was really going on, and we want to upset them because this is wrong and we need to change it.'"

It was the kind of internal debate about photo usage that goes on at newspapers and TV news institutions. "So to hear it from first graders," says Share, "this is the seed that we're planting."

It's all about questioning. "The purpose is to teach them how to analyze and be critical of other media," Share says. "Because it's in the process of creating that they really recognize that, 'Wait a second, I shouldn't take this at face value. Look, I'm making all these decisions; other people are doing the same thing.'" That, Share hopes, will lead these young kids to "where we've never gone, and they will say, 'Well, wait a second, I should be questioning my textbook in the classroom. I should be questioning my teacher.'"

Many will view that as a threat, if not as a step toward anarchy in the classroom. But Share believes that media literacy and the present technological revolution are perfectly matched partners to lead the way toward "getting at the social construction of knowledge that we've never really had at school."

This is visionary thinking. And when applied it to both traditional and instant new media? Not being distracted and looking past the speed and glitz straight into the soul of the beast can yield the kind of knowledge that will smarten and empower us to meet many of the challenges of our throw-it-at-you-as-fast-as-it-comes-in news culture.

Whether media literacy happens in a meaningful way is hardly a sure thing, and something that even the crystal ball–gazing news swamis covered in this book would not want to predict. But if it does, like consumers of Happy Meals, we'll be lovin' it.

Afterword

You won't have ink on your fingers and old unread newspapers in the driveway.
—blogger Daniel Langendorf, touting an advantage of news delivered via mobile phones

In researching and writing this book, we found ourselves continually looking back over our shoulders, trying to stay ahead of a techno-driven avalanche of media happenings that threatened to overtake us. A classic line from Stepin Fetchit came to mind: "Feets, don't fail me now!"

The worry was justified. Quite clearly, this book is predicated on epic changes in the delivery of news and information, and the impact of those changes—much of it problematic—not only in the United States but across the planet. When planning the book, however, we could not have predicted the swiftness of this transformation—a metamorphoses whose very catalyst is speed. And this relentless surge continued even as we turned off the lights and locked the door after putting the preceding portion of this book to bed.

Summing up . . .

Stop the presses! On June 3, as votes were cast in the campaign's final Democratic Primaries, in South Dakota and Montana, Barak Obama finally became his party's presumptive nominee.

"I'm getting that new year's eve feeling," gushed a giddy Chris Matthews on MSNBC. So he and his colleagues had been right from the start about Obama winning—just five months premature in uncorking the bubbly.

Not that everyone had learned from past mistakes. The Associated Press reported on June 3 that Hillary Clinton would make a concession speech that night. *Wrong*. Plus, CBS News carried a story saying she would acknowledge Obama had gained enough delegates to secure the nomination. *Wrong*.

And speaking of stopping the presses, five weeks earlier they had done just that at the *Capital Times* in Madison, Wisconsin, after 90 years of publishing.

The newspaper that for generations was delivered to doorsteps and available on the street did what many newspapers had done: It ceased to exist. The banner headline didn't end there, however, for the *Capital Times* made history also by achieving something that had not been matched by a metropolitan daily previously. It morphed into a standalone website, a *Stepford Wives* cyber-version of its former wood pulp self, not an Internet adjunct to the newspaper but, in fact, a URL (Uniform Resource Locator) that *is* the newspaper.

As an evening publication in a two-newspaper town, the *Capital Times* had been facing a death sentence for some time due to a steady circulation freefall of more than 50 percent since the 1960s. Yet its demise as a traditional newspaper and resurrection online are a fitting coda to a book about wide-ranging new media changes that cut deeply into our very intellectual fabric, many of them on the print front.

The *Capital Times* reimagined is not just the way of the future, it's increasingly the way of the present, with newspapers as we have known them surely destined to become the extinct dodos of media and communication in an age when *fast and faster, brief and briefer* are commandments carved into stone.

Some of this evokes wistfulness, as in Leon Wieseltier, veteran literary editor of the *New Republic,* lamenting that book reviews "must now be short and pert and helpful and explain—like many of the books themselves, alas—only how or why something does or does not work."

Some of it has pragmatic resonance, showing that Internet double duty, for example, can be more than just a nuisance to print journalists; it can be potentially hazardous to their health.

Ask Barry Bearak. The seasoned *New York Times* reporter was assigned to cover the March 2008 elections in Zimbabwe, where ruthless dictator Robert Mugabe was clinging tenaciously to power. Because covering news there without government approval (rarely given to foreigners) is dangerous, reporters must go to extreme lengths to protect their sources and themselves. And Bearak did just that, even destroying his notes after first emailing them to himself at a place where they could not be found should his laptop ever be confiscated and its hard drive searched.

Even so, Bearak was arrested and charged with "committing journalism." What had gone wrong? Possibly that he'd been compromised by his obligation to serve his newspaper's online function.

Writing of his ordeal after being freed following his brief imprisonment, Bearak explained what happened: "Necessity numbed my own caution. My articles required continuous updating for the *Times*'s website, so there I'd be in downtown Harare, a backpack slung over my shoulder, dictating quotes from my notebook and spelling names into the wavering connection of the mobile phone."

Which was no way to remain incognito in a nation that regards "journalism" as criminal, but he did what he had to do.

Bearak recalled what he had jokingly told his wife after being arrested—that he could handle prison in Zimbabwe because "anything is better than having to file four stories a day for the website."

Or perhaps he wasn't joking, for just as economic hardship has eroded newspaper profits (the *New York Times* joined other publications and announced its own staff reductions two months later) and made them rethink their roles in our media universe, the Internet compounds that pressure by forcing print journalists to redefine what they do.

As in the *Los Angeles Times* setting up a fifth-floor video studio "to ramp up our ability to do quick turnaround, in house-video" for the newspaper's website.

And as summer 2008 approached, a number of newspapers joined with the Associated Press to establish the Mobile News

Network. Its mission: to bring local news to cellphones, smart phones, and the like based on users' zip codes. In other words, news in the palm of your hand, not exactly a revolutionary concept, but one now taking hold.

A prototype on the Associated Press website featured six categories of print and video news along with a set of newspaper headlines. "So," gushed a video voice, "the next time your favorite star elopes to Vegas or your home team wins the game, you can be the first tell your friends." Why you could mistake this for your hometown newspaper . . . if your hometown newspaper was several inches long.

Not only "news at your fingertips," as the Associated Press promises, but news the size of your fingertips.

And news and faux news that continued to fly like the wind.

Soaring through cyberspace in late April was a photo that seemed to show Chinese paramilitary forces carrying monks' robes—conclusive evidence, a chorus of bloggers and emailers insisted, that Chinese police had staged the previous month's riots in Tibet. One very slight glitch, though. The photo turned out to be seven years old and apparently taken during a film shoot.

"In this politically charged environment, people throw any kind of thing out there without checking," Xiao Qiang, director of the China Internet Project at University of California Berkeley, told the *Los Angeles Times*. "It's just part of the crazy Internet world."

Wild and crazy—which is why we love it, right?

But how to match that appealing wildness and craziness if your competing media? Cable's 24-hour news dragsters proved they knew the score as they continued their quest to increase the speed of news by reporting it before it happened. Two minutes—*two minutes*—before Hillary Clinton was scheduled to address a national TV audience after the North Carolina and Indiana primaries on May 6, MSNBC's Keith Olbermann asked Brian Williams, "What on earth could she say?"

Why on earth would he ask?

And on CNN that evening, after Clinton had been trounced in North Carolina by Barak Obama and barely edged him in Indiana, David Gergen put on his mind-reading swami robes and disclosed that a post-speech embrace by Hillary and Bill Clinton had been "genuine." As for their daughter, Chelsea, said Gergen (who had worked in the Clinton White House), despite her happy face he could see clearly that her "heart was breaking."

We won't know about that until Chelsea publishes her inevitable memoir, probably after writing it on a cellphone.

Not that media accuracy was a salable commodity in the run-up to the November 4 election. "It's difficult to say definitely that the press and pundits covering the 2008 campaign have missed the mark more often, and by a wider margin, than in elections past—though given everything from 'McCain's done' to 'It's all about Iowa,' it's hard not to believe," the *Columbia Journalism Review* editorialized. "What one *can* say definitely is that conventional wisdom is vulnerable in large part because it is often based on imperfect and incomplete information; and that the source of the vast majority of that information—reporting by mainstream news outlets—is under assault as never before."

In its latest state-of-media report, the Project for Excellence in Journalism found that all across the media landscape, "less is being devoted to original newsgathering, especially the bearing witness and monitoring of the basic news."

In fact, *opinion disguised as news and analysis* continued to spread across and seep deeply into presidential election coverage as we wrapped up this book. That scourge was typified by Karl Rove, President Bush's former confidante, surfacing on the Fox News Channel as a purported neutral observer. Wrote Jim Rutenberg and Jacques Steinberg in the *New York Times*: "At times clearly partisan, at others apparently offering down-the-middle analysis, Mr. Rove in his new role as media star marks another step in the evolution of mainstream journalism, where opinion, 'straight news' reporting and unmistakable spin increasingly mingle, especially on television." Added Marvin Kalb, a former correspondent for CBS and NBC: "We now have reached a point particularly in 24/7 cable where it is not the journalist who is the preferred participant, but the politician, the political activist, the Karl Rove type." To say nothing of the Democratic activist type.

Arguably even more disturbing was a *New York Times* expose that several dozen retired high-ranking officers who made thousands of appearances on TV and radio as military analysts since 2002, we're actually front men for the Pentagon's campaign to generate rosy coverage of the Bush administration's wartime performances in Iraq and Afghanistan.

"The analysts, many with undisclosed ties to military contractors, have been wooed in hundreds of private briefings with senior government officials, given access to classified information and taken on Pentagon-sponsored trips to Iraq and Guantanamo Bay in Cuba," the *Times* reported.

This means either that the TV news community was in too much of a rush to properly vet these poseurs (which is bad enough) or that their true agendas were known to media executives who didn't care (which is worse) because they were happy to pump anything available into the bottomless black hole they call editorial space. Yes, again, feeding the God-damned beast.

There's a natural segue from this reporting by the *Times* to our favorite crusader-saviors, the *Onward Citizen Soldiers* of the Internet.

Good news/bad news scenario: Notably, it was a citizen reporter—a 61-year-old "Off the Buser" for the HuffingtonPost and a self-proclaimed Obama supporter—not the *Times* or any other traditionalist media top gun who first reported Obama's statements about the "bitter" feelings of small-town Americans that earned him waves of criticism less than six months before the 2008 election. Thumbs up for her all the way.

However, the same woman should have known not to give money (she said she contributed $2,500) to Obama's campaign while covering it. How basic is that?

And let's do get serious here, heart of hearts. Can anyone really envision citizen journalists ever uncovering, assembling, and reporting a story of the magnitude, say, of that expose of Pentagon surrogates posing on TV as independent military analysts? Or matching the jobs that traditional journalists slog away at day in, day out?

Citizen journalists are "an army of average Joes, equipped with cell phones, laptops, and video cameras, [that] has commandeered our news media," Ted Gup, who teaches journalism at Case Western Reserve University, wrote in the *Chronicle of Higher*

Education. "The mantra of 'We want to hear from you!' is all the rage, from CNN to NPR; but although invigorating and democratizing, it has failed to supplant the provision of essential facts, generating more heat than light."

Not that "essential facts" seem to matter to students whom Gup encounters. "Despite their Blackberrys, cell phones, and WiFi," he says, "they are, in their own way, as isolated as the remote tribes of New Guinea. They disprove the notion that technology fosters engagement, that connectivity and community are synonymous."

Or perhaps that speed and multi-tasking equal illumination.

A study released in June 2008 found that young adults fail to give full attention to news because they are simultaneously engaged in other activities, such as reading email. Commissioned by the Associated Press, the research showed that persons 18 to 34 in six cities in the United States, United Kingdom, and India experience news fatigue and have difficulty accessing in-depth stories because of being bombarded by facts and updates in headlines and news snippets.

This brings us full circle, all the way back the *no-time-to-thinkness* that underpins nearly everything written here. Now, the hard part.

By clicking a mouse or punching a master remote device we filter out what we don't wish to see or hear and can select instead from a menu offering only choices that please us or are familiar. Yes, the echo chamber again, and if only real-life quandaries were that easily fixed. They're not.

So no easy panaceas from us, no neatly tying up of loose ends before the final credits, only a dose of hope. If you've read this far, presumably you *have* taken the time to think, and are aware that this book is ultimately far less a plea for slowness or slowerness as an antidote to speed—that launched spaceship is already circling the planet—than for providing our children with tools to cope with the blistering pace of new media. In doing that, perhaps we'll teach ourselves.

Bibliography

Auletta, Ken. *Media Man*, Atlas Books, 2004.

Benkler, Yochai. *The Wealth of Networks*, Yale University Press, 2006.

Bibb, Porter, *It Ain't as Easy as It Looks*, Crown Publishers Inc., 1993.

Bowman, Shayne and Willis, Chris. *We Media: How Audiences Are Shaping the Future of News and Information*, the Media Center at the American Press Institute, 2003.

Campbell, Alastair. *The Blair Years*, Alfred A. *Knopf*, 2007.

Cloud, Stanley and Olson, Lynne. *The Murrow Boys*, Houghton Mifflin Company, 1996.

Davies, Nick. *Flat Earth News*, Chatto & Windus, Random House, 2008.

Downie Jr., Leonard and Kaiser, Robert G. *The News About the News: American Journalism in Peril*, Alfred A. Knopf, 2002.

Gillmor, Dan. *We the Media: Grassroots Journalism by the People for the People*, O'Reilly Media Inc., 2004.

Gladwell, Malcolm. *blink*, Back Bay Books, 2005.

Gleick, James. *Faster: The Acceleration of Just About Everything*, Abacus, 1999.

Goldberg, Robert and Goldberg, Jay. *Citizen Turner*, Harcourt Brace & Company, 1995.

Gore, Al. *The Assault on Reason*, Penguin Press, 2007.

Greenfield, Jeff. *Oh, Waiter! One Order of Crow!*, G.P. Putnam's Sons, 2001.

Groopman, Jerome. *How Doctors Think*, Houghton Mifflin Company, 2007.

Honore, Carl. *In Praise of Slowness*. HarperOne, 2004.

Jacoby, Susan. *The Age of American Unreason*, Pantheon Books, 2008.

Keen, Andrew. *The Cult of the Amateur*, Doubleday, 2007.

Kovach, Bill and Rosenstiel, Tom. *Warp Speed*, the Century Foundation Press, 1999.

Marlane, Judith. *Women in Television News Revisited*, University of Texas Press, 1999.

May, Ernest R. and Zelikow, Philip D. *The Kennedy Tapes*, W.W. Norton & Company Ltd., 2002.

McKay, Charles. *Extraordinary Popular Delusions and the Madness of Crowds (1841)*, Harmony Books, 1980.

Patterson, Thomas E. *Out of Order*, Alfred A. Knopf, 1993.

Persico, Joseph E. *Edward R. Murrow: An American Original*, McGraw-Hill Publishing Co., 1988.

Rosenberg, Howard. *Not So Prime Time: Chasing the Trivial on American Television*, Ivan R. Dee, 2004.

Schechter, Danny. *The More You Watch, The Less You Know*, Seven Stories Press, 1997.

Schroeder, Alan. *Presidential Debates*, Columbia University Press, 2000.

Shirky, Clay. *Here Comes Everybody: The Power of Organizing Without Organizations*, Penquin Press, 2008.

Sites, Kevin. *In the Hot Zone*, Harper Perennial, 2007.

Sorensen, Ted. *Counselor*, HarperCollins, 2008.

Sperber, A.M. *Murrow: His Life and Times*, Freundlich Books, 1986.

Stephens, Mitchell. *A History of News*, Oxford University Press, 2007.

Talese, Gay. *The Kingdom and the Power*, World Publishing, 1969.

Toobin, Jeffrey. *The Nine: Inside the Secret World of the Supreme Court*, Doubleday, 2007.

Trippi, Joe. *The Revolution Will Not Be Televised*, Regan, 2004.

Virilio, Paul. *The Information Bomb*, Verso, 2000.

Whittemore, Hank. *CNN: The Inside Story*, Little Brown and Company, 1990.

Index